Mastering Japanese Kanji

The Innovative Visual Method for Learning Japanese Characters

Volume 1

Mastering Japanese Kanji

The Innovative Visual Method for Learning Japanese Characters

Volume 1

By Glen Nolan Grant

Illustrations by Ya-Wei Lin

TUTTLE PUBLISHING

Tokyo • Rutland, Vermont • Singapore

ACKNOWLEDGMENTS

This book is the result of a collaborative effort. Sincere thanks to Eric Oey of Periplus Editions for steering everything in the right direction, as well as to Sandra Korinchak, Bob Graham, William Notte, and the entire editorial and design departments of Tuttle Publishing for their stellar work with the manuscript. Watai Yuko, Niimi Emiko, Nakano Mariko, Watai Fumiko, Murray Grant, Cathy Grant, Damon Vignale, and Shaun Culham all offered welcome assistance. Special thanks are also owed to Junko Lucas, for lending her voice to the sound recordings, Matt Pinneo, for his excellent job designing the CD-ROM, and to the very talented Ya-Wei Lin, whose wonderful illustrations helped bring each of the stories to life.

This book is dedicated to Mr. H.B. (Henry Barrie) and Mrs. Wilma Grant, for their incredible support and encouragement.

Published by Tuttle Publishing, an imprint of Periplus Editions (HK) Ltd., with editorial offices at 364 Innovation Drive, North Clarendon, Vermont 05759 U.S.A.

Library of Congress Cataloging-in-Publication Data

Grant, Glen Nolan.
Mastering Japanese kanji : the innovative visual method for learning Japanese characters / by Glen Nolan Grant ;
illustrations by Ya-Wei Lin
v. <1-> ; cm.
Includes bibliographical references and index.
ISBN 978-4-8053-0992-6 (pbk. : alk. paper)
1. Chinese characters--Study and teaching. 2. Japanese language--Orthography and spelling. I. Lin, Ya-Wei. II. Title.
PL528.G73 2009
495.6'82421--dc22
2008045831

ISBN: 978-4-8053-0992-6

Distributed by:

North America, Latin America & Europe
Tuttle Publishing
364 Innovation Drive
North Clarendon, VT 05759-9436 U.S.A
Tel: 1 (802) 773 8930
Fax: 1 (802) 773 6993
info@tuttlepublishing.com
www.tuttlepublishing.com

Japan
Tuttle Publishing
Yaekari Building, 3rd Floor
5-4-12 Osaki, Shinagawa-ku
Tokyo 141 0032
Tel: (81) 3 5437-0171
Fax: (81) 3 5437-0755
tuttle-sales@gol.com

Asia-Pacific
Berkeley Books Pte Ltd
61 Tai Seng Avenue #02-12
Singapore 534167
Tel: (65) 6280-3320
Fax: (65) 6280-6290
inquiries@periplus.com.sg
www.periplus.com

First edition
13 12 11 10 09 10 9 8 7 6 5 4 3 2 1

Printed in Singapore

Contents

Introduction 8

Chapter 1
1. Mountain (山) 12
2. Person (人) 13
3. One (一) 14
4. Two (二) 15
5. Three (三) 16
6. Sun (日) 17
7. White (白) 18
8. Mouth (口) 19
9. Rotate (回) 20
10. Four (四) 21
11. Moon (月) 22
12. Bright (明) 23
13. Tree (木) 24
14. Five (五) 25
15. Eye (目) 26
16. Woman (女) 27
17. Large (大) 28
18. Middle (中) 29
19. Eight (八) 30
20. Small (小) 31

Chapter 1 Review Exercises 32

Chapter 2
21. Shellfish (貝) 34
22. Six (六) 35
23. King (王) 36
24. Jewel (玉) 37
25. Heart (心) 38
26. Country (国) 39
27. Complete (全) 40
28. Ten (十) 41
29. Early (早) 42
30. Upper (上) 43
31. Lower (下) 44
32. Rice (米) 45
33. Self (自) 46
34. Inside (内) 47
35. Right (右) 48
36. Have (有) 49
37. Meat (肉) 50
38. Half (半) 51
39. Nine (九) 52
40. Spring (春) 53

Chapter 2 Review Exercises 54

Chapter 3
41. Capital (京) 56
42. See (見) 57
43. Stop (止) 58
44. Seven (七) 59
45. Few (少) 60
46. South (南) 61
47. Craft (工) 62
48. Left (左) 63
49. Tall (高) 64
50. Buy (買) 65
51. Hundred (百) 66
52. Circle (円) 67
53. Basis (元) 68
54. Neck (首) 69
55. Walk (歩) 70
56. Child (子) 71
57. Like (好) 72
58. Old (古) 73
59. Fire (火) 74
60. Winter (冬) 75

Chapter 3 Review Exercises 76

Chapter 4
61. Water (水) 78
62. Ease (安) 79
63. Strength (力) 80
64. Summer (夏) 81
65. Thousand (千) 82
66. Rest (休) 83
67. Hand (手) 84
68. Main (本) 85
69. Change (化) 86
70. River (川) 87
71. Body (体) 88
72. North (北) 89

73. Rice field (田) 90
74. Man (男) 91
75. House (家) 92
76. East (東) 93
77. Think (思) 94
78. Ear (耳) 95
79. Father (父) 96
80. Say (言) 97
Chapter 4 Review Exercises 98

Chapter 5

81. Dry (干) 100
82. Gold (金) 101
83. Words (語) 102
84. Gentleman (士) 103
85. Morning (朝) 104
86. Blue (青) 105
87. Earth (土) 106
88. Hang (掛) 107
89. Ten thousand (万) 108
90. Rain (雨) 109
91. Electric (電) 110
92. Sell (売) 111
93. Individual (者) 112
94. Enter (入) 113
95. Snow (雪) 114
96. Gate (門) 115
97. Interval (間) 116
98. Exit (出) 117
99. Life (生) 118
100. Cow (牛) 119
Chapter 5 Review Exercises 120
Cumulative Review Exercises for Chapters 1-5 122

Chapter 6

101. Beautiful (美) 125
102. Island (島) 126
103. Tiny (寸) 127
104. Temple (寺) 128
105. Precede (先) 129
106. Open (開) 130
107. Bird (鳥) 131
108. Evening (夕) 132
109. Outside (外) 133
110. Tongue (舌) 134
111. Diagram (図) 135
112. Stand (立) 136
113. Parent (親) 137
114. Star (星) 138
115. Autumn (秋) 139
116. West (西) 140
117. Sword (刀) 141
118. Cut (切) 142
119. Day of the week (曜) 143
120. Around (周) 144
Chapter 6 Review Exercises 145

Chapter 7

121. Read (読) 147
122. Road (道) 148
123. Heaven (天) 149
124. Part (分) 150
125. Thing (物) 151
126. Axe (斤) 152
127. New (新) 153
128. Flower (花) 154
129. Name (名) 155
130. Mother (母) 156
131. Private (私) 157
132. Night (夜) 158
133. Before (前) 159
134. Many (多) 160
135. Hold (持) 161
136. Write (書) 162
137. Sound (音) 163
138. Meet (会) 164
139. Hear (聞) 165
140. Center (央) 166
Chapter 7 Review Exercises 167

Chapter 8

141. Near (近) 169
142. Lose (失) 170
143. Bow (弓) 171
144. Horse (馬) 172
145. Week (週) 173
146. Pull (引) 174
147. Second (秒) 175
148. Shell (甲) 176
149. Spirit (気) 177
150. Time (時) 178
151. Speak (話) 179

152. English (英) ... 180
153. Instruction (訓) ... 181
154. Push (押) ... 182
155. Year (年) ... 183
156. Come (来) ... 184
157. Study (学) ... 185
158. Mind (意) ... 186
159. Again (又) ... 187
160. Red (赤) ... 188
Chapter 8 Review Exercises ... 189

Chapter 9

161. Public (公) ... 191
162. Goods (品) ... 192
163. City (市) ... 193
164. Primary (主) ... 194
165. Block (丁) ... 195
166. Friend (友) ... 196
167. Group (団) ... 197
168. Every (毎) ... 198
169. Empty (空) ... 199
170. Town (町) ... 200
171. Dog (犬) ... 201
172. Death (死) ... 202
173. Go (行) ... 203
174. Take (取) ... 204
175. Village (村) ... 205
176. Character (字) ... 206
177. Tool (具) ... 207
178. Pour (注) ... 208
179. Cherry tree (桜) ... 209
180. Hamlet (里) ... 210
Chapter 9 Review Exercises ... 211

Chapter 10

181. Grove (林) ... 213
182. Forest (森) ... 214
183. Cloud (雲) ... 215
184. Black (黒) ... 216
185. Mix (交) ... 217
186. Not (不) ... 218
187. After (後) ... 219
188. Most (最) ... 220
189. Fat (太) ... 221
190. Car (車) ... 222
191. Receive (受) ... 223
192. Evil (凶) ... 224
193. Sea (海) ... 225
194. School (校) ... 226
195. Leg (足) ... 227
196. Thread (糸) ... 228
197. Same (同) ... 229
198. Noon (午) ... 230
199. Love (愛) ... 231
200. Separate (離) ... 232
Chapter 10 Review Exercises ... 233

Cumulative Review Exercises for Chapters 1-10 ... 235
Answer Key for Exercises ... 238

Appendices

Index 1: Stroke Count ... 241
Index 2: Kanji Names ... 242
Index 3: Romaji Reading ... 244
Index 4: Hiragana and Katakana Reading ... 248
On-yomi Keyword Table ... 252

INTRODUCTION

This book can help you greatly reduce the time and effort involved in learning to read Japanese. It does so by introducing a method that is both effective and easy to use in memorizing the meanings and pronunciations of *kanji*, the array of characters that are used in the language to symbolize everything from abstract ideas to concrete nouns.

Learning any of the kanji, you will find, is a two-step process, requiring that you remember both the *visual* aspect of a character (so you can recognize it when you see it) and the *aural* aspect (so you will know how to say and, thus, read it). The method presented here will show you how to tackle both of these aspects from the outset, and by so doing enable you to immediately get down to the practical (and fun!) business of recognizing and reading kanji on everything from street signs to newspapers. By the time you finish this book, in fact, you will be able to boast of a Japanese vocabulary numbering in the thousands of words.

Kanji and the Japanese Writing System

Kanji (literally, "Chinese characters") arrived in Japan along with Buddhism and other aspects of Chinese culture approximately 1,500 years ago. As with many concepts introduced into the country from abroad, this writing system was gradually shaped and modified over the centuries to better suit the Japanese themselves. Kanji today comprise one part of written Japanese, being used alongside a pair of much simpler phonetic syllabaries, *katakana* and *hiragana.* Katakana are generally employed to denote foreign words, as well as various technical and scientific terms. Hiragana, on the other hand, have a largely grammatical function, and are used for everything from verb endings to particles. As you can see from the examples below, katakana and hiragana are visually similar; they never contain more than four strokes. Kanji, however, are more varied; they can have anywhere from one to more than 20 strokes.

Hirigana:	か	き	く	け	こ
Katakana:	カ	キ	ク	ケ	コ
Kanji:	東	曜	秋	語	意

Written Japanese is thus a mixture of three elements, and a single sentence can have all three present, as in the following example.

アフリカで水牛とキリンを見ました。
I saw a water buffalo and a giraffe in Africa.

Number and Frequency of Kanji

As katakana and hiragana can be learned quickly (there are only around fifty of each), this book will focus exclusively on mastering kanji. It's worth keeping in mind that the Japanese Ministry of Education has stipulated that high school students in Japan are expected to learn 1,945 characters (the so-called "general-use" kanji) by the time they graduate. Magazines and newspapers can employ upwards of 3,000 kanji, although these "extra" characters are often accompanied by hiragana showing how they are to be pronounced; without; this, most Japanese would often be unsure of both the meaning of the character in question and its pronunciation.

Despite there being so many kanji, it is important to understand that some are used far more frequently than others. The 500 most common, for example, make up approximately 80% of the kanji you will see. The 1,000 most common bring this figure to over 90%. Learning the 200 kanji presented in this volume, therefore, will offer great immediate benefit.

The Composition of Kanji

In general, kanji dictionaries divide characters into groups that share a common part (call a "radical"). As you can see below, the kanji in the first row all share the same left-hand radical 亻. The kanji in the second row share the same top 宀, while the radical in the third row (夂) appears in various positions.

休　化　体
安　家　字
冬　夏　愛

At times this book will break kanji apart into fragments smaller than radicals. To keep things simple, all radicals and parts that make up a kanji – *but are not themselves kanji* – are called components, and will always be presented in a separate text box immediately before the first character in which they appear.

Stroke Order

Stroke order refers to the sequence of lines that are used to correctly write out a kanji. Knowing this order is important for several reasons. First, it will help train you to quickly count the number of strokes in a character, and thus make it easier to locate unfamiliar kanji (or those for which pronunciations may have been forgotten) in a kanji dictionary. It will also aid you in breaking down characters visually, making it easier to see the components that will help you recall a kanji's meaning. Stroke order diagrams accompany each entry in this book. The accompanying CD-ROM, in addition, provides an animated graphic showing each character being written in its proper order.

An Overview of *On-yomi* and *Kun-yomi*

On-yomi and **kun-yomi** are the two main branches of pronunciation (or "readings", as they are called) that are present in modern day Japanese. **On-yomi** are sometimes called the "Chinese readings" of the kanji, as these were the initial pronunciations attached to the characters when they first arrived from China. The **kun-yomi**, on the other hand, developed from within Japan, and are thus referred to as "Japanese readings". This, along with the fact that different **on-yomi** for the same character sometimes arrived from China centuries later, helps explain how a single kanji in Japanese can sometimes have more than one of each type of reading.

Clearly, memorizing these various pronunciations and knowing when to use them are two of the most difficult tasks in learning Japanese. There are, however, reasons to be optimistic. Over 60% of the kanji have only a single **on-yomi**, or one **on-yomi** and one **kun-yomi**. In addition, when multiple **on-** or **kun-yomi** are present, there is usually only one dominant reading for each. This book will help you determine the most important pronunciations to be learned by classifying every reading as either "common" or "less common". Those less common do not merit being learned at this stage of your language study; they are presented only for future reference.

An interesting aspect of Japanese (and an unlucky one for us in this volume!) is that the most complex kanji in terms of pronunciation are often amongst the most simple to write. Do not get discouraged, therefore, when thorny characters such as "person" (Entry 2), "one" (Entry 3), "sun" (Entry 6), and "large" (Entry 17) all show up in the first chapter, as these can be classified with the most difficult in the language. Be patient with such characters, and take comfort in knowing that by the time you finish this book you will have dealt with the trickiest entries in the entire range of the general-use kanji.

Some Rules for Using *On-yomi* and *Kun-yomi*

There are some useful ground rules that you should keep in mind when learning to read single kanji and compounds (words formed from several kanji put together):

1. Kanji in most compounds are usually read with their **on-yomi**. Note, incidentally, that when the pronunciations for **on-yomi** are given, these are conventionally written in katakana, and indicated by uppercase letters in English.

KANJI	PRONUNCIATION	MEANING
火山	**KA·ZAN** カ·ザン	*volcano*
家具	**KA·GU** カ·グ	*furniture*
弓道	**KYŪ·DŌ** キュウ·ドウ	*(Japanese) archery*
同時	**DŌ·JI** ドウ·ジ	*simultaneous*

2. Compounds only rarely mix **on-yomi** and **kun-yomi**. Note here that **kun-yomi** are conventionally written in hiragana, and indicated by lowercase letters in English.

KANJI	PRONUNCIATION	MEANING
中古車	**CHŪ·KO·SHA** チュウ·コ·シャ	*used car*
十二月	**JŪ·NI·GATSU** ジュウ·ニ·ガツ	*December*
小春	**ko·haru** こ·はる	*Indian summer*
花見	**hana·mi** はな·み	*cherry blossom viewing*

3. Kanji in compounds that are accompanied by hiragana are almost always read with their **kun-yomi**.

KANJI (+ HIRIGANA)	PRONUNCIATION	MEANING
切り下げる	**ki·ri sa·geru** き·り さ·げる	*to devalue*
売り家	**u·ri ie** う·り いえ	*"House for sale"*
名高い	**na daka·i** な だか·い	*renowned*
立ち止まる	**ta·chi do·maru** た·ち ど·まる	*to stand still*

4. Kanji that appear alone (that is, they are not part of a compound in a sentence) are usually read with their **kun-yomi**.

KANJI (+ HIRIGANA)	PRONUNCIATION	MEANING
小さい	**chii·sai** ちい・さい	*small*
犬	**inu** いぬ	*dog*
東	**higashi** ひがし	*east*
来る	**ku·ru** く・る	*to come*

You may have noticed words such as "usually" and "almost always" in the above rules. One thing you will soon learn about kanji is that they seem to take delight in turning up exceptions to every rule. The best thing to do is make use of these exceptions as a means to memorize the words in which they appear. Put another way, you will be much further ahead if you learn to love headstrong words that live by their own rules!

Voiced and Unvoiced Sounds

An important consideration in learning to read Japanese is understanding the difference between voiced and unvoiced consonant sounds. Think of this difference by saying aloud the English words "brink" and "bring"; the "k" of "brink" is unvoiced, while the "g" of "bring" is voiced (you need to vibrate your vocal cords to say it). This is the same distinction, for example, between the Japanese sounds "**ka**" and "**ga**" (か and が). What you need to know is that certain kanji can turn from being unvoiced to voiced, depending on where they appear in a compound. The first entry under Table 1 above provides an example: the unvoiced **on-yomi** **SAN** (サン) changes to the voiced **ZAN** (ザン) in the first sample word shown. Although there are an assortment of rules that explain when such changes take place, it is best to develop a "feel" for when these phonetic transformations might occur. Once this happens, your ear will develop to the point where certain compounds begin sounding more natural with one of their kanji voiced.

Irregular Readings

It sometimes occurs in Japanese that a kanji compound has an irregular reading. Known as *jukujikun*, such readings have no relation to the normal **on-** or **kun-yomi** of their component kanji. Rather, these irregular readings are assigned to entire compounds rather than to their component kanji.

You will encounter the first of these in Entry 2. In all three such irregular readings shown there, the reading of the kanji "人" is completely different from what we would expect it to be normally. In a sense, this is much like the problem foreigners face when learning English; the pronunciation of the word "cough", for example, has little connection with the normal sound of the letters from which it is made. Fortunately there are not many irregular readings to be learned (less than thirty appear in this book), but as they are all in common use it is best to come to grips with them the moment they are encountered, by memorizing them as individual words. All irregular readings in this book will be presented separately from the "Common words and compounds" section, to make it clear that these are some truly oddball pronunciations.

A Method for Memorizing the Visual and Aural Aspects of Kanji

As we have seen, kanji are typically more visually complex than hiragana and katakana. Because of this, a good way to simplify the task of committing kanji to memory is to look at their constituent parts. We will do just that, breaking the characters down piece-by-piece and assigning meanings to these components based exclusively on *how they look*. When these various components then join together to build kanji, we will make use of short stories featuring the pieces as "actors", accompanied by drawings to help solidify the appearance of the characters in a unique way. This part of our memorization approach, therefore, will focus exclusively on the visual aspect of each kanji.

For the aural side of the equation, we need to take one other difference between the **on-** and **kun-yomi** into account when devising our memorization strategy: there are far fewer **on-yomi** to learn than **kun-yomi**. This is because **on-yomi** are not often complete words on their own – it helps to think of them as short "blocks" of sound that in most cases form words only when they are strung together. (It is worth keeping in mind, though, that the kanji for numbers are a notable exception to this). Given that roughly 300 **on-yomi** suffice to cover the entire range of Japan's 1,945 general-use characters, a single reading can be attached to many different kanji. **SHŌ** (ショウ), for example, is an **on-yomi** for more that 60 characters. We will be taking advantage of this aspect of Japanese to cut down on the work involved in memorizing these readings.

Our basic plan for committing both the **on-yomi** and **kun-yomi** to memory will be to come up with English keywords that approximate their sounds as closely as possible, and to use these in sentences that also contain a word encompassing the general meaning of the character.

As an example, the kanji for "two" has an **on-yomi** of **NI** (ニ), and a **kun-yomi** of **futa** (ふた). If we choose the word "knee" to suggest **NI**, and the phrase "**who tans**" for **futa**, a possible sentence might be the following: "TWO **knee**s? **Who tan**s only those?". This second side to our approach, therefore, will focus exclusively on the aural aspect of a kanji.

A useful shortcut will involve using the same **on-yomi** keyword every time a kanji having that reading appears (recall that many kanji can share the same **on-yomi**). In the preceding example, therefore, the word "knee" will be used each time a kanji with the **on-yomi** "**NI**" crops up, and will simply be combined with the different **kun-yomi** and meaning of the new kanji. A major advantage of this approach is that it will make easily confused **on-yomi** such as **HŌ** (ホウ) and **HO** (ホ) absolutely distinctive in your mind, as you will have assigned different keywords to each of these. Given their importance (they will need to be used over and over again with different kanji), the creation of **on-yomi** keywords will be left up to you once a few examples have been provided at the beginning of Chapter 1 – your sentences will be more memorable if these words have a distinct personal meaning for you. The **On-Yomi** *Keyword Table* at the end of the book will help you manage your list of these keywords as it grows, and is designed to be filled in as you encounter each **on-yomi** in the pages ahead. By keeping all these readings in one place, you can refer to them quickly when needed.

The **kun-yomi**, on the other hand, are far greater in number, and therefore best learned individually. Fortunately, they tend to be more distinctive than the **on-yomi**, and are, as a result, often easier to remember once a unique keyword phrase has been created. In order to help with the workload in this respect, suggestions for **kun-yomi** keywords are provided with each kanji throughout the book. But you should not hesitate to use an idea of your own should one spring immediately to mind.

Presentation of the Entries In This Book

Each entry will offer one kanji along with a word embracing its broadest possible meaning, followed by a grid showing its stroke order. Next, you'll see a list of the components making up the character, together with reference numbers indicating the points at which these have been introduced earlier in the book. After a short background section describes the various shades of meaning the character conveys, a story (when required) and illustration are presented to help you memorize the kanji visually. A pronunciation section then lists the most common **on-** and **kun-yomi** for the character followed by readings that you will encounter less frequently. Entries conclude with a section showing the character's use in a number of common Japanese words, and a sample sentence in which the kanji is featured. Where space permits, a table for writing practice is also included.

There is an important point to keep in mind with respect to the "Common words and compounds" table in each entry: any word or compound consisting of kanji you have already learned will be shown in **bold face** and in a larger font than the other kanji in the table. This will allow you to focus on reviewing those words you have previously encountered. One useful way to review would involve covering up the right-hand columns in the table with your hand or a piece of paper, then drawing it back to reveal the individual kanji meanings, pronunciation, and the overall meaning of the word in question.

In order to make your task a bit more manageable – you'll be mastering 200 of the most important kanji in Japanese, after all! – the book is divided into chapters of 20 entries each. This will allow you to periodically review a reasonable number of characters before proceeding onward. Short review sections at the end of each chapter will help you check your learning, along with cumulative exercises following Chapters 5 and 10. Use these reviews to see exactly how far you've come in your mastery of the kanji, and to find out which entries to return to for more practice, if you need it. You'll find answer keys, along with indices listing kanji by stroke count, **on-yomi**, **kun-yomi**, and English meaning, at the end of the book. Remember that all of the **on-yomi** are presented in katakana and employ upper-case Roman letters for romaji. The **kun-yomi** are written with hiragana, and have lower-case Roman letters for romaji.

To add an audio aspect to your kanji learning, the accompanying CD-ROM contains pronunciations for all the **on-** and **kun-yomi** found in this book, as well as for the sample sentences and common words in each entry; it will be particularly useful in helping you to select your **on-yomi** keywords. An animated graphic is also provided to show you how each kanji is written using the proper stroke order.

Learning to read kanji is fascinating; the characters, so different from those used in our own writing system, have a mysterious quality that attracts everyone who studies Japanese. As you progress through this book and see how kanji are easily able to present even the most complex ideas, it is worth keeping in mind that you are not only setting out to learn a new means of written communication, but another way of conceptualizing the world around you. It's an exciting task, and by using the present book as your guide you will find this process to be not only interesting, but fun. So let's jump right in – and start mastering Japanese kanji!

CHAPTER 1 (KANJI 1-20)

KANJI 1

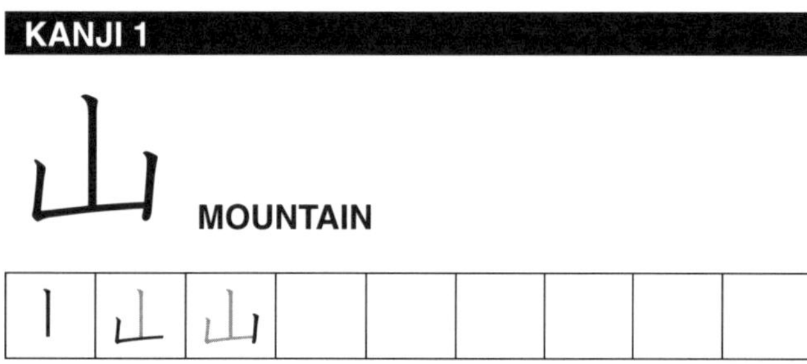

MEANING
Mountain. Our first kanji is one of those wonderful characters whose meaning is obvious at a glance. As kanji such as these are best learned from a simple picture, there is no need for an accompanying story. A number of characters in the book will fall into this category.

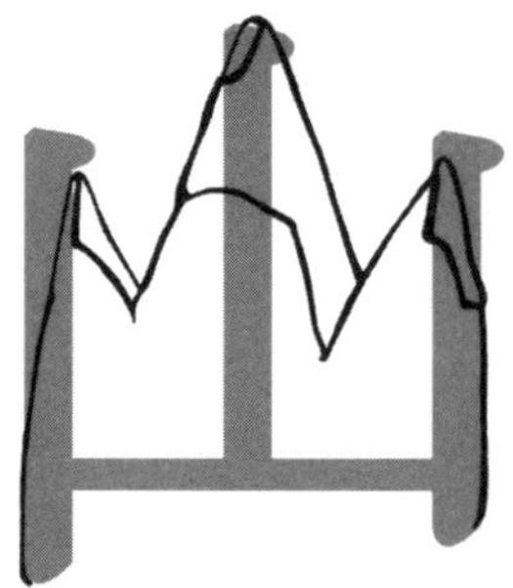

COMMON PRONUNCIATIONS
Common **ON** reading: **SAN** (サン)
Common **kun** reading: **yama** (やま)

This kanji has only one **on-yomi** and one **kun-yomi** (the pronunciation of which – together with all others in this book – can be heard on the accompanying CD-ROM). To suggest these sounds, let's use the word "**SAN**DWICH" for **SAN**, and "**yam a**ttack" for **yama**. As "sandwich" will now be a permanent keyword for all kanji sharing the reading **SAN**, turn to the **on-yomi** table in the back of the book and write "Sandwich" in the space next to **SAN**. Remember that only **on-yomi** (not **kun-yomi**) should be entered in the table.

We now need to link the *meaning* of the kanji to its *sounds* by using the words "mountain", "sandwich", and "yam attack" in a sentence. Let's try this: "On the Mountain I had a **yam a**ttack, so I ate a **SAN**DWICH". For future review, write this sentence in the box below.

Now for some common words that make use of this kanji. There's no need to worry for the moment about being unable to recognize the other characters, as they will all be learned over the course of the book; at this stage, try to see how the meanings of individual kanji combine to form more complex words (look especially at the fourth example below). This is a useful skill, as it will help foster an intuitive feel for the meanings of unfamiliar compounds that you encounter in the future. It is also one of the most rewarding aspects of learning to read the language. Understanding the logic that went into the formation of a compound not only makes it easier to remember, but offers fascinating insight into the minds of the people who devised it hundreds – if not thousands – of years earlier.

Remember that the uppercase letters and *katakana* here indicate **on-yomi**, with lowercase letters and *hiragana* indicating **kun-yomi**. Recall as well from the introduction that this is our first instance of a character whose unvoiced reading can sometimes become voiced (in examples 3 - 4, where the **on-yomi** changes from **SAN** to **ZAN**). Note how the first entry below is presented in bold face — indicating that this is a word you now know.

COMMON WORDS AND COMPOUNDS		
山	*mountain*	**yama** やま
一山	one + mountain = *a pile of something*	hito·**yama** ひと·やま
高山	tall + mountain = *alpine*	**KŌ·ZAN** コウ·ザン
火山	fire + mountain = *volcano*	**KA·ZAN** カ·ザン
山村	mountain + village = *mountain village*	**SAN**·SON サン·ソン

Each entry concludes with a sample sentence featuring the character under discussion; any unfamiliar kanji in these sentences are introduced later in the book.

SAMPLE SENTENCE

山 に 木 が ありません。
yama ni ki ga arimasen.
mountain tree are not
= *There are no trees on the mountain.*

KANJI 2

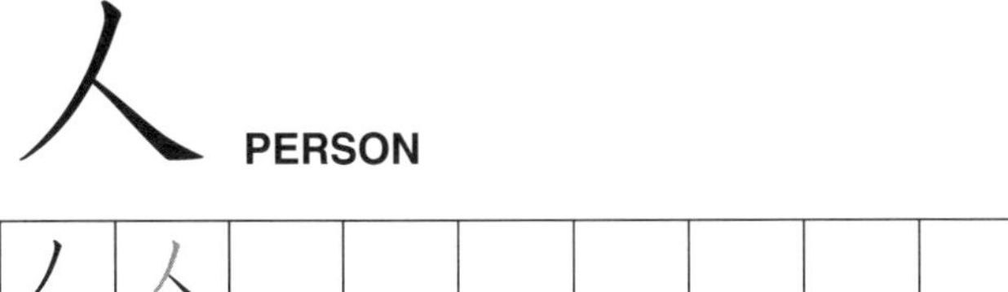

人 PERSON

MEANING
Person/Human being. Another visually simple kanji for which no story is required. When appearing at the end of country names, this kanji denotes an individual's nationality.

COMMON PRONUNCIATIONS
Common **ON** reading: **JIN** (ジン); **NIN** (ニン)
Common **kun** reading: **hito** (ひと)

As mentioned in the introduction, 人 is a character that challenges every student of Japanese. As there are few patterns to its distribution of readings, words containing it often need to be memorized individually. **JIN**, however, tends to signify that a person belongs to a certain subgroup of humanity, while **NIN** indicates a person engaged in an activity specified by the kanji preceding it. Look for **JIN** in the first position and at the end of words signifying countries, and be aware that the **kun-yomi** is always voiced (changes from **hito** to **bito**) when it appears outside of the first position, as it does in the sixth compound below.

We now need our keywords and sentence for the three readings. For **JIN** and **NIN** let's choose "**JEANS**" and "**NIN**COMPOOP". As you did in the previous entry for 山, turn to the **on-yomi** table at the end of the book, but this time write "Jeans" in the space next to **JIN** and "Nincompoop" in the space next to **NIN**. For the **kun-yomi** "**hito**" we'll use "**heat o**pen". We can now throw everything together into the sentence "That Person is a **NIN**compoop because they **heat o**pen their **JEANS**". Remember to write this sentence in the box below so that you can review it later.

Here are our initial encounters with irregular readings. Note that the irregular reading in the first two examples belongs to 人; as you will learn in the next two entries, "一" and "二" are read with their normal **kun-yomi**. In the final compound, both readings are irregular. All three of these words are best thought of as special cases, and memorized individually.

IRREGULAR READINGS		
一人	one + person = *one person*	**hito·ri** ひと·り
二人	two + person = *two people*	**futa·ri** ふた·り
大人	large + person = *adult*	**otona** おとな

COMMON WORDS AND COMPOUNDS		
人	*person*	**hito** ひと
白人	white + person = *caucasian*	HAKU·**JIN** ハク·ジン
人口	person + mouth = *population*	**JIN**·KŌ ジン·コウ
三人	three + person = *three people*	SAN·**NIN** サン·ニン
四人	four + person = *four people*	yo·**NIN** よ·ニン
村人	village + person = *villager*	mura·**bito** むら·びと
外国人	outside + country + person = *foreigner*	GAI·KOKU·**JIN** ガイ·コク·ジン

SAMPLE SENTENCE
あの	人	の	手	は	小さい	です。
ano	**hito**	**no**	**te**	**wa**	**chii·sai**	**desu.**
that	person		hand		small	

= *That person's hands are small.*

WRITING PRACTICE

KANJI 3

一

ONE

一								

MEANING

One. It's hard to find an easier kanji to remember than this!

REMEMBERING THIS KANJI

Despite its simplicity, we need to complicate things a little in order to make use of this character in other kanji. As a result, this character will mean the "top of a hamburger bun" when appearing over all other parts of another character, and the "bottom of a hamburger bun" when it shows up beneath them. But what of a horizontal line found in the middle of a character? Well, that would be the patty (which vegetarians may wish to picture being made of tofu).

"*In the beginning, there was* ONE *shapeless... bun.*"

COMMON PRONUNCIATIONS

Common **ON** readings: **ICHI** (イチ); **ITSU** (イツ)

Common **kun** reading: **hito** (ひと)

Though this is the simplest kanji in a visual sense, knowing when to use which of its readings can be tricky. Now that we have some understanding of the difference between voiced and unvoiced consonant sounds, however, it's much easier for us to make sense of it all. Basically, whenever this kanji appears as the first character in a compound it is almost always read with its **on-yomi**, and its pronunciation of **ICHI** or **ITSU** will depend on whether the initial sound of the following kanji is voiced or voiceless (look closely at the sixth compound of the common words section below to see how the sound of **ITSU** "doubles up" with the sound of the next kanji in this situation). Don't worry if this sounds complicated for now; rest assured it will soon become intuitive as compounds begin sounding more natural with one reading or the other.

We now need a sentence with all three common readings together with the word "one". To suggest the sounds **ICHI** and **ITSU**, let's use "**EACH EEL**" and "**EAT SOUP**". Write these in their respective places in the **on-yomi** table at the back of the book. For the **kun-yomi** "**hito**", we'll use "**he told**". Let's choose the following sentence: "One," **he told** us, "**EACH EEL** must **EAT SOUP**." As before, write this sentence in the box below for future reference.

LESS COMMON PRONUNCIATIONS

Less common **ON** reading: none

Less common **kun** reading: none

Here is another irregular reading; the word "day" appears in brackets to make the logic behind the compound clearer by indicating a secondary meaning of 日 (Entry 6).

IRREGULAR READING		
一日	one I sun (day) = *first day of the month*	**tsuitachi** ついたち

Note that the same compound is shown below with a different pronunciation and meaning. Context will determine which is the appropriate reading to apply; when 一日 is seen at the top of a newspaper page, for example, it clearly refers to the first day of the month and would thus be read "**tsuitachi**" (ついたち).

COMMON WORDS AND COMPOUNDS		
一	*one*	**ICHI** イチ
一つ	*one (general counter)*	**hito**·tsu ひと·つ
一日	one + sun (day) = *one day*	**ICHI**·NICHI イチ·ニチ
一月	one + moon (month) = *January*	**ICHI**·GATSU イチ·ガツ
同一	same + one = *identical*	DŌ·**ITSU** ドウ·イツ
一回	one + rotate = *once*	**IK**·KAI イッ·カイ
一時	one + time = *one o'clock*	**ICHI**·JI イチ·ジ

SAMPLE SENTENCE

一時 に 会いましょう。

ICHI·JI **ni** **a·imashō.**

One o'clock let's meet

= *Let's meet at one o'clock.*

KANJI 4

二 TWO

一	二							

BUILDING THIS KANJI
one 一(3) + **one** 一(3) = 二

MEANING
All things to do with two, including the ideas of "double" and "bi-", etc. Note that the top line is drawn slightly shorter.

REMEMBERING THIS KANJI
On day TWO, things began to emerge in the form of a hamburger-like object.

COMMON PRONUNCIATIONS
Common **ON** reading: **NI** (ニ)
Common **kun** reading: **futa** (ふた)

After that bruising encounter with the pronunciation of 一, things become much simpler with 二, although as you can see below there are also three irregular readings that need to be learned with this character. To suggest our **on-yomi**, let's use "**KNEE**", and for our **kun-yomi**, "**who tans**". After entering KNEE in your **on-yomi** table, write the following sentence in the box below: "Two **KNEES**? **Who tans** only those?"

LESS COMMON PRONUNCIATIONS
Less common **ON** reading: none
Less common **kun** reading: none

Here are three irregular readings that will be frequently encountered. The final kanji in the third example (歳), incidentally, is not covered in this book; such characters will be included only when they form common words in which the pronunciation of the character we are considering has an irregular reading. Irregular readings containing these kanji will be identified with an asterisk (*).

IRREGULAR READINGS		
二日	two + sun (day) = *second day of the month*	**futsuka** ふつか
二十日	two + ten + sun (day) = *twentieth day of the month*	**hatsuka** はつか
二十歳*	two + ten + annual = *twenty years old*	**hatachi** はたち

COMMON WORDS AND COMPOUNDS		
二	*two*	**NI** ニ
二つ	*two (general counter)*	**futa**·tsu ふた·つ
二月	two + moon (month) = *February*	**NI**·GATSU ニ·ガツ
二十	two + ten = *twenty*	**NI**·JŪ ニ·ジュウ
二百	two + hundred = *two hundred*	**NI**·HYAKU ニ·ヒャク
二時	two + time = *two o'clock*	**NI**·JI ニ·ジ
二週間	two + week + interval = *two weeks*	**NI**·SHŪ·KAN ニ·シュウ·カン

SAMPLE SENTENCE

二月 の オーストラリア は 美しい。
NI·GATSU no ōsutoraria wa utsuku·shii.
February Australia beautiful
= *Australia is beautiful in February.*

WRITING PRACTICE

KANJI 5

三 THREE

一	二	三						

BUILDING THIS KANJI
one 一(3) + **one** 一(3) + **one** 一(3) = 三

MEANING
Three/Triple/Tri-, etc.

REMEMBERING THIS KANJI
On day THREE, the full hamburger - in all its glory - came into being.

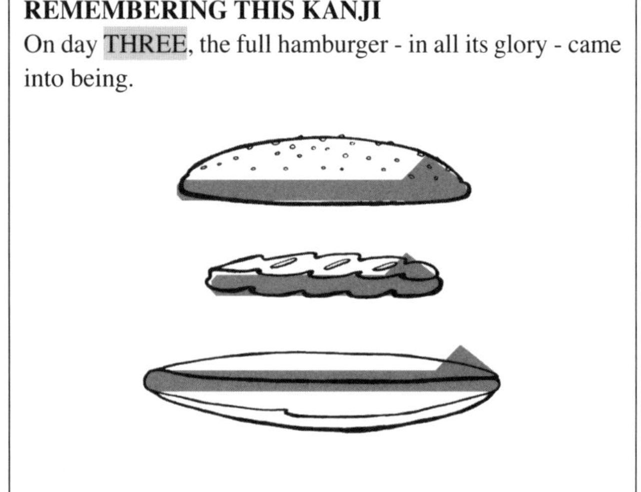

COMMON PRONUNCIATIONS
Common **ON** reading: **SAN** (サン)
Common **kun** reading: none

It's now time to begin making use of our key shortcut for learning the **on-yomi**. As we have already created a keyword for **SAN** (recall the **on-yomi** for "山" in Entry 1), we will now use that same word here. Let's keep things simple and have "Three **SAN**DWICHES" as our phrase. As always, write this in the box below.

LESS COMMON PRONUNCIATIONS
Less common **ON** reading: none
Less common **kun** readings: **mi-** (みっ); **mi** (み)

Here we have our first examples of some less common readings, in this case the two **kun-yomi** "**mi-**" and "**mi**". Keep in mind that "less common" does not equate with "unimportant," as to read Japanese fluently these pronunciations will all have to be learned in time. At this stage, however, it is far more useful to solidify the common readings in your memory and take up the others when they are encountered in the future. When you reach that stage, the appropriate phrase for the respective kanji (e.g. "Three **SAN**DWICHES") can simply be extended to accommodate additional mnemonic words.

In the present example, the first **kun-yomi** appears in only two words, and always "doubles up" in the same way "**ITSU**" (the **on-yomi** for "一") does when preceding voiceless consonant sounds (this is indicated by the short dash after mi). In a sense, this reading is unusual enough to merit the words being learned as if they were irregular readings: 三日 [**mik·ka** (みっ·か)] "the third day of the month", and 三つ [**mit·tsu** (みっ·つ)] the general counter for "three". The second less common reading is more typical of the pronunciations you will find in this section. The words in which it occurs are obscure; it is enough to be aware that such less common readings exist for some of the kanji in this book, but that you don't need to worry about them for now.

COMMON WORDS AND COMPOUNDS		
三	*three*	**SAN** サン
三人	three + person = *three people*	**SAN**·NIN サン·ニン
三月	three + moon (month) = *March*	**SAN**·GATSU サン·ガツ
三時	three + time = *three o'clock*	**SAN**·JI サン·ジ
三十	three + ten = *thirty*	**SAN**·JŪ サン·ジュウ
三千	three + thousand = *three thousand*	**SAN**·ZEN サン·ゼン

SAMPLE SENTENCE

三人 が 早く 来ました。
SAN·NIN ga haya·ku ki·mashita.
Three people early came.
= *Three people came early.*

WRITING PRACTICE

KANJI 6

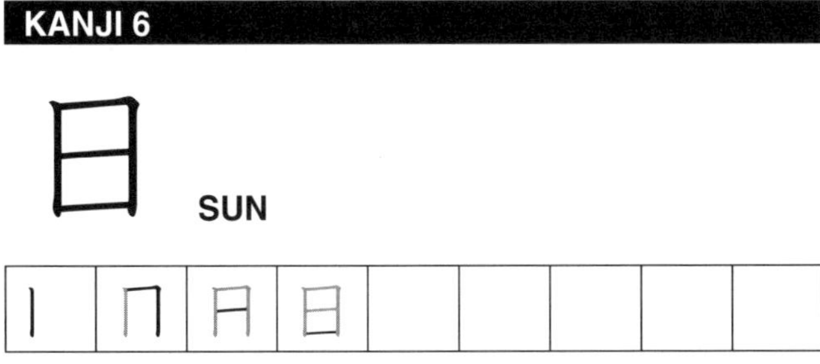

MEANING

This is a kanji with two primary meanings that are clearly related: "sun" and "day". The character will become most familiar to you through its use in the days of the week, and as the initial kanji in the compound for Japan.

This is another character, incidentally, for which we do not need to make use of a story.

COMMON PRONUNCIATIONS

Common **ON** readings: **NICHI** (ニチ); **JITSU** (ジツ)
Common **kun** reading: **hi** (ひ)

日 is another example of a simple-looking kanji that can cause a bit of trouble when it comes to pronunciation. As all three of these readings occur frequently, the best approach is to look for patterns: **NICHI** will be encountered overwhelmingly in the first position (**hi** makes only a few appearances), **JITSU** in the second, and **hi** in the third – where it becomes voiced and pronounced **bi** (び). A perfect example of this odd behavior can be seen in the word Sunday, the final example below. Note also that **NICHI** acts like **ITSU** (from 一) by doubling up any unvoiced consonant sounds that follow it, as can be seen in the more formal rendering of the pronunciation for "Japan", **NIP·PON** (ニッ·ポン), from which the more common **NI·HON** (ニ·ホン) has been derived.

At this point we will now start building our own sentences to memorize pronunciations. First, think of a word to approximate the **on-yomi NICHI** (a German philosoper, perhaps?) and the **on-yomi JITSU** (a martial art, maybe?). Whichever words you decide to use, don't forget to write them in the **on-yomi** table at the back of the book. When it comes to the **kun-yomi**, suggestions will be provided for each one ahead (they can be tough to dream up at times). Don't hesitate, however, to use your own ideas if another word springs immediately to mind. For the present character, try "**he**lium"; use this together with "sun" and your **on-yomi** keywords to create the sentence you will write in the box below.

LESS COMMON PRONUNCIATIONS

Less common **ON** reading: none
Less common **kun** reading: **ka** (か)

ka is used only to identify the days of the month from 2-10, 14, 17, 20, 24 and 27.

Here are four irregular readings (the most that will appear for any character in this book). You've already seen the first.

IRREGULAR READINGS		
一日	one + day = *first day of the month*	**tsuitachi** ついたち
昨日*	past + day = *yesterday*	**kinō** きのう
今日*	now + day = *today*	**kyō** きょう
明日	bright + day = *tomorrow*	**asu** あす **ashita** あした

COMMON WORDS AND COMPOUNDS		
日	*sun; day*	**hi** ひ
一日	one + day = *one day*	ICHI·**NICHI** イチ·ニチ
日本	sun + main = *Japan*	**NI**·HON ニ·ホン **NIP**·PON ニッ·ポン
休日	rest + day = *holiday*	KYŪ·**JITSU** キュウ·ジツ
毎日	every + day = *daily*	MAI·**NICHI** マイ·ニチ
朝日	morning + sun = *morning sun*	asa·**hi** あさ·ひ
日曜日	sun + day of the week + day = *Sunday*	**NICHI**·YŌ·**bi** ニチ·ヨウ·び

SAMPLE SENTENCE

毎日	日本語	の	本	を読みます。
MAI·NICHI	**NI·HON·GO**	**no**	**HON**	**o yo·*mimasu.***
daily	Japanese		book	read

= *(I) read Japanese books every day.*

COMPONENT 7

JELLY BEAN 

Here we have our initial "component". These will always be introduced directly before the first character in which they appear, and will be set apart in a separate text box to indicate that they are **not** themselves kanji on their own.

This little guy, incidentally, can appear at various places and on various angles in a kanji. It can also show up with not only one friend, as in Entry 60, but with two, as in Entry 25.

KANJI 7

WHITE

BUILDING THIS KANJI
Jelly Bean ㇏ + **Sun** 日(6) = 白

MEANING
White. To the Japanese, this color symbolizes cleanliness and purity (which helps explain the presence of so many white cars in the country!). As a result, the kanji can appear in words with this shade of meaning. The fourth compound is an example.

REMEMBERING THIS KANJI
As this kanji is composed of a separate character and a component, our first story will help you to memorize it:

I think it's safe to say that any **jelly bean**, no matter what color it is, will turn WHITE if thrown into the **sun**.

COMMON PRONUNCIATIONS
Common **ON** reading: **HAKU** (ハク)
Common **kun** reading: **shiro** (しろ)

kun-yomi suggestion: "**she wro**te"

Create your **on-yomi** keyword and enter it in the table at the back of the book. After that, write your sentence to remember the **on-yomi** and **kun-yomi** readings in the box below.

LESS COMMON PRONUNCIATIONS
Less common **ON** reading: **BYAKU** (ビャク)
Less common **kun** reading: **shira** (しら)

COMMON WORDS AND COMPOUNDS		
白	*white (noun)*	**shiro** しろ
白い	*white (adjective)*	**shiro·i** しろ·い
白人	white + person = *caucasian*	**HAKU**·JIN ハク·ジン
明白	bright + white = *obvious*	MEI·**HAKU** メイ·ハク
白鳥	white + bird = *swan*	**HAKU**·CHŌ ハク·チョウ
白米	white + rice = *polished rice*	**HAKU**·MAI ハク·マイ

SAMPLE SENTENCE

この 白い 馬 の 名前 は "雪" です。
kono shiro·i uma no na·mae wa "yuki" desu.
this white horse name "snow"
= *This white horse's name is "Snow".*

WRITING PRACTICE

KANJI 8

MOUTH

丨	冂	口						

MEANING

Along with the literal meaning of "mouth" and things oral, the kanji also relates to openings in general, from caves and harbors to taps and bottles, for instance.

REMEMBERING THIS KANJI

Has there ever been a more famous MOUTH than that of Dracula? We will use this image of a vampire to suggest the word "mouth" in our stories from now on; a few other simple characters will be treated like this as well.

COMMON PRONUNCIATIONS

Common **ON** reading: **KŌ** (コウ)
Common **kun** reading: **kuchi** (くち)

Note how the **kun-yomi** for this kanji can become voiced when it appears in the second position, as it does in the fifth example below.

kun-yomi suggestion: "**coochie** coochie coo"

Create your **on-yomi** keyword and enter it in the table at the back of the book. After that, write your sentence to remember the **on-yomi** and **kun-yomi** readings in the box below.

LESS COMMON PRONUNCIATIONS

Less common **ON** reading: **KU** (ク)
Less common **kun** reading: none

COMMON WORDS AND COMPOUNDS		
口	*mouth*	**kuchi** くち
人口	person + mouth = *population*	JIN·**KŌ** ジン·コウ
早口	early (fast) + mouth = *rapid speaking*	haya·**kuchi** はや·くち
口語	mouth + words = *colloquial language*	**KŌ**·GO コウ·ゴ
出口	exit + mouth = *exit*	de·**guchi** で·ぐち
口先	mouth + precede = *lip service*	**kuchi**·saki くち·さき

SAMPLE SENTENCE

この 国 の 人口 は 少ない。
kono kuni no JIN·KŌ wa suku·nai.
this country population few
= *This country has a small population.*

WRITING PRACTICE

COMPONENT 9

PRISON 囗

Though it looks similar to the kanji for "mouth", this component is larger and always completely surrounds whatever happens to be inside it (like a prison should!); this difference can be seen clearly in Entry 9.

KANJI 9

ROTATE

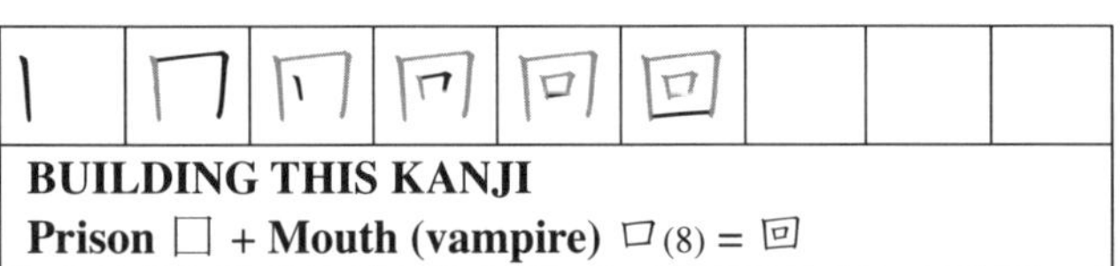

BUILDING THIS KANJI
Prison 囗 + **Mouth (vampire)** 口 (8) = 回

MEANING

Here we see the difference between the "prison" component and the kanji for "mouth". Note that the interior part of this kanji is written following the first two strokes of the prison walls, and becomes enclosed by the final stroke at the bottom. All characters of this type have the same pattern.

The general sense of this kanji relates to the ideas of rotation and going around in both space and time. It can also refer to the vicinity of things (neighborhoods and surroundings, etc), and is well-known to Japanese baseball fans as the character used to denote innings.

REMEMBERING THIS KANJI

It was a great relief for everyone when the **vampire** was finally put in **prison**. It soon became obvious, though, that he could not be kept with the rest of the cons; his offer to "ROTATE the blood" of everyone made them suspicious. The end result, as might be expected, was solitary confinement, a bad enough development for the **vampire** that became even worse when he turned into a bat; flying in endless ROTATIONS apparently brought on some nasty dizzy spells.

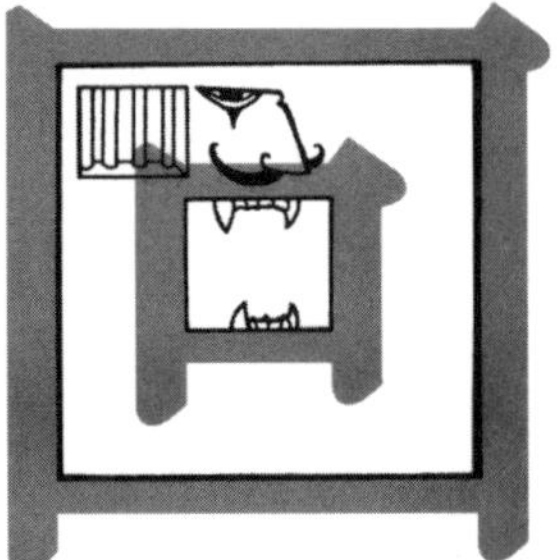

COMMON PRONUNCIATIONS

Common **ON** reading: **KAI** (カイ)
Common **kun** reading: **mawa** (まわ)

kun-yomi suggestion: "lla**ma wa**gon"

Create your **on-yomi** keyword and enter it in the table at the back of the book. After that, write your sentence to remember the **on-yomi** and **kun-yomi** readings in the box below.

LESS COMMON PRONUNCIATIONS

Less common **ON** reading: none
Less common **kun** reading: none

This is a good place to highlight another important aspect of Japanese: the difference between intransitive (intr) and transitive (tr) verbs. Basically, an intransitive verb does not require an object, whereas a transitive verb does. This can be more easily understood by comparing the first two examples given below; a person or thing "goes around" on their own (intransitive), but must have an object to "send around" (transitive). As many Japanese verbs come in such intransitive/transitive pairs (the same kanji accompanied by different *hiragana* attached to the end), it is worth noticing how certain endings often indicate the type of verb; for "**-ru**/**-su**" pairs such as in the example here, the **-su** verb will always be the transitive.

COMMON WORDS AND COMPOUNDS		
回る (intr)	*to go around*	**mawa**·ru まわ·る
回す (tr)	*to send around*	**mawa**·su まわ·す
一回	one + rotate = *one time*	IK·**KAI** イッ·カイ
二回	two + rotate = *twice*	NI·**KAI** ニ·カイ
引き回す	pull + rotate = *to pull around*	hi·ki **mawa**·su ひ·き まわ·す
言い回し	say + rotate = *(turn of) expression*	i·i **mawa**·shi い·い まわ·し

SAMPLE SENTENCE

私 は 二回 カナダ へ 行きました。
watashi wa NI·KAI Canada e i·kimashita.
I twice Canada went.
= *I went to Canada twice.*

COMPONENT 10

BALLET  

We'll be using this component to mean anything to do with the world of ballet.

KANJI 10

 **FOUR**

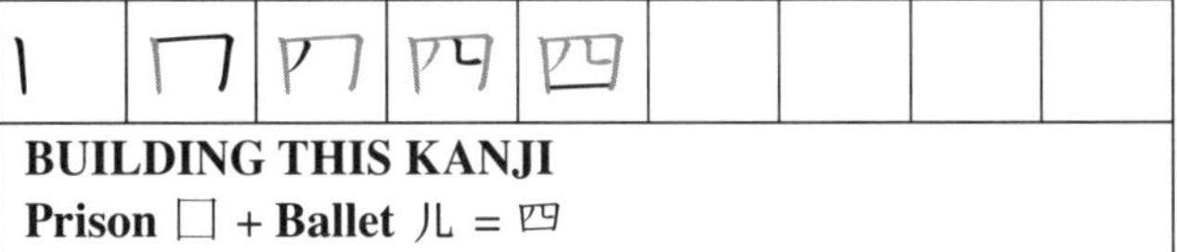

BUILDING THIS KANJI
Prison 口 + **Ballet** 儿 = 四

MEANING
Four/Quad-, etc. Recall what was noted in Entry 9 regarding the proper stroke order for such characters: the inner part is written after the first two strokes of the prison walls, and enclosed by the final line at the bottom.

REMEMBERING THIS KANJI
Look, I'm not able to say for certain why they threw the **ballet** dancer into **prison**, but I do know one thing: they didn't break him. How could I tell? Well, every afternoon during our exercise period, while the rest of us inmates were either pumping iron or sharpening our shivs, there he'd be, dancing to the FOUR corners of the **prison** walls. We all respected him for it, I suppose; not a single con in those FOUR corners ever laughed at his tights.

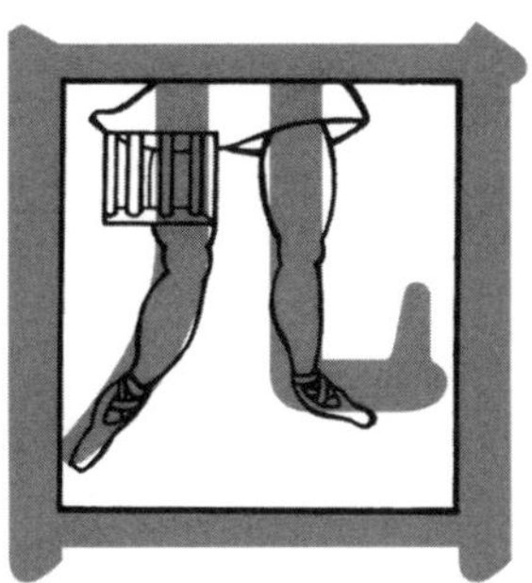

COMMON PRONUNCIATIONS
Common **ON** reading: **SHI** (シ)
Common **kun** readings: **yon** (よん); **yo** (よ)

Do not choose the word "SHE" for your **on-yomi**, as we will be needing it far more for **kun-yomi**, and a word less abstract (try to think of things, places or people) will always be more memorable and make your sentences easier to create. As you can see from the examples below, this character has a tendency to appear in compounds having a mix of **kun-yomi** and **on-yomi**; this makes it a little trickier than the other kanji for numbers.

kun-yomi suggestions: "l**ie** **on**ly"; "**yo**del"

Create your **on-yomi** keyword and enter it in the table at the back of the book. After that, write your sentence to remember the **on-yomi** and **kun-yumi** readings in the box below.

LESS COMMON PRONUNCIATIONS
Less common **ON** reading: none
Less common **kun** reading: **yo-** (よっ)

This reading is like the less common **kun-yomi** for "three" in that it appears in only two words: 四日 [**yok·ka** (よっ·か)] "the fourth day of the month", and 四つ [**yot·tsu** (よっ·つ)] the general counter for "four". These words are best learned as if they were ateji.

COMMON WORDS AND COMPOUNDS		
四	*four*	**SHI** シ
四人	four + person = *four*	**yo**·NIN よ·ニン
四月	four + moon (month) = *April*	**SHI**·GATSU シ·ガツ
四時	four + time = *four o'clock*	**yo**·JI よ·ジ
四十	four + ten = *forty*	**yon**·JŪ よん·ジュウ
四百	four + hundred = *four hundred*	**yon**·HYAKU よん·ヒャク

SAMPLE SENTENCE

四月 には 雨 が 多い。
SHI·GATSU ni wa ame ga ō·i.
April rain many.
= *There's a lot of rain in April.*

KANJI 11

月 MOON

ノ	刀	月	月					

MEANING

As with the kanji for "sun", this character carries two meanings that are clearly related, in this case "moon" and "month". You will become very familiar with this kanji through its use in the names of the months. This is another visually simple character for which no story is required.

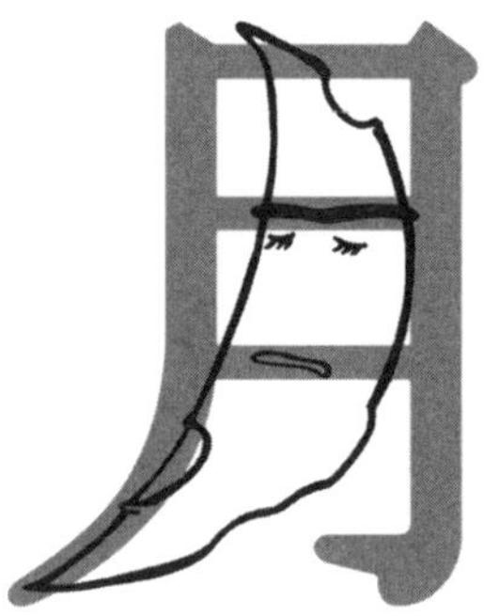

COMMON PRONUNCIATIONS

Common **ON** readings: **GETSU** (ゲツ); **GATSU** (ガツ)
Common **kun** reading: **tsuki** (つき)

Like **ITSU** (with the kanji "一") and other readings ending in "**-TSU**", the two **on-yomi** double up any unvoiced consonant sounds that follow. You will encounter **GATSU** primarily in the names of the months.

kun-yomi suggestion: "bough**t** **Sioux** **kee**psakes"

Create your **on-yomi** keyword and enter it in the table at the back of the book. After that, write your sentence to remember the **on-yomi** and **kun-yomi** readings in the box below.

LESS COMMON PRONUNCIATIONS

Less common **ON** reading: none
Less common **kun** reading: none

COMMON WORDS AND COMPOUNDS		
月	*moon; month*	**tsuki** つき
一月	one + month = *January*	ICHI·**GATSU** イチ·ガツ
二月	two + month = *February*	NI·**GATSU** ニ·ガツ
三月	three + month = *March*	SAN·**GATSU** サン·ガツ
四月	four + month = *April*	SHI·**GATSU** シ·ガツ
先月	precede + month = *last month*	SEN·**GETSU** セン·ゲツ
月見	moon + see = *moon viewing*	**tsuki**·mi つき·み

SAMPLE SENTENCE

九月 に 月見 に 行きました。
KU·GATSU ni tsuki·mi ni i·kimashita.
September moon viewing went
= *I went moon viewing in September.*

WRITING PRACTICE

KANJI 12

BRIGHT

BUILDING THIS KANJI
Sun 日 (6) + **Moon** 月 (11) = 明

MEANING
Bright/Clear/Light.

REMEMBERING THIS KANJI
"I'm far more BRIGHT than you are," said the **moon**.
"Really?" answered the **sun**, smiling. "I find that hard to believe. I'm so BRIGHT people have to wear shades; how many people do you notice wearing **moon**glasses."
The **moon** looked confused. "What are you talking about?" he said. "There's no such thing as **moon**glasses."
"You know," sighed the **sun**, "you're even less BRIGHT than I thought."

COMMON PRONUNCIATIONS
Common **ON** reading: **MEI** (メイ)
Common **kun** readings: **a** (あ); **aka** (あか)

kun-yomi suggestions: "**a**pt"; "st**ack a**…".

Write your sentence to remember the readings below.

LESS COMMON PRONUNCIATIONS
Less common **ON** readings: **MYŌ** (ミョウ); **MIN** (ミン)
Less common **kun** reading: **aki** (あき)

COMMON WORDS AND COMPOUNDS		
明るい	*bright*	**aka**·rui あか·るい
明かり	*clearness*	**a**·kari あ·かり
明白	bright + white = *obvious*	**MEI**·HAKU メイ·ハク
不明	not + bright = *unclear*	FU·**MEI** フ·メイ

SAMPLE SENTENCE

月　は　明るい　です。
tsuki　wa　aka·rui　desu.
moon　　bright
= *The moon is bright.*

WRITING PRACTICE

KANJI 13

TREE

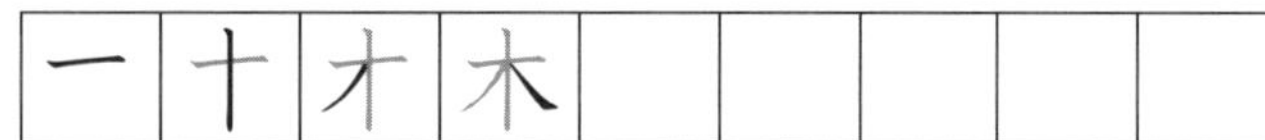

MEANING
Tree/Wood. No story required.

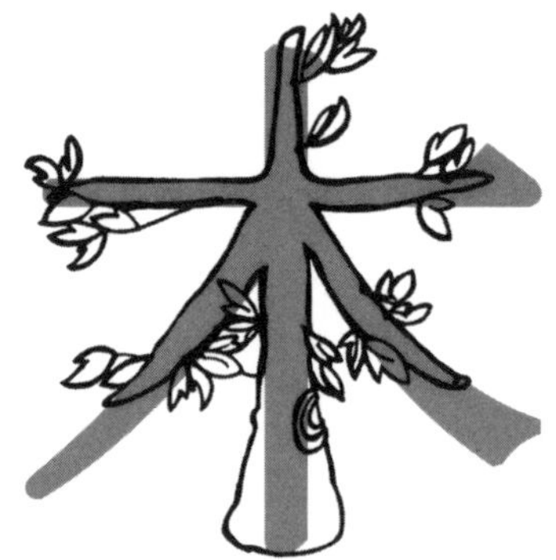

COMMON PRONUNCIATIONS
Common **ON** readings: **MOKU** (モク); **BOKU** (ボク)
Common **kun** reading: **ki** (き)

This is another kanji that will require patience to learn. Look for **MOKU** to show up in the first position, however, and **BOKU** in the second. **ki** occurs less often, but appears with equal frequency in the first or second position.

kun-yomi suggestion: "**kee**l" (do not use "key", as this will have far more value as an **on-yomi** keyword).

Create your **on-yomi** keyword and enter it in the table at the back of the book. After that, write your sentence to remember the **on-yomi** and **kun-yomi** readings in the box below.

LESS COMMON PRONUNCIATIONS
Less common **ON** reading: none
Less common **kun** reading: **ko** (こ)

Here is a common irregular reading you will often see on clothing tags, etc.

IRREGULAR READING		
木綿*	tree + cotton = *cotton (cloth)*	**mo·MEN** も·メン

COMMON WORDS AND COMPOUNDS		
木	*tree*	**ki** き
木曜日	tree + day of the week + sun (day) = *Thursday*	**MOKU**·YŌ·bi モク·ヨウ·び
木星	tree + star = *Jupiter (planet)*	**MOKU**·SEI モク·セイ
大木	large + tree = *large tree*	TAI·**BOKU** タイ·ボク
土木	earth + tree = *civil engineering*	DO·**BOKU** ド·ボク

SAMPLE SENTENCE

あの 高い 木 の 名前 が 分かります か。
ano taka·i ki no na·mae ga wa·karimasu ka.
that tall tree name understand
= *Do you know the name of that tall tree?*

WRITING PRACTICE

KANJI 14

FIVE

MEANING
Five.

REMEMBERING THIS KANJI
This is how most people feel when their work day ends at FIVE o'clock.

COMMON PRONUNCIATIONS
Common **ON** reading: **GO** (ゴ)
Common **kun** reading: none

Create your **on-yomi** keyword and enter it in the table at the back of the book. After that, write your sentence to remember the **on-yomi** reading in the box below.

LESS COMMON PRONUNCIATIONS
Less common **ON** reading: none
Less common **kun** reading: **itsu** (いつ)

As you might expect, this reading is of most use because of its appearance in two words: 五日 [**itsu·ka** (いつ·か)] "the fifth day of the month", and 五つ [**itsu·tsu** (いつ·つ)] the general counter for "five".

COMMON WORDS AND COMPOUNDS

五	*five*	**GO** ゴ
五人	five + person = *five people*	**GO**·NIN ゴ·ニン
五月	five + moon (month) = *May*	**GO**·GATSU ゴ·ガツ
五十	five + ten = *fifty*	**GO**·JŪ ゴ·ジュウ
五時	five + time = *five o'clock*	**GO**·JI ゴ·ジ

SAMPLE SENTENCE

五十人 で 山 へ 行きました。
GO·JŪ·NIN de yama e i·kimashita.
fifty people mountain went
= *Fifty (of us) went to the mountain.*

WRITING PRACTICE

KANJI 15

目 EYE

丨	冂	月	月	目				

MEANING

The general meaning is eye. An important secondary usage of the character, however, can be seen when it comes at the end of a number compound such as in the third example below. In these instances it is read with its **kun-yomi** and indicates the "-th" suffix in words such as "fourth" and "seventh" (it also expresses the related endings of "first", "second" and "third" in such compounds).

REMEMBERING THIS KANJI

In the interests of full disclosure, it should be said that the Cyclops lobbied long and hard to be this book's representative for "EYE". Well, it looks like his efforts – which included a few thoughtfully chosen gifts – have paid off. Cyclops, you have been placed on an equal footing with Dracula!

COMMON PRONUNCIATIONS

Common **ON** reading: **MOKU** (モク)
Common **kun** reading: **me** (め)

me is the more common of the two readings. Remember to use the keyword for **MOKU** that you entered into the **on-yomi** table earlier (from the kanji "木", Entry 13).

kun-yomi suggestion: "**ma**te"

Create your **on-yomi** keyword and enter it in the table at the back of the book. After that, write your sentence to remember the **on-yomi** and **kun-yomi** readings in the box below.

LESS COMMON PRONUNCIATIONS

Less common **ON** reading: **BOKU** (ボク)
Less common **kun** reading: **ma** (ま)

COMMON WORDS AND COMPOUNDS		
目	*eye*	**me** め
目玉	eye + jewel = *eyeball*	**me**·dama め·だま
八回目	eight + rotate + eye = *the eighth time*	HACHI·KAI·**me** ハチ·カイ·め
目立つ	eye + stand = *to stand out*	**me** da·tsu め だ·つ
注目	pour + eye = *notice*	CHŪ·**MOKU** チュウ·モク

SAMPLE SENTENCE

王子 の 目 は 青い です。
Ō·JI no me wa ao·i desu.
prince eye blue
= *The prince's eyes are blue.*

WRITING PRACTICE

KANJI 16

女 WOMAN

𠃋	𡿨	女						

MEANING
Woman/Female. No story required.

COMMON PRONUNCIATIONS
Common **ON** reading: **JO** (ジョ)
Common **kun** reading: **onna** (おんな)

kun-yomi suggestion: "**own NASA**"

Create your **on-yomi** keyword and enter it in the table at the back of the book. After that, write your sentence to remember the **on-yomi** and **kun-yomi** readings in the box below.

LESS COMMON PRONUNCIATIONS
Less common **ON** readings: **NYO** (ニョ); **NYŌ** (ニョウ)
Less common **kun** reading: **me** (め)

COMMON WORDS AND COMPOUNDS		
女	*woman*	**onna** おんな
女王	woman + king = *queen*	**JO·Ō** ジョ·オウ
少女	few + woman = *girl*	SHŌ·**JO** ショウ·ジョ
女心	woman + heart = *a woman's heart*	**onna**·gokoro おんな·ごころ
雪女	snow + woman = *snow fairy*	yuki·**onna** ゆき·おんな
男女	man + woman = *men and women*	DAN·**JO** ダン·ジョ

SAMPLE SENTENCE

女 の 人 は 木 の 下 で 止まりました。
onna no hito wa ki no shita de to·marimashita.
woman person tree under stopped
= *The woman stopped under a tree.*

WRITING PRACTICE

KANJI 17

LARGE

一	ナ	大						

MEANING

Large/Big. The meanings of "important" and "great (not always in a positive sense)" can also be implied in words containing this kanji.

REMEMBERING THIS KANJI

Not many things are LARGER than a sumo wrestler, so we'll use this image as our connection to the character from now on.

COMMON PRONUNCIATIONS

Common **ON** readings: **DAI** (ダイ); **TAI** (タイ)

Common **kun** reading: **ō** (おお)

As **DAI** and **TAI** occur with equal frequency (**ō** much less often) when this kanji appears in the first position, this character presents a special challenge for students of Japanese. When it occupies other positions in a compound, however, **DAI** is far and away the more common reading.

kun-yomi suggestion: "**o**boe"

Create your **on-yomi** keywords and enter them in the table at the back of the book. After that, write your sentence to remember the **on-yomi** and **kun-yomi** readings in the box below.

LESS COMMON PRONUNCIATIONS

Less common **ON** reading: none

Less common **kun** reading: none

Here is the irregular reading we met earlier in Entry 2.

IRREGULAR READING		
大人	large + person = *adult*	**otona** おとな

COMMON WORDS AND COMPOUNDS		
大きい	*large*	**ō**·kii おお·きい
大木	large + tree = *large tree*	**TAI**·BOKU タイ·ボク
大好き	large + like – *to really like*	**DAI** su·ki ダイ す·き
大体	large + body = *in general*	**DAI**·TAI ダイ·タイ
大雨	large + rain = *heavy rain*	**ō**·ame おお·あめ
大切	large + cut = *important*	**TAI**·SETSU タイ·セツ
大学	large + study = *university*	**DAI**·GAKU ダイ·ガク

SAMPLE SENTENCE

あの 森 には 大木 が 多い。

ano mori ni wa TAI·BOKU ga ō·i.

that forest large trees many

= *There are many large trees in that forest.*

WRITING PRACTICE

COMPONENT 18

POLE

KANJI 18

MIDDLE

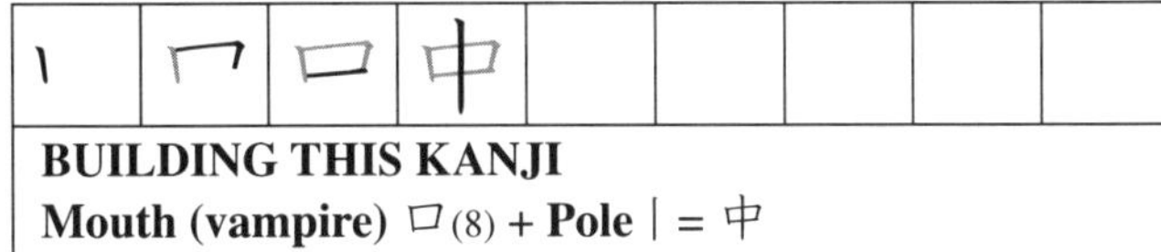

BUILDING THIS KANJI

Mouth (vampire) 口(8) + **Pole** 丨 = 中

MEANING

A versatile character that expresses the ideas of "middle", "medium", and "average", etc. This kanji can also serve as an abbreviation for China; " 日 " is used as the equivalent with respect to Japan.

REMEMBERING THIS KANJI

I approached the sleeping **vampire** with the **pole** shaking in my hands: it was now or never. Raising the weapon over his feet I prepared to bring it down, but at the last moment the master's words came back: "How many times must we go over this? Drive it through the MIDDLE of the **vampire**! The MIDDLE!" Yes, I thought, placing the **pole** over the **vampire's** stomach, it would all go perfectly now.

COMMON PRONUNCIATIONS

Common **ON** reading: **CHŪ** (チュウ)
Common **kun** reading: **naka** (なか)

kun-yomi suggestion: "**knack 'a**"

Create your **on-yomi** keyword and enter it in the table at the back of the book. After that, write your sentence to remember the **on-yomi** and **kun-yomi** readings in the box below.

LESS COMMON PRONUNCIATIONS

Less common **ON** reading: **JŪ** (ジュウ)
Less common **kun** reading: none

COMMON WORDS AND COMPOUNDS		
中	*middle*	**naka** なか
中心	middle + heart = *center*	**CHŪ**·SHIN チュウ·シン
中米	middle + rice (America) = *Central America*	**CHŪ**·BEI チュウ·ベイ
中国	middle + country = *China*	**CHŪ**·GOKU チュウ·ゴク
中立	middle + stand = *neutrality*	**CHŪ**·RITSU チュウ·リツ
中古	middle + old = *secondhand*	**CHŪ**·KO チュウ·コ
水中	water + middle = *underwater/in the water*	SUI·**CHŪ** スイ·チュウ

SAMPLE SENTENCE

車 の 中 に なに が あります か。
kuruma no naka ni nani ga arimasu ka.
car middle what is
= *What is in your car?*

WRITING PRACTICE

KANJI 19

八 EIGHT

ノ	八							

MEANING
Eight.

REMEMBERING THIS KANJI
This is another kanji in the manner of "one" and "mouth" for which it is useful to assign an external meaning, in this case, a volcano:
"I can't be sure, but I think the Krakatoa volcano (which erupted in the 1880's) was one of the EIGHT *wonders of the ancient world."*

COMMON PRONUNCIATIONS
Common **ON** reading: **HACHI** (ハチ)
Common **kun** reading: none

Create your **on-yomi** keyword and enter it in the table at the back of the book. After that, write your sentence to remember the **on-yomi** reading in the box below.

LESS COMMON PRONUNCIATIONS
Less common **ON** reading: none
Less common **kun** readings: **yō** (よう); **ya-** (やっ); **ya** (や)

Interestingly, the first two **kun-yomi** readings are like the less common **kun-yomi** for "three" and "four" (Entries 5 and 10, respectively), and are found in only one word each: 八日 [**yō·ka** (よう·か)] "the eighth day of the month", and 八つ [**yat·tsu** (やっ·つ)] the general counter for "eight".

COMMON WORDS AND COMPOUNDS

八	*eight*	**HACHI** ハチ
八月	eight + moon (month) = *August*	**HACHI**·GATSU ハチ·ガツ
八人	eight + person = *eight people*	**HACHI**·NIN ハチ·ニン
八円	eight + circle (yen) = *eight yen*	**HACHI**·EN ハチ·エン
八時	eight + time = *eight o'clock*	**HACHI**·JI ハチ·ジ

SAMPLE SENTENCE

八月	に	秋田	へ	行きましょう。
HACHI·GATSU	**ni**	**Aki·ta**	**e**	**i·kimashō.**
August		Akita		let's go

= Let's go to Akita in August.

WRITING PRACTICE

COMPONENT 20

HARPOON 亅 

Note how the barbed hook on the bottom of this component distinguishes it from the pole (Component 18).

KANJI 20

小 SMALL

亅	小	小						

BUILDING THIS KANJI
Harpoon 亅 **+ Eight (volcano)** 八(19) = 小

MEANING
Small/Little.

REMEMBERING THIS KANJI
The dwarf spoke, his words SMALL comfort: "If you be going after the miniature lava whale," he said, "you'd best toss your **harpoon** in that there **volcano** over yonder. Your chances of landing him are SMALL, though, given that he's so… SMALL."

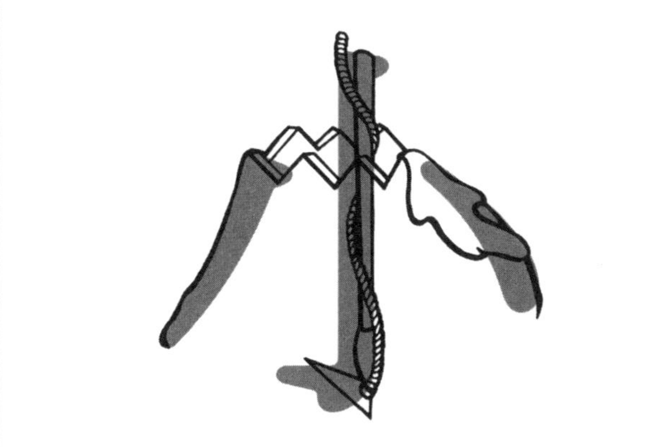

COMMON PRONUNCIATIONS
Common **ON** reading: **SHŌ** (ショウ)
Common **kun** readings: **chii** (ちい); **ko** (こ)

SHŌ and **ko** are the readings most often found in compounds, **chii** only being used in the first example below.

kun-yomi suggestions: "**cheeee**se!"; "**co**at"

Create your **on-yomi** keyword and enter it in the table at the back of the book. After that, write your sentence to remember the **on-yomi** and **kun-yomi** readings in the box below.

LESS COMMON PRONUNCIATIONS
Less common **ON** reading: none
Less common **kun** reading: **o** (お)

COMMON WORDS AND COMPOUNDS		
小さい	*small*	**chii**·sai ちい·さい
小春	small + spring = *Indian summer*	**ko**·haru こ·はる
小国	small + country = *small country*	**SHŌ**·KOKU ショウ·コク
小高い	small + tall = *slightly elevated*	**ko** daka·i こ だか·い
最小	most + small = *smallest*	SAI·**SHŌ** サイ·ショウ

SAMPLE SENTENCE

あの 車 は とても 小さい です ね。
ano kuruma wa totemo chii·sai desu ne.
that car really small isn't it
= *That car is really small, isn't it?*

WRITING PRACTICE

CHAPTER 1 REVIEW EXERCISES

A. Please match the following kanji to their meanings.

1. 人	a. Rotate
2. 女	b. Large
3. 月	c. Woman
4. 木	d. Mouth
5. 大	e. Person
6. 二	f. Two
7. 回	g. Moon
8. 小	h. Three
9. 三	i. Tree
10. 口	j. Small

B. Please match the following meanings to their kanji, and these to their **on** or **kun-yomi**.

1. Bright	a. 白	1. **yama** (やま)
2. Five	b. 目	2. **ICHI** (イチ)
3. White	c. 山	3. **me** (め)
4. Four	d. 八	4. **hi** (ひ)
5. Eye	e. 日	5. **GO** (ゴ)
6. Middle	f. 一	6. **HACHI** (ハチ)
7. Mountain	g. 明	7. **SHI** (シ)
8. One	h. 中	8. **aka** (あか)
9. Eight	i. 四	9. **naka** (なか)
10. Sun	j. 五	10. **HAKU** (ハク)

C. Please choose the best answer(s) to the following questions.

1. Which of the following readings apply to the kanji 人?
   a. **Ō** (オウ)
   b. **hito** (ひと)
   c. **NIN** (ニン)
   d. **JIN** (ジン)
   e. **hi** (ひ)

2. Where is the most appropriate place to go in a spaceship?
   a. 人
   b. 目
   c. 月
   d. 口
   e. 木

3. Which of the following readings apply to the kanji 女?
   a. **ZEN** (ゼン)
   b. **SHUN** (シュン)
   c. **uchi** (うち)
   d. **JO** (ジョ)
   e. **onna** (おんな)

4. Which of the following readings apply to the kanji 口?
   a. **KŌ** (コウ)
   b. **haru** (はる)
   c. **SHI** (シ)
   d. **kuchi** (くち)
   e. **Ō** (オウ)

5. Which of the following readings apply to the kanji 日?
   a. **hi** (ひ)
   d. **to** (と)
   b. **KOKU** (コク)
   e. **JITSU** (ジツ)
   c. **NICHI** (ニチ)

D. Please answer the following questions.

1. Which is the correct reading of 回る?
   a. **mi·ru** (み·る)
   b. **sube·ru** (すべ·る)
   c. **haka·ru** (はか·る)
   d. **mawa·ru** (まわ·る)

2. What is the reading for 一日 when it indicates the first day of a month?
   a. **tama** (たま)
   b. **kuni** (くに)
   c. **uchi** (うち)
   d. **kuchi** (くち)
   e. **tsuitachi** (ついたち)

3. Given that **hitori** (ひとり) is the reading for 一人, what is the reading for 二人?
   a. **hatsuka** (はつか)
   b. **futari** (ふたり)
   c. **hatachi** (はたち)
   d. **futsuka** (ふつか)

4. Which of the following does not belong with the others?
   a. 一
   b. 八
   c. 四
   d. 小
   e. 三

5. Which is the correct reading of 白い?
   a. **furu·i** (ふる·い)
   b. **shiro·i** (しろ·い)
   c. **maru·i** (まる·い)
   d. **hiro·i** (ひろ·い)

E. Please match the following compounds and words to their meanings and pronunciations.

1. 三月	a. Twice	1. **hito·tsu** (ひと·つ)
2. 白人	b. Obvious	2. **JIN·KŌ** (ジン·コウ)
3. 二回	c. White	3. **shiro·i** (しろ·い)
4. 小さい	d. Five people	4. **SAN·GATSU** (サン·ガツ)
5. 明白	e. Small	5. **chii·sai** (ちい·さい)
6. 人口	f. March	6. **NI·KAI** (ニ·カイ)
7. 一つ	g. Large tree	7. **GO·NIN** (ゴ·ニン)
8. 五人	h. One	8. **TAI·BOKU** (タイ·ボク)
9. 白い	i. Population	9. **HAKU·JIN** (ハク·ジン)
10. 大木	j. Caucasian	10. **MEI·HAKU** (メイ·ハク)

CHAPTER 2 (KANJI 21-40)

KANJI 21

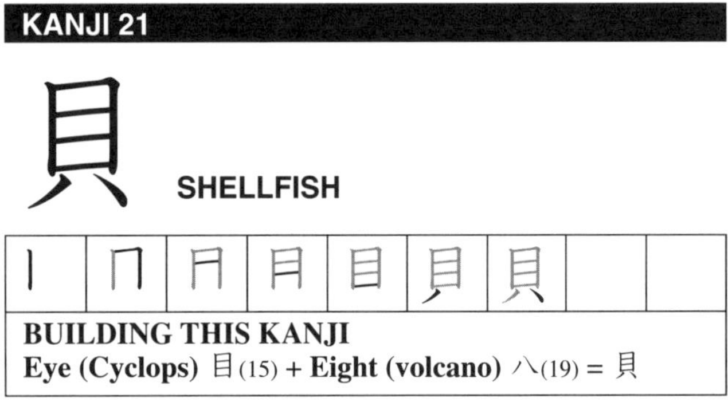

BUILDING THIS KANJI
Eye (Cyclops) 目(15) + **Eight (volcano)** 八(19) = 貝

MEANING

Shellfish/Seashell. As the lack of common words and compounds in the table indicates, this is not the most useful character to learn for its own sake. It often appears as a component in other kanji, however, and for this reason needs to be learned here.

REMEMBERING THIS KANJI

Celebrating his inclusion in this book, the **Cyclops** decided to throw an enormous SHELLFISH barbecue for all his friends. Minotaurs, griffins, nymphs and satyrs… even the sirens showed up (after agreeing to refrain from singing, of course). It was quite a crowd, but the grill the **Cyclops** stretched over a nearby **volcano** was more than enough to accommodate the food. And what a variety of SHELLFISH there was! Oysters, mussels, abalone, scallops…everyone agreed it was the best spread since Zeus' clambake on Mt. Etna.

COMMON PRONUNCIATIONS

Common **ON** reading: none
Common **kun** reading: **kai** (かい)

This character is always unvoiced (**kai**) in the first position, and becomes voiced (**gai**) elsewhere.

kun-yomi suggestion: "**Kai**ser roll". If you are choosing your own keywords for the **kun-yomi**, do not use the same word you selected for **KAI** (カイ), the **on-yomi** for "回" in Entry 9; it is best to keep the two types of readings separate. Create your sentence to remember the **kun-yomi** reading in the box below.

LESS COMMON PRONUNCIATIONS

Less common **ON** reading: **BAI** (バイ)
Less common **kun** reading: none

COMMON WORDS AND COMPOUNDS		
貝	*shellfish*	**kai** かい
生貝	life + shellfish = *raw shellfish*	nama·**gai** なま·がい
赤貝	red + shellfish = *ark shell*	aka·**gai** あか·がい

SAMPLE SENTENCE

このレストランの 赤貝 は 有名 です。
kono resutoran no aka·gai wa YŪ·MEI desu.
this restaurant ark shell famous is
= *The ark shell in this restaurant is famous.*

WRITING PRACTICE

COMPONENT 22

POLICE  

Our hat will symbolize the police, or any other authority from sheriffs to park rangers.

KANJI 22

 **SIX**

BUILDING THIS KANJI
Police 亠 **+ Eight (volcano)** 八(19) = 六

MEANING
Six.

REMEMBERING THIS KANJI
Something tells me that if you throw a police hat into a volcano, it will burn. Don't ask me how I know this; it's my SIXTH sense.

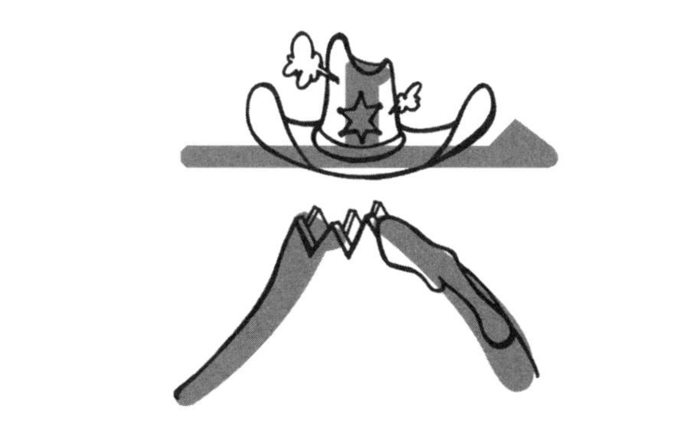

COMMON PRONUNCIATIONS
Common **ON** reading: **ROKU** (ロク)
Common **kun** reading: none

Create your **on-yomi** keyword and enter it in the table at the back of the book. After that, write your sentence to remember the **on-yomi** reading in the box below.

LESS COMMON PRONUNCIATIONS
Less common **ON** reading: **RIKU** (リク)
Less common **kun** readings: **mui** (むい); **mu-** (むっ); **mu** (む)

You may have guessed that these first two **kun-yomi** are found in only one word each: 六日 [**mui·ka** (むい·か)] "the sixth day of the month", and 六つ [**mut·tsu** (むっ·つ)] the general counter for "six".

COMMON WORDS AND COMPOUNDS		
六	*six*	**ROKU** ロク
六人	six + person = *six people*	**ROKU**·NIN ロク·ニン
六月	six + moon (month) = *June*	**ROKU**·GATSU ロク·ガツ
六円	six + circle (yen) = *six yen*	**ROKU**·EN ロク·エン
六時	six + time = *six o'clock*	**ROKU**·JI ロク·ジ

SAMPLE SENTENCE

六人 は 日本 へ 行きました。
ROKU·NIN wa NI·HON e i·kimashita.
six people Japan went
= *The six people went to Japan.*

WRITING PRACTICE

KANJI 23

KING

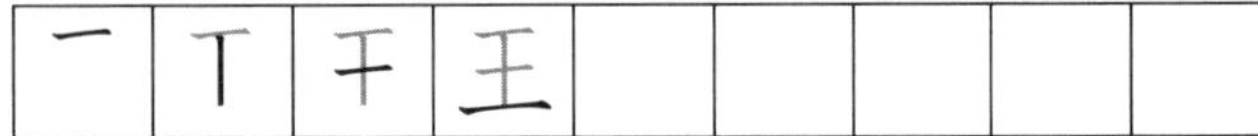

MEANING

Crowns, scepters, long purple robes…think of kings and royalty when you see this kanji. No story required.

COMMON PRONUNCIATIONS

Common **ON** reading: **Ō** (オウ)
Common **kun** reading: none

Only one reading to deal with here — wouldn't it be nice if all the kanji were this well-behaved? Create your **on-yomi** keyword and enter it in the table at the back of the book. After that, write your sentence to remember the **on-yomi** reading in the box below.

LESS COMMON PRONUNCIATIONS

Less common **ON** reading: none
Less common **kun** reading: none

COMMON WORDS AND COMPOUNDS		
女王	women + king = *queen*	JO·**Ō** ジョ·オウ
王国	king + country = *kingdom*	**Ō**·KOKU オウ·コク
王朝	king + morning = *dynasty*	**Ō**·CHŌ オウ·チョウ
王子	king + child = *prince*	**Ō**·JI オウ·ジ
海王星	sea + king + star = *Neptune (planet)*	KAI·**Ō**·SEI カイ·オウ·セイ

SAMPLE SENTENCE

女王 が 日本 へ 行きました。
JO·Ō ga NIHON e i·kimashita.
Queen Japan went.
= *The queen went to Japan.*

WRITING PRACTICE

KANJI 24

JEWEL

一	T	干	王	玉				
BUILDING THIS KANJI **King** 王(23) + **Jelly Bean** ヽ = 玉								

MEANING

This character appears in the names of a variety of precious stones, including the compounds for rubies, sapphires, and emeralds. It also incorporates the sense of a "ball-like" object, a meaning evident in the final examples below.

Take note of the correct stroke order for this kanji ("King" + "Jelly bean"); the three horizontal lines are **not** written first.

REMEMBERING THIS KANJI

"I wish to reward you for your faithful service," the **king** said to his minister. "There is a **jelly bean** for you at my feet; you may take it if you wish." The man was a little confused by this, of course, until he bent down and saw a JEWEL shaped like a **jelly bean** next to the **king's** shoes. "You might not want to eat that," smiled the **king**. "After all, JEWELS aren't particularly tasty."

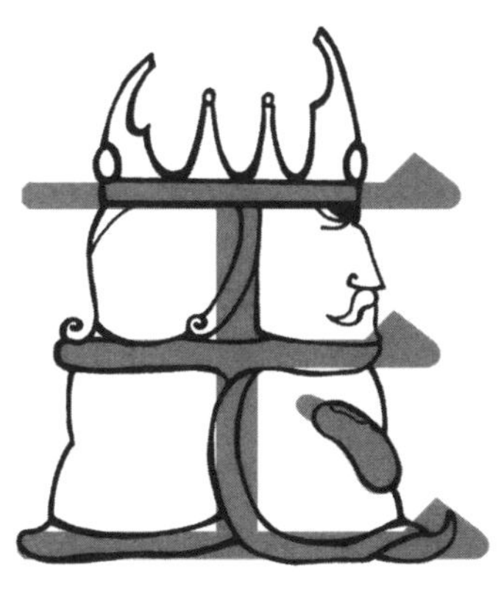

COMMON PRONUNCIATIONS

Common **ON** reading: none
Common **kun** reading: **tama** (たま)

Note how often this character changes from the voiceless "**tama**" (たま) to its corresponding voiced form "**dama**" (だま) when in the second position.

kun-yomi suggestion: "hot **tama**le"

Create your sentence to remember the **kun-yomi** reading in the box below.

LESS COMMON PRONUNCIATIONS

Less common **ON** reading: **GYOKU** (ギョク)
Less common **kun** reading: none

COMMON WORDS AND COMPOUNDS		
玉	*jewel*	**tama** たま
玉ねぎ	*onion*	**tama**·negi たま·ねぎ
目玉	eye + jewel = *eyeball*	me·**dama** め·だま
水玉	water + jewel = *drop of water*	mizu·**tama** みず·たま
火玉	fire + jewel = *fireball*	hi·**dama** ひ·だま
雪玉	snow + jewel = *snowball*	yuki·**dama** ゆき·だま

SAMPLE SENTENCE

玉ねぎ を 切って 下さい。
tama·negi o ki·tte kuda·sai.
onion(s) cut please
= *Please cut the onions.*

WRITING PRACTICE

COMPONENT 25

HOOK 乚

KANJI 25

HEART

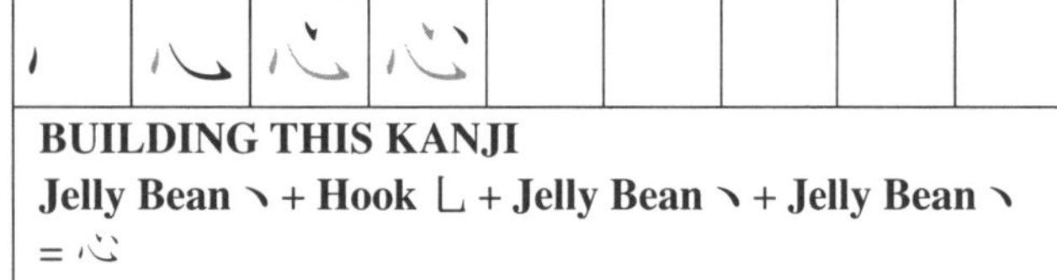

BUILDING THIS KANJI
Jelly Bean ㇏ + Hook 乚 + Jelly Bean ㇏ + Jelly Bean ㇏
= 心

MEANING
This unique-looking character conveys the idea of heart in all its shades of meaning, be it the actual physical organ, the sense of "feelings", or the concept of something's "core".

REMEMBERING THIS KANJI
There are a couple of ways to capture a HEART. The first is by using kindness; giving gifts such as a trio of **jelly beans** is an example of this method. The second is to simply use a **hook**.

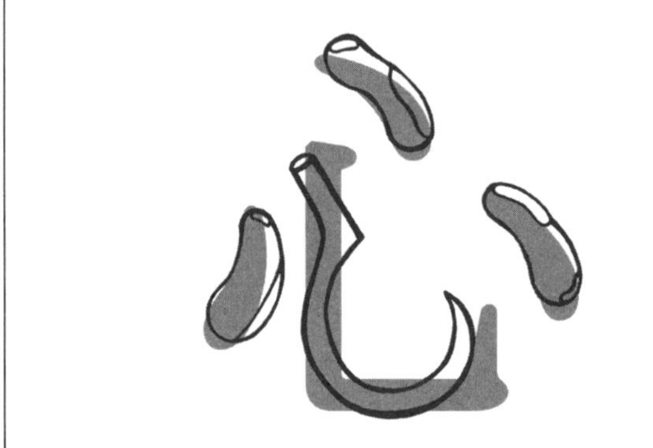

COMMON PRONUNCIATIONS
Common **ON** reading: **SHIN** (シン)
Common **kun** reading: **kokoro** (こころ)

The **kun-yomi** for this kanji always becomes voiced (**gokoro**) when not in the first position (as in the second and fourth examples).

kun-yomi suggestion: "**cocoa ro**ast"

Create your **on-yomi** keyword and enter it in the table at the back of the book. After that, write your sentence to remember the **on-yomi** and **kun-yomi** readings in the box below.

LESS COMMON PRONUNCIATIONS
Less common **ON** reading: none
Less common **kun** reading: none

Here is a common irregular reading containing this character, composed of both **kun** and **on-yomi**.

IRREGULAR READING		
心地*	heart + ground = *feeling*	**koko·CHI** ここ·チ

COMMON WORDS AND COMPOUNDS		
心	*heart*	**kokoro** こころ
女心	woman + heart = *a woman's heart*	onna·**gokoro** おんな·ごころ
中心	middle + heart = *center*	CHŪ·**SHIN** チュウ·シン
下心	lower + heart = *ulterior motive*	shita·**gokoro** した·ごころ
安心	ease + heart = *peace of mind*	AN·**SHIN** アン·シン
愛国心	love + country + heart = *patriotism*	AI·KOKU·**SHIN** アイ·コク·シン

SAMPLE SENTENCE

女王 に よる と 愛国心 は 大切
JO·Ō ni yoru to AI·KOKU·SHIN wa TAI·SETSU
queen according to patriotism important
だ そう です。
da sō desu.
= *According to the queen, patriotism is important.*

WRITING PRACTICE

KANJI 26

COUNTRY

BUILDING THIS KANJI
Prison 囗 + **Jewel** 玉(24) = 国

MEANING

Think of "country" here in the sense of a nation state.

REMEMBERING THIS KANJI

Most folks will state that their COUNTRY is like a **jewel**, one that must be protected from external dangers. And so they build walls. But is there a difference between being protected and being in **prison**? It's a thorny question, but perhaps the philosopher Epicurus answered it best: "There may be a **jewel** of a COUNTRY within **prison** walls somewhere, but I'd be willing to bet they'd have lousy food."

COMMON PRONUNCIATIONS

Common **ON** reading: **KOKU** (コク)
Common **kun** reading: **kuni** (くに)

kun-yomi suggestion: "ty**coon** era"

Create your **on-yomi** keyword and enter it in the table at the back of the book. After that, write your sentence to remember the **on-yomi** and **kun-yomi** readings in the box below.

LESS COMMON PRONUNCIATIONS

Less common **ON** reading: none
Less common **kun** reading: none

COMMON WORDS AND COMPOUNDS		
国	*country*	**kuni** くに
王国	king + country = *kingdom*	Ō·**KOKU** オウ·コク
全国	complete + country = *the whole country/ nationwide*	ZEN·**KOKU** ゼン·コク
入国	enter + country = *to enter a country*	NYŪ·**KOKU** ニュウ·コク
国内	country + inside = *domestic*	**KOKU**·NAI コク·ナイ
外国人	outside + country + person = *foreigner*	GAI·**KOKU**·JIN ガイ·コク·ジン
愛国心	love + country + heart = *patriotism*	AI·**KOKU**·SHIN アイ·コク·シン

SAMPLE SENTENCE

あの 国 には 外国人 が 多い。
ano kuni ni wa GAI·KOKU·JIN ga ō·i.
that country foreigners many
= *There are many foreigners in that country.*

WRITING PRACTICE

KANJI 27

COMPLETE

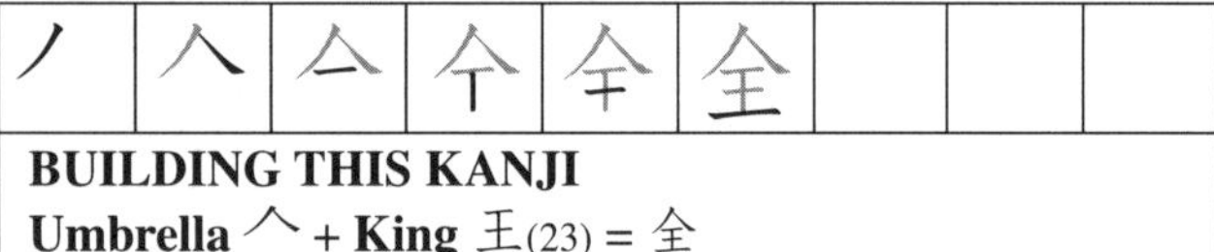

BUILDING THIS KANJI
Umbrella 𠆢 + **King** 王(23) = 全

MEANING

This kanji expresses the idea of wholeness and completion. Note in the sample compounds how both the first and third entries can have different connotations. Although the context will usually make the meaning clear, such ambiguity is a common feature of Japanese.

REMEMBERING THIS KANJI

"You might imagine that the ***king's umbrella*** *bearer has a job that even a* COMPLETE *idiot could do. Well, you're wrong, because you'd better not let the* ***king*** *get wet. Sadly, I learned this the hard way, for one afternoon the* ***umbrella*** *I chose had a hole, and a drop of moisture sprinkled the* ***king's*** *robe. That was enough to leave me dangling in the dungeon for a week. A tyrant* ***king****, you say? Perhaps, but the lesson I learned that day has remained with me forever: the* ***umbrella*** *must* COMPLETELY *cover the* ***king****."*

COMMON PRONUNCIATIONS

Common **ON** reading: **ZEN** (ゼン)
Common **kun** reading: none

Given that "Zen" (as in Buddhism) is one of the few Japanese words to have entered the English language, feel free to take advantage of this by using it to remember this reading. For the sentence, then, you might employ some Zen-like simplicity: "Complete **ZEN**".

Create your **on-yomi** keyword and enter it in the table at the back of the book. After that, write your sentence to remember the **on-yomi** reading in the box below.

LESS COMMON PRONUNCIATIONS

Less common **ON** reading: none
Less common **kun** readings: **matta** (まった); **matto** (まっと)

COMMON WORDS AND COMPOUNDS		
全国	complete + country = *the whole country/ nationwide*	**ZEN**·KOKU ゼン·コク
安全	ease + complete = *safety*	AN·**ZEN** アン·ゼン
全校	complete + school = *the whole school/ all schools*	**ZEN**·KŌ ゼン·コウ
全力	complete + strength = *all one's power*	**ZEN**·RYOKU ゼン·リョク
全体	complete + body = *the whole*	**ZEN**·TAI ゼン·タイ
全部	complete + part = *all*	**ZEN**·BU ゼン·ブ

SAMPLE SENTENCE

田中さん は 全国 を 回る。
Ta·naka-san wa ZEN·KOKU o mawa·ru.
Tanaka-san whole country go around
= *Tanaka-san is going around the whole country.*

WRITING PRACTICE

KANJI 28

十 TEN

一	十							

MEANING
Ten. The first two examples of Entry 176 show another use for this character, an interesting application based entirely on its shape.

REMEMBERING THIS KANJI
This is another simple character for which we will assign an external meaning: scarecrow.

In case you're wondering why this particular scarecrow was chosen, the answer is simple: he was rated a perfect TEN in terms of style and poise.

COMMON PRONUNCIATIONS
Common **ON** reading: **JŪ** (ジュウ)
Common **kun** reading: none

Say hello to the first character for which you should know all the compounds in the main table below. You've already come a long way!

Create your **on-yomi** keyword and enter it in the table at the back of the book. After that, write your sentence to remember the **on-yomi** reading in the box below.

LESS COMMON PRONUNCIATIONS
Less common **ON** reading: **JITSU** (ジツ)
Less common **kun** readings: **tō** (とお); **to** (と)

tō appears with only one word, 十日 [**tō·ka** (とお·か)] "the tenth day of the month".

Two common irregular readings, found earlier with the kanji 二.

IRREGULAR READINGS		
二十日	two + ten + sun (day) = *twentieth day of the month*	**hatsuka** はつか
二十歳*	two + ten + annual = *twenty years old*	**hatachi** はたち

COMMON WORDS AND COMPOUNDS		
十	*ten*	**JŪ** ジュウ
十月	ten + moon (month) = *October*	**JŪ**·GATSU ジュウ·ガツ
十一月	ten + one + moon (month) = *November*	**JŪ**·ICHI·GATSU ジュウ·イチ·ガツ
十二月	ten + two + moon (month) = *December*	**JŪ**·NI·GATSU ジュウ·ニ·ガツ
十六	ten + six = *sixteen*	**JŪ**·ROKU ジュウ·ロク
十八	ten + eight = *eighteen*	**JŪ**·HACHI ジュウ·ハチ

SAMPLE SENTENCE

十月	に	は	あの	木	は	美しく
JŪ·GATSU	**ni**	**wa**	**ano**	**ki**	**wa**	**utsuku·shiku**
October			that	tree		beautiful

なります。
narimasu.
becomes

= *That tree becomes beautiful in October.*

WRITING PRACTICE

KANJI 29

EARLY

丨	冂	日	日	旦	早			

BUILDING THIS KANJI
Sun 日(6) + **Ten (scarecrow)** 十(28) = 早

MEANING
Early/Fast. It is important to remember that this kanji expresses both of these ideas.

REMEMBERING THIS KANJI
There isn't much a **scarecrow** can do for exercise, but ours is determined to stay in shape. How so? Well, EARLY each day, once the **sun** is up, he'll launch into a vigorous routine of finger stretches, toe curls, and head rolls. As it's too hot to do this later on, it's fortunate he's an EARLY riser.

COMMON PRONUNCIATIONS
Common **ON** reading: **SŌ** (ソウ)
Common **kun** reading: **haya** (はや)

Note the intransitive/transitive verb pair in the table.

kun-yomi suggestion: "**hi ya**!"

Create your **on-yomi** keyword and enter it in the table at the back of the book. After that, write your sentence to remember the **on-yomi** and **kun-yomi** readings in the box below.

LESS COMMON PRONUNCIATIONS
Less common **ON** reading: **SATSU** (サツ)
Less common **kun** reading: none

COMMON WORDS AND COMPOUNDS		
早い	*early; fast*	**haya**·i はや·い
早まる (intr)	*to be in a hurry*	**haya**·maru はや·まる
早める (tr)	*to hurry (something)*	**haya**·meru はや·める
早口	fast + mouth = *rapid speaking*	**haya**·kuchi はや·くち
早春	early + spring = *early spring*	**SŌ**·SHUN ソウ·シュン
早朝	early + morning = *early morning*	**SŌ**·CHŌ ソウ·チョウ

SAMPLE SENTENCE

どうして そんな に 早く 来た の です か。
dōshite sonna ni haya·ku ki·ta no desu ka.
why so early come
= *Why did you come so early?*

WRITING PRACTICE

COMPONENT 30

GOOD FIGURE SKATER ⺊

A good figure skater always keeps her leg straight in this position.

KANJI 30

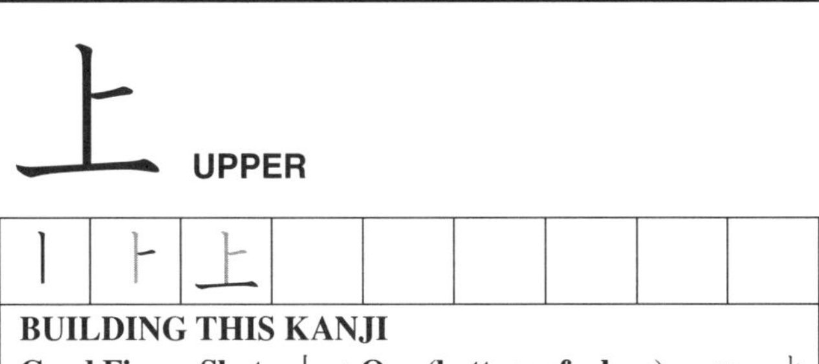

上 **UPPER**

丨	⺊	上						

BUILDING THIS KANJI
Good Figure Skater ⺊ + One (bottom of a bun) 一(3) = 上

MEANING
This simple-looking character expresses a broad range of ideas relating to the words "upper", "on", and "over", among others; it can refer to anything from goods of high quality to superiors at work. It's a fascinating kanji that is widely used, and one that rewards patient study.

REMEMBERING THIS KANJI
Look at the beautiful posture, with the outstretched leg held perfectly straight; this is a **good figure skater** with complete confidence in her abilities, skating as if the ice were the **bottom of a bun** that would not hurt her if she fell. This is clearly an UPPER-class athlete.

COMMON PRONUNCIATIONS
Common **ON** reading: **JŌ** (ジョウ)
Common **kun** readings: **kami** (かみ); **ue** (うえ); **nobo** (のぼ); **a** (あ); **uwa** (うわ)

Take a deep breath, as this kanji contains the second largest number of common readings for any character you will encounter in Japanese (you won't have long to wait for the one with the most!). The **on-yomi JŌ**, however, is by far the most frequently used, and the **kun-yomi** readings will often appear with **hiragana** accompaniment (which will offer a clue as to which pronunciation should be used for the kanji).

The verb **a·geru** (あ·げる) in example 5 below, incidentally, is almost always used in a transitive sense (that is, it "lifts" some object in either a physical or symbolic way), and is best thought of as being paired with the intransitive **a·garu** (あ·がる).

Before proceeding with your sentence, it is useful now to consider one of the most important benefits of the **on-yomi** table: because you will have chosen different keywords for each of the readings, there will be no danger of confusing pronunciations differing only in their use of a "long" versus "short" vowel sound. We encounter the first example of this here, with **JŌ** sounding much like **JO** (the **on-yomi** for "女" in Entry 16), but needing to be memorized as a separate reading.

kun-yomi suggestions: "**ma**k**e a me**al"; "**tr**u**e a**ge"; "**no bo**nes"; "**a**naconda"; "**n**e**w wo**k"

Write your sentence to remember the readings below.

LESS COMMON PRONUNCIATIONS
Less common **ON** reading: **SHŌ** (ショウ)
Less common **kun** reading: none

COMMON WORDS AND COMPOUNDS		
上	*upper*	**kami** かみ
上	*over; on*	**ue** うえ
上る (intr)	*to climb*	**nobo**·ru のぼ·る
上がる (intr)	*to rise*	**a**·garu あ·がる
上げる (tr/intr)	*to lift*	**a**·geru あ·げる
上手	upper + hand = *skillful*	**JŌ·ZU** ジョウ·ズ

SAMPLE SENTENCE

肉 は テーブル の 上 に あります。
NIKU wa TĒBURU no ue ni arimasu.
meat table on is
= *The meat is on the table.*

COMPONENT 31

POOR FIGURE SKATER

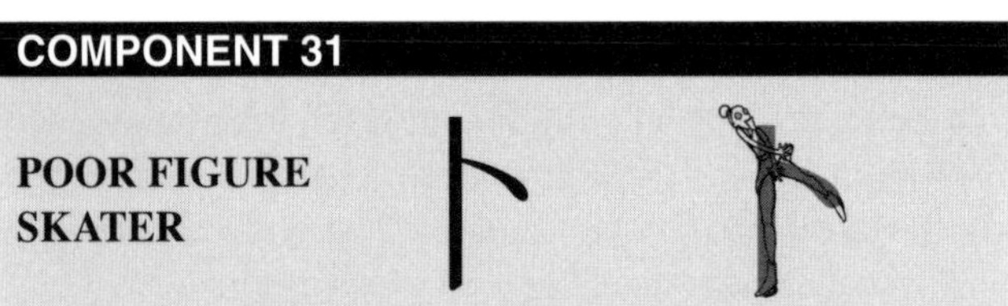

A poor figure skater lets her leg droop in this position.

KANJI 31

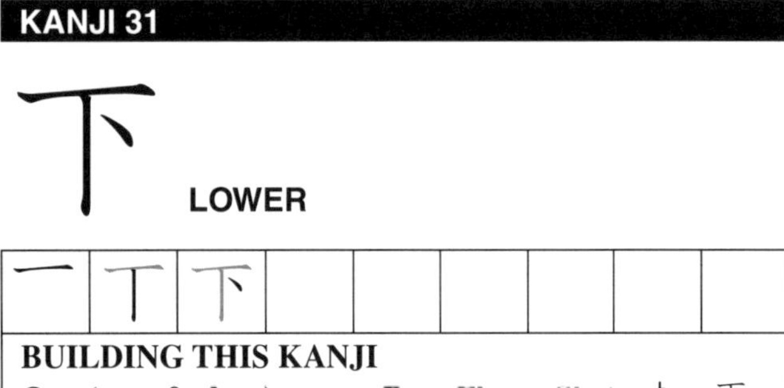

下 LOWER

一	丅	下						

BUILDING THIS KANJI
One (top of a bun) 一(3) + **Poor Figure Skater** ⺊ = 下

MEANING

This obvious partner to the preceding kanji expresses a similarly wide range of ideas, with words in this case relating to the notions of "lower", "under", and "below".

REMEMBERING THIS KANJI

No doubt about it: figure skating crowds are tough, and will not tolerate LOWER-class skaters. In one competition, all it took was a **poor figure skater**'s drooping leg to make the audience hurl the **tops of their buns** at her in disgust.

COMMON PRONUNCIATIONS

Common **ON** readings: **KA** (カ); **GE** (ゲ)
Common **kun** readings: **shita** (した); **shimo** (しも); **o** (お); **sa** (さ); **kuda** (くだ)

Here it is: the kanji with the most common readings of all. Although it can be a bit of work trying to come to grips with this character's many angles, keep in mind that the final three **kun-yomi** above are all verb stems, and will thus be accompanied by **hiragana** hinting at the correct pronunciation. When it comes to the readings used for compounds, **KA** or **GE** will be encountered far more than the others, although there are no easily discernible patterns as to when each of these is used.

This kanji illustrates well the difference between intransitive/transitive verb pairs. Refer back to "早" and "上" (Entries 29 and 30). Notice a similarity between the verbs presented there and examples four and five shown here.

kun-yomi suggestions: "**she ta**ckled"; "**she mo**ped"; "**o**rangutan"; "**sa**t"; "barra**cuda**"

Write your sentence to remember the readings below.

LESS COMMON PRONUNCIATIONS

Less common **ON** reading: none
Less common **kun** reading: **moto** (もと)

IRREGULAR READING		
下手	lower + hand = *to be poor at (something)*	**he·ta** へ·た

COMMON WORDS AND COMPOUNDS		
下	*low; below; under*	**shita** した
下りる (intr)	*to come down*	**o**·riru お·りる
下ろす (tr)	*to take down*	**o**·rosu お·ろす
下がる (intr)	*to hang down (on one's own)*	**sa**·garu さ·がる
下げる (tr)	*to lower (something)*	**sa**·geru さ·げる
下さる	*to oblige*	**kuda**·saru くだ·さる
上下	upper + lower = *high and low*	JŌ·**GE** ジョウ·ゲ
天下	heaven + lower = *the whole land*	TEN·**KA** テン·カ

SAMPLE SENTENCE

木 から 下りて 下さい。
ki kara o·rite kuda·sai.
tree from come down please
= *Please come down from the tree.*

COMPONENT 32

KANJI 32

 RICE

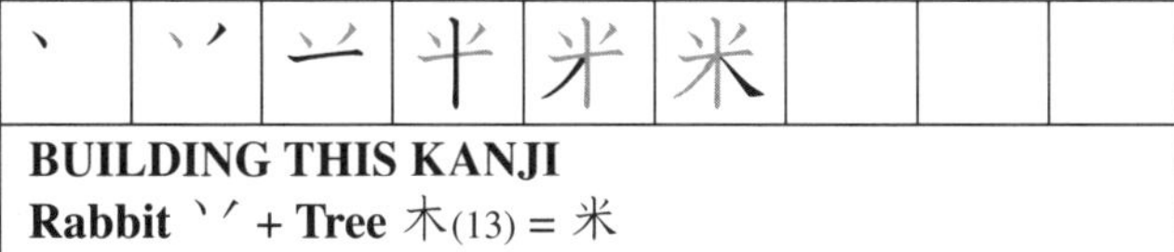

BUILDING THIS KANJI
Rabbit 丷 + **Tree** 木(13) = 米

MEANING
(Uncooked) rice. As can be seen in the last five compounds below, this character is used, curiously, to symbolize the Americas (recall how 中 is used in a similar way for China, and 日 for Japan). Note how the fourth example combines two such characters; this occurs frequently in written Japanese.

REMEMBERING THIS KANJI
Interesting fact: Japan has the equivalent of an Easter Bunny! The difference is that this **rabbit** will sneak around behind **trees** until he can dart out and hide RICE for children to find. Unfortunately, as the grains are really small and a lot less interesting than colored eggs, many kids have grown bored with the custom. As a result of this, the tradition of the Japanese RICE **rabbit** is not well-known today.

COMMON PRONUNCIATIONS
Common **ON** readings: **MAI** (マイ); **BEI** (ベイ)
Common **kun** reading: **kome** (こめ)

BEI is used as the reading in compounds when this kanji relates to the Americas, with **MAI** the primary choice when it refers to rice.

kun-yomi suggestion: "**comb a**cres"

Create your **on-yomi** keyword and enter it in the table at the back of the book. After that, write your sentence to remember the **on-yomi** and **kun-yomi** readings in the box below.

LESS COMMON PRONUNCIATIONS
Less common **ON** reading: none
Less common **kun** reading: none

COMMON WORDS AND COMPOUNDS		
米	*rice (uncooked)*	**kome** こめ
白米	white + rice = *polished rice*	HAKU·**MAI** ハク·マイ
米国	rice (America) + country = *the United States*	**BEI**·KOKU ベイ·コク
日米	sun + rice (America) = *Japan – U.S.*	NICHI·**BEI** ニチ·ベイ
中米	middle + rice (America) = *Central America*	CHŪ·**BEI** チュウ·ベイ
北米	north + rice (America) = *North America*	HOKU·**BEI** ホク·ベイ
南米	south + rice (America) = *South America*	NAN·**BEI** ナン·ベイ

SAMPLE SENTENCE

米国 の 牛肉 は 高い。
BEI·KOKU no GYŪ·NIKU wa taka·i.
United States beef expensive
= *U.S. beef is expensive.*

WRITING PRACTICE

KANJI 33

SELF

㇒	丿	冂	白	自	自			

BUILDING THIS KANJI
Jelly Bean ㇏ + Eye (Cyclops) 目(15) = 自

MEANING

This character conveys the important idea of self. Its function becomes clearer if you think of such English words as "self-confidence" and "self-government". When these and other words beginning with "self-" are translated into Japanese, the resulting compound will usually begin with this kanji.

REMEMBERING THIS KANJI

Everyone is aware of a **Cyclops'** weakness for **jelly beans**. It was this, in fact, that saved Hercules; dangling a **jelly bean** over the **Cyclops'** head was enough to make the monster drop his club and lose all sense of SELF. "It was sad, actually," Hercules said at a later press conference.

"No SELF-respecting **Cyclops** should act that way. He needs more SELF-control."

COMMON PRONUNCIATIONS

Common **ON** reading: **JI** (ジ)
Common **kun** reading: none

Write your sentence to remember the reading below.

LESS COMMON PRONUNCIATIONS

Less common **ON** reading: **SHI** (シ)
Less common **kun** reading: **mizuka** (みずか)

SHI appears only in the compound 自然 (Self/Suchlike*), the Japanese word for "nature": **SHI·ZEN** (シ·ゼン).

COMMON WORDS AND COMPOUNDS		
自国	self + country = *one's homeland*	**JI**·KOKU ジ·コク
自立	self + stand = *independence*	**JI**·RITSU ジ·リツ
自分	self + part = *oneself*	**JI**·BUN ジ·ブン
自体	self + body = *in itself*	**JI**·TAI ジ·タイ

SAMPLE SENTENCE

自分 の 車 が 買いたい。
JI·BUN no kuruma ga ka·itai.
oneself car want to buy
= *I want to buy my own car.*

WRITING PRACTICE

COMPONENT 34

GORILLA 冂 

KANJI 34

内 INSIDE

丨	冂	内	内					

BUILDING THIS KANJI
Gorilla 冂 + **Person** 人(2) = 内

MEANING

Inside/Interior/Within. This character can also convey the idea of "home".

REMEMBERING THIS KANJI

*"You can know nothing of the **gorilla**'s ways unless you are* INSIDE *its world. To truly understand, each **person** must get* INSIDE *an Acme™ **gorilla** suit – available for a limited time at this low introductory price – and head immediately into the jungle. It is then a simple matter of being accepted by a **gorilla** pod; once this has been done, a **person** can delve easily* INSIDE *the consciousness of our greatest primate."*

COMMON PRONUNCIATIONS

Common **ON** reading: **NAI** (ナイ)
Common **kun** reading: **uchi** (うち)

kun-yomi suggestion: "**ooh, chee**tahs"

Create your **on-yomi** keyword and enter it in the table at the back of the book. After that, write your sentence to remember the **on-yomi** and **kun-yomi** readings in the box below.

LESS COMMON PRONUNCIATIONS

Less common **ON** reading: **DAI** (ダイ)
Less common **kun** reading: none

COMMON WORDS AND COMPOUNDS

内	*inside*	**uchi** うち
国内	country + inside = *domestic*	KOKU·**NAI** コク·ナイ
市内	city + inside = *within the city*	SHI·**NAI** シ·ナイ
内海	inside + sea = *inland sea*	**NAI**·KAI ナイ·カイ
車内	car + inside = *inside the car*	SHA·**NAI** シャ·ナイ
町内	town + inside = *in the town*	CHŌ·**NAI** チョウ·ナイ

SAMPLE SENTENCE

その 人 は 国内 で 有名 です。
sono hito wa KOKU·NAI de YŪ·MEI desu.
that person domestic famous
= *That person is famous domestically.*

WRITING PRACTICE

COMPONENT 35

SUPERHERO ナ 

KANJI 35

右 RIGHT

ノ	ナ	ナ	右	右				

BUILDING THIS KANJI
Superhero ナ + **Mouth (vampire)** 口(8) = 右

MEANING
Right/Right-hand side.

REMEMBERING THIS KANJI
Vampires are extremely RIGHT wing, demanding unconditional obedience to their authority and strict adherence to traditional ways. Even **superheroes** can turn to the RIGHT under their hypnotic influence; they invariably develop a tougher stance on crime and become less likely to wear skin-tight costumes.

COMMON PRONUNCIATIONS
Common **ON** reading: none
Common **kun** reading: **migi** (みぎ)

kun-yomi suggestion: "foa**my gee**se"

Create your sentence to remember the **kun-yomi** reading in the box below.

LESS COMMON PRONUNCIATIONS
Less common **ON** readings: **YŪ** (ユウ); **U** (ウ)
Less common **kun** reading: none

COMMON WORDS AND COMPOUNDS		
右	*right*	**migi** みぎ
右回り	right + rotate = *clockwise*	**migi** mawa·ri みぎ まわ·り
右上	right + upper = *upper right*	**migi**·ue みぎ·うえ
右下	right + lower = *lower right*	**migi**·shita みぎ·した
右手	right + hand = *right hand*	**migi**·te みぎ·て
右足	right + leg = *right leg*	**migi**·ashi みぎ·あし

SAMPLE SENTENCE

山口さん は 右 の 目 が かゆい。
Yama·guchi-san wa migi no me ga kayui.
Yamaguchi-san right eye itchy
= *Yamaguchi-san's right eye is itchy.*

WRITING PRACTICE

KANJI 36

HAVE

ノ	ナ	冇	有	有	有			

BUILDING THIS KANJI
Superhero ナ + **Moon** 月 (11) = 有

MEANING
Have/Possess.

REMEMBERING THIS KANJI
"Help me!" yelled the **moon**. "I'm going down!"
And indeed he was. But just then a **superhero** arrived on the scene.
"I HAVE you, **moon**," he said, flying him higher into the sky before returning to Earth with a smile. "Citizens," he declared before us, "you HAVE your **moon** back."
"Geez," I heard someone whisper, "how many times should we tell this guy that the **moon's** *supposed* to go down?"

COMMON PRONUNCIATIONS
Common **ON** reading: **YŪ** (ユウ)
Common **kun** reading: **a** (あ)

kun-yomi suggestion: "**A**tilla"

Create your **on-yomi** keyword and enter it in the table at the back of the book. After that, write your sentence to remember the **on-yomi** and **kun-yomi** readings in the box below.

LESS COMMON PRONUNCIATIONS
Less common **ON** reading: **U** (ウ)
Less common **kun** reading: none

COMMON WORDS AND COMPOUNDS		
有る	*to have*	**a**·ru あ·る
有力	have + strength = *powerful*	**YŪ**·RYOKU ユウ·リョク
有名	have + name = *famous*	**YŪ**·MEI ユウ·メイ
私有	private + have = *privately owned*	SHI·**YŪ** シ·ユウ
公有	public + have = *publicly owned*	KŌ·**YŪ** コウ·ユウ
国有化	country + have + change = *nationalization*	KOKU·**YŪ**·KA コク·ユウ·カ

SAMPLE SENTENCE

エジプト の ピラミッド は 有名 です。
Ejiputo no piramiddo wa YŪ·MEI desu.
Egypt pyramids famous
= *The Egyptian pyramids are famous.*

WRITING PRACTICE

KANJI 37

MEAT

丨	冂	冂	内	肉	肉			

BUILDING THIS KANJI
Inside 内(34) + **Person** 人(2) = 肉

MEANING

Meat/Flesh. In addition to its literal meaning, this kanji also has a sexual connotation through its appearance in words such as "lust" and "sensuality".

REMEMBERING THIS KANJI

"What is really **inside** a **person**?" Troubled by this question, I embarked on an extended spiritual quest that eventually led me to a remote Himalayan summit. There I fasted, growing weak and delirious until a talking leopard appeared one day and laid a paw on my shoulder. "What are you, nuts?" it said. "Take it from me: there's nothing but MEAT in there."

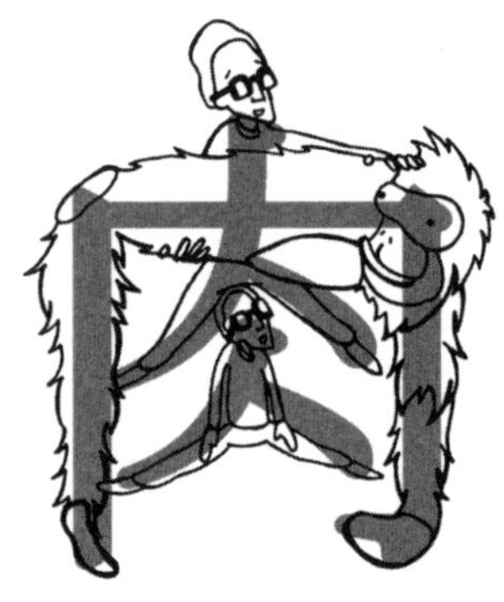

COMMON PRONUNCIATIONS

Common **ON** reading: **NIKU** (ニク)
Common **kun** reading: none

Create your **on-yomi** keyword and enter it in the table at the back of the book. After that, write your sentence to remember the **on-yomi** reading in the box below.

LESS COMMON PRONUNCIATIONS

Less common **ON** reading: none
Less common **kun** reading: none

COMMON WORDS AND COMPOUNDS		
肉	*meat*	**NIKU** ニク
人肉	person + meat = *human flesh*	JIN·**NIKU** ジン·ニク
牛肉	cow + meat = *beef*	GYŪ·**NIKU** ギュウ·ニク
肉親	meat + parent = *blood relative*	**NIKU**·SHIN ニク·シン
肉体	meat + body = *the body*	**NIKU**·TAI ニク·タイ

SAMPLE SENTENCE

あの 四人 は 牛肉 が 大好き です。
ano yo·NIN wa GYŪ·NIKU ga DAI su·ki desu.
those four people beef really like.
= *Those four people really like beef.*

WRITING PRACTICE

KANJI 38

HALF

丶	丶丿	䒑	兰	半				

BUILDING THIS KANJI
Rabbit 丷 + **Two** 二(4) + **Pole** 丨 = 半

MEANING

Half. This character also incorporates a sense of "partial", forming many words that English conveys with the prefix "semi-".

REMEMBERING THIS KANJI

I remember a chef answering a question I once posed. "Yes," she said, "a **pole** *could* split a **rabbit** into **two** HALF sections." I also recall her noting that there would only be HALF the **rabbit** left if it were prepared in such a ridiculous way.

COMMON PRONUNCIATIONS

Common **ON** reading: **HAN** (ハン)
Common **kun** reading: none

Create your **on-yomi** keyword and enter it in the table at the back of the book. After that, write your sentence to remember the **on-yomi** reading in the box below.

LESS COMMON PRONUNCIATIONS

Less common **ON** reading: none
Less common **kun** reading: **naka** (なか)

COMMON WORDS AND COMPOUNDS		
上半	upper + half = *upper half*	JŌ·**HAN** ジョウ·ハン
下半	lower + half = *lower half*	KA·**HAN** カ·ハン
半日	half + sun (day) = *half a day*	**HAN**·NICHI ハン·ニチ
半分	half + part = *half*	**HAN**·BUN ハン·ブン
九時半	nine + time + half = *nine-thirty*	KU·JI·**HAN** ク·ジ·ハン
半円	half + circle = *semicircle*	**HAN**·EN ハン·エン

SAMPLE SENTENCE

木口さん は 半日 ぐらい 新聞 を
Ki·guchi-san wa HAN·NICHI gurai SHIN·BUN o
Kiguchi-san half a day about newspaper
読みました。
yo·mimashita.
read
= *Kiguchi-san read the newspaper for about half a day.*

WRITING PRACTICE

KANJI 39

NINE

ノ	九							

MEANING
Nine.

REMEMBERING THIS KANJI
This is clearly someone dressed to the NINES.

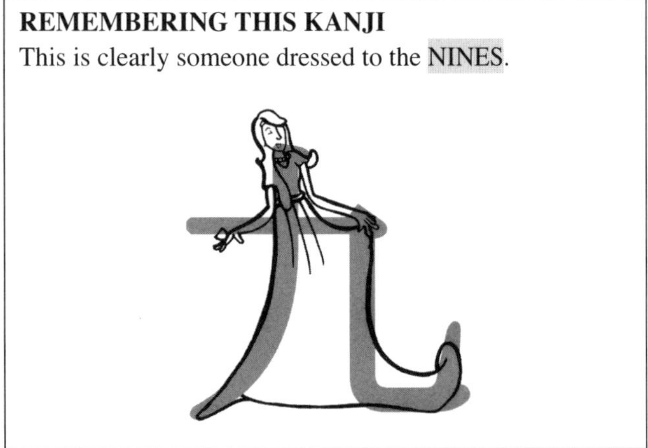

COMMON PRONUNCIATIONS
Common **ON** readings: **KYŪ** (キュウ); **KU** (ク)
Common **kun** reading: none

KYŪ is the general reading for this kanji. You are only likely to encounter **KU** in the third and fourth examples below.

Create your **on-yomi** keyword and enter it in the table at the back of the book. After that, write your sentence to remember the **on-yomi** reading in the box below.

LESS COMMON PRONUNCIATIONS
Less common **ON** reading: none
Less common **kun** reading: **kokono** (ここの)

This is another reading of most use because of its appearance in two words: 九日 [**kokono·ka** (ここの·か)] "the ninth day of the month", and 九つ [**kokono·tsu** (ここの·つ)] the general counter for "nine".

COMMON WORDS AND COMPOUNDS		
九	*nine*	**KYŪ** キュウ
九十	nine + ten = *ninety*	**KYŪ·JŪ** キュウ·ジュウ
九月	nine + moon (month) = *September*	**KU·GATSU** ク·ガツ
九時	nine + time = *nine o'clock*	**KU·JI** ク·ジ

SAMPLE SENTENCE

中山さん は 九月 に 日本 へ
Naka·yama-san wa KU·GATSU ni NI·HON e
Nakayama-san September Japan
行きました。
i·kimashita.
went
= *Nakayama-san went to Japan in September.*

WRITING PRACTICE

KANJI 40

SPRING

一	二	三	夫	夫	表	春	春	春

BUILDING THIS KANJI
Three (full hamburger) 三(5) + **Person** 人(2) + **Sun** 日(6) = 春

MEANING
This elegant-looking character refers to the season of spring. Interestingly, it also carries a hint of sexuality and amorousness, a meaning apparent by its presence in the Japanese word for "puberty", as well as in one of the compounds below. Make sure in writing this kanji to follow the order of the components as they are listed above (three + person + sun).

REMEMBERING THIS KANJI
It's doubtful any **person** looks forward to SPRING more than I do. As a matter of fact, on the first day of the season you'll surely see me in the backyard before dawn, firing up my barbecue to make the most enormous **full hamburger** possible. And why do I do that? Well, it's simple: I'm a **person** who wants to welcome the SPRING **sun** properly when it rises!

COMMON PRONUNCIATIONS
Common **ON** reading: **SHUN** (シュン)
Common **kun** reading: **haru** (はる)

kun-yomi suggestion: "**haru**mph"

Create your **on-yomi** keyword and enter it in the table at the back of the book. After that, write your sentence to remember the **on-yomi** and **kun-yomi** readings in the box below.

LESS COMMON PRONUNCIATIONS
Less common **ON** reading: none
Less common **kun** reading: none

COMMON WORDS AND COMPOUNDS		
春	*spring*	**haru** はる
小春	small + spring = *Indian summer*	ko·**haru** こ·はる
青春	blue + spring = *youth*	SEI·**SHUN** セイ·シュン
売春	sell + spring = *prostitution*	BAI·**SHUN** バイ·シュン
春分	spring + part = *vernal equinox*	**SHUN**·BUN シュン·ブン
来春	come + spring = *next spring*	RAI·**SHUN** ライ·シュン

SAMPLE SENTENCE

日本 の 春 は 美しい。
NI·HON no haru wa utsuku·shii.
Japan spring beautiful.
= *Japan's spring is beautiful.*

WRITING PRACTICE

CHAPTER 2 REVIEW EXERCISES

A. Please match the following kanji to their meanings.

1. 玉 — a. Ten
2. 全 — b. Country
3. 米 — c. Jewel
4. 貝 — d. Right
5. 肉 — e. Meat
6. 十 — f. Rice
7. 心 — g. Upper
8. 上 — h. Shellfish
9. 右 — i. Heart
10. 国 — j. Complete

B. Please match the following meanings to their kanji, and these to their **on** or **kun-yomi**.

1. Nine	a. 内	1. **HAN** (ハン)
2. Have	b. 春	2. **uchi** (うち)
3. Inside	c. 早	3. **haru** (はる)
4. King	d. 九	4. **YŪ** (ユウ)
5. Half	e. 下	5. **ROKU** (ロク)
6. Spring	f. 有	6. **haya** (はや)
7. Self	g. 自	7. **shita** (した)
8. Lower	h. 半	8. **JI** (ジ)
9. Early	i. 六	9. **Ō** (オウ)
10. Six	j. 王	10. **KYŪ** (キュウ)

C. Please choose the best answer(s) to the following questions.

1. Which of the following readings apply to the kanji 米?
   a. **MAI** (マイ)
   b. **kome** (こめ)
   c. **SHŪ** (シュウ)
   d. **BEI** (ベイ)
   e. **to** (と)

2. Which of the following readings apply to the kanji 上?
   a. **nobo** (のぼ)
   b. **ue** (うえ)
   c. **naka** (なか)
   d. **JŌ** (ジョウ)
   e. **kami** (かみ)

3. Which of the following readings apply to the kanji 心?
   a. **migi** (みぎ)
   b. **SHIN** (シン)
   c. **tsuki** (つき)
   d. **kokoro** (こころ)
   e. **HAN** (ハン)

4. Which of the following is a sushi chef most likely to put on rice?
   a. 王
   b. 自
   c. 早
   d. 貝
   e. 国

5. Which of the following readings apply to the kanji 下?
   a. **kuda** (くだ)
   b. **KA** (カ)
   c. **shita** (した)
   d. **o** (お)
   e. **GE** (ゲ)

D. Please choose the best answer to the following questions.

1. Which is the correct reading of 上がる?
   a. **to·garu** (と·がる)
   b. **a·garu** (あ·がる)
   c. **ma·garu** (ま·がる)
   d. **sa·garu** (さ·がる)

2. Which answer best captures the meaning of the compound 米国?
   a. Wednesday
   b. Vampire
   c. The United States
   d. Oatmeal
   e. Heart failure

3. Which is the correct reading for 九月?
   a. **KU·GATSU** (ク·ガツ)
   b. **kokono·GATSU** (ここの·ガツ)
   c. **KYŪ·GATSU** (キュウ·ガツ)
   d. **kokono·tsuki** (ここの·つき)

4. Which of the following does not belong with the others?
   a. 十
   b. 九
   c. 六
   d. 右

5. Which is the correct reading of 早い?
   a. **aru·i** (ある·い)
   b. **maru·i** (まる·い)
   c. **haya·i** (はや·い)
   d. **ara·i** (あら·い)

E. Please match the following compounds and words to their meanings and pronunciations.

1. 六月	a. Rapid speaking	1. **ROKU·GATSU** (ロク·ガツ)
2. 中国	b. Ulterior motive	2. **JO·Ō** (ジョ·オウ)
3. 早口	c. Queen	3. **GO·JŪ** (ゴ·ジュウ)
4. 五十	d. Early spring	4. **migi·ue** (みぎ·うえ)
5. 中米	e. Upper right	5. **SŌ·SHUN** (ソウ·シュン)
6. 女王	f. Fifty	6. **CHŪ·GOKU** (チュウ·ゴク)
7. 上下	g. June	7. **CHŪ·BEI** (チュウ·ベイ)
8. 早春	h. High and low	8. **shita·gokoro** (した·ごころ)
9. 下心	i. Central America	9. **JŌ·GE** (ジョウ·ゲ)
10. 右上	j. China	10. **haya·kuchi** (はや·くち)

CHAPTER 3 (KANJI 41-60)

KANJI 41

京 CAPITAL

'	亠	亡	亣	古	亨	京	京	

BUILDING THIS KANJI
Police 亠 + **Mouth (vampire)** 口(8) + **Small** 小(20) = 京

MEANING

Think of "capital" in the sense of a large metropolis. Though it's not the most common of characters, it is useful to learn this kanji because of its appearance in the compound for Tokyo and other cities.

REMEMBERING THIS KANJI

The CAPITAL can be a pretty intimidating place if you don't know it, and as a **police** officer here I'm always having to help folks with directions. Even **vampires**, who normally wouldn't go near anyone in a **police** uniform, come up to me now and then. It's not surprising, I suppose, that they're overwhelmed by all the buildings and traffic after having come from such **small** Transylvanian villages. But then, it's only natural that everyone – **vampires** included – feels a bit **small** in the CAPITAL.

COMMON PRONUNCIATIONS

Common **ON** reading: **KYŌ** (キョウ)
Common **kun** reading: none

Create your **on-yomi** keyword and enter it in the table at the back of the book. After that, write your sentence to remember the **on-yomi** reading in the box below.

LESS COMMON PRONUNCIATIONS

Less common **ON** reading: **KEI** (ケイ)
Less common **kun** reading: none

COMMON WORDS AND COMPOUNDS		
上京	upper + capital = *come/go to Tokyo*	JŌ·**KYŌ** ジョウ·キョウ
東京	east + capital = *Tokyo*	TŌ·**KYŌ** トウ·キョウ

SAMPLE SENTENCE

中山さん は 上京 しました。
Naka·yama-san wa JŌ·KYŌ shimashita.
Nakayama-san went to Tokyo
= *Nakayama-san went to Tokyo.*

WRITING PRACTICE

KANJI 42

SEE

丨	冂	冃	冃	目	貝	見		

BUILDING THIS KANJI
Eye (Cyclops) 目 (15) + **Ballet** 儿 = 見

MEANING

See/Watch. The idea of "show" can also be expressed. Make sure you notice the difference between this kanji and "貝" (Entry 21).

REMEMBERING THIS KANJI

"I'm tired of living a lie," said the **Cyclops**, throwing down his club before emerging in a tutu. "People need to SEE me for who I really am. They need to SEE I'm not some slob who lounges around belching in a cave littered with sailor bones. They need to SEE the truth: that I…am a **ballerina**!"

COMMON PRONUNCIATIONS

Common **ON** reading: **KEN** (ケン)
Common **kun** reading: **mi** (み)

Expect to use the **kun-yomi** when this kanji appears in the first position. The **on-yomi** occurs more often in the second.

kun-yomi suggestion: "**me**an"

Write your sentence to remember the readings below.

LESS COMMON PRONUNCIATIONS

Less common **ON** reading: none
Less common **kun** reading: none

COMMON WORDS AND COMPOUNDS		
見える (intr)	*to be visible*	**mi**·eru み·える
見る (tr)	*to see; to watch*	**mi**·ru み·る
見せる (tr)	*to show (something)*	**mi**·seru み·せる
見上げる	see + upper = *to look up (to/at)*	**mi** a·geru み あ·げる
月見	moon + see = *moon viewing*	tsuki·**mi** つき·み
見失う	see + lose = *to lose sight of*	**mi** ushina·u み うしな·う
外見	outside + see = *external appearance*	GAI·**KEN** ガイ·ケン

SAMPLE SENTENCE

山 の 上 に 小さい 木 が 見えます。
yama no ue ni chii·sai ki ga mi·emasu.
mountain upper small tree is visible
= *A small tree is visible on top of the mountain.*

WRITING PRACTICE

KANJI 43

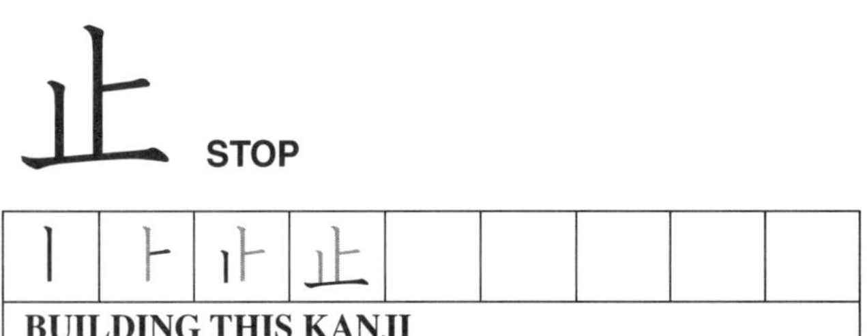

BUILDING THIS KANJI
Good Figure Skater ⺊ + Pole 丨 + One (bottom of a bun) 一(3) = 止

MEANING
All senses of the meaning "stop". Take care with the stroke sequence of this kanji; the components should be written in the order shown above.

REMEMBERING THIS KANJI
"STOP! STOP!" the audience screamed.
It was horrible. The **good figure skater's** posture was perfect, she was skating as if on the **bottom of a bun**, yet was oblivious to the **pole** sticking out of the ice in front of her. To be sure, no one could figure out what a **pole** was doing there in the first place, but no matter; the story must STOP here, as what happened next is too painful to relate.

COMMON PRONUNCIATIONS
Common **ON** reading: **SHI** (シ)
Common **kun** reading: **to** (と)

Remember to use the **on-yomi** keyword for **SHI** that you applied to the kanji "四" (Entry 10). Note also how the **kun-yomi** can become voiced when it is used (as in the fourth and fifth examples) in second position, something that occurs frequently with this kanji.

kun-yomi suggestion: "**to**tal"

Create your **on-yomi** keyword and enter it in the table at the back of the book. After that, write your sentence to remember the **on-yomi** and **kun-yomi** readings in the box below.

LESS COMMON PRONUNCIATIONS
Less common **ON** reading: none
Less common **kun** reading: none

COMMON WORDS AND COMPOUNDS		
止まる (intr)	*to stop*	**to**·maru と·まる
止める (tr)	*to stop (an object)*	**to**·meru と·める
中止	middle + stop = *discontinue*	CHŪ·**SHI** チュウ·シ
立ち止まる	stand + stop = *to stand still*	ta·chi **do**·maru た·ち ど·まる
車止め	car + stop = *closed to vehicles*	kuruma **do**·me くるま ど·め

SAMPLE SENTENCE

こちら に 止まって 下さい。
kochira ni to·matte kuda·sai.
here stop please
= *Please stop here.*

WRITING PRACTICE

COMPONENT 44

COMET 

Much like a wandering comet, our friend can appear in a variety of locations: as a slanted or curved line (as opposed to the horizontal "one") on top of a character, at the bottom, or right through the middle. One thing worth keeping in mind is that you should always draw this component from its head to its tail (i.e., in this case, from left to right).

KANJI 44

 **SEVEN**

一	七							

BUILDING THIS KANJI
Comet 一 + **Hook** L = 七

MEANING
Seven. Only two strokes here, but they should be written as the components are listed.

REMEMBERING THIS KANJI
Using a **comet** as his guide, Captain **Hook** sailed the SEVEN seas.

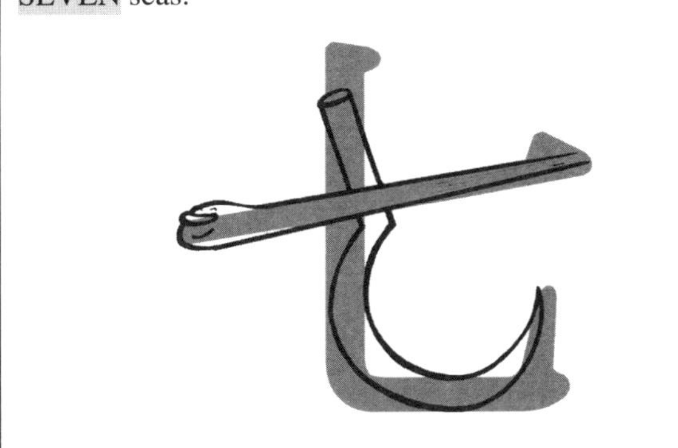

COMMON PRONUNCIATIONS
Common **ON** reading: **SHICHI** (シチ)
Common **kun** reading: **nana** (なな)

Note the mix of **on** and **kun** readings in the fourth and fifth examples.

kun-yomi suggestion: "**Nana**"

Create your **on-yomi** keyword and enter it in the table at the back of the book. After that, write your sentence to remember the **on-yomi** and **kun-yomi** readings in the box below.

LESS COMMON PRONUNCIATIONS
Less common **ON** reading: none
Less common **kun** reading: **nano** (なの)

This reading appears with only one word (any guesses?): 七日 [**nano·ka** (なの·か)] "the seventh day of the month".

COMMON WORDS AND COMPOUNDS		
七	*seven*	**SHICHI** シチ
七つ	*seven (general counter)*	**nana**·tsu なな·つ
七月	seven + moon (month) = *July*	**SHICHI**·GATSU シチ·ガツ
十七	ten + seven = *seventeen*	JŪ·**nana** ジュウ·なな
七十	seven + ten = *seventy*	**nana**·JŪ なな·ジュウ
七時	seven + time = *seven o'clock*	**SHICHI**·JI シチ·ジ

SAMPLE SENTENCE

高木さん が 七月 に 中米
Taka·gi-san ga SHICHI·GATSU ni CHŪ·BEI
Takagi-san July Central America
から 来ます。
kara ki·masu.
will come
= *Takagi-san will come from Central America in July.*

WRITING PRACTICE

KANJI 45

FEW

丨	小	小	少					

BUILDING THIS KANJI
Small 小(20) + **Comet** 一 = 少

MEANING
Few/Little (in terms of quantity).

REMEMBERING THIS KANJI
"That's not true," said the **comet**. "I mean, let's face it: I'm **small**, and have only a FEW opportunities to meet others. Everyone knows a planet because of its size and where it lives, but I move all over the place; that's why I have so FEW friends. It's got nothing to do with my tail leaving a mess on people's carpets."

COMMON PRONUNCIATIONS
Common **ON** reading: **SHŌ** (ショウ)
Common **kun** readings: **suku** (すく); **suko** (すこ)

SHŌ will appear in compounds. **Suku** and **suko** are only found in the first and second examples below. Note the special symbol in example three; Japanese uses this to indicate that a kanji is repeated.

kun-yomi suggestion: "**scoo**ter"; "**sco**ld"

Create your **on-yomi** keyword and enter it in the table at the back of the book. After that, write your sentence to remember the **on-yomi** and **kun-yomi** readings in the box below.

LESS COMMON PRONUNCIATIONS
Less common **ON** reading: none
Less common **kun** reading: none

COMMON WORDS AND COMPOUNDS		
少ない	*few*	**suku**·nai すく·ない
少し	*a little; a few*	**suko**·shi すこ·し
少々	few + few = *a little*	**SHŌ**·**SHŌ** ショウ·ショウ
少女	few + woman = *girl*	**SHŌ**·JO ショウ·ジョ
少年	few + year = *boy*	**SHŌ**·NEN ショウ·ネン
最少	most + few = *fewest*	SAI·**SHŌ** サイ·ショウ

SAMPLE SENTENCE

この 家 には 物 が 少ない。
kono ie ni wa mono ga suku·nai.
this house thing few
= *There are few things in this house.*

WRITING PRACTICE

COMPONENT 46

SNOWBOARD 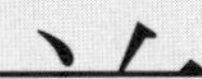 

KANJI 46

 **SOUTH**

BUILDING THIS KANJI
Ten (scarecrow) 十(28) + **Gorilla** 冂 + **Snowboard** 䒑 + **Ten (scarecrow)** 十(28) = 南

MEANING
South.

REMEMBERING THIS KANJI
Stepchildren can often be a problem. The **gorilla** knew this, of course, when she married the **scarecrow**, for all the **scarecrow's** son wanted to do was **snowboard**. Because of this, there was a predictable response when the **gorilla** suggested they travel SOUTH for their vacation.

"I don't want to go SOUTH," said Junior, pouting. "How can I **snowboard** there?"

"Now don't be like that, son," said his father. "You know **gorillas** like warm weather. We're going SOUTH, and that's all there is to it."

Junior said nothing to this, but the **gorilla** knew very well what he was thinking: "I wish Dad had married the polar bear."

COMMON PRONUNCIATIONS
Common **ON** reading: **NAN** (ナン)
Common **kun** reading: **minami** (みなみ)

kun-yomi suggestion: "**mean a meal**"

Create your **on-yomi** keyword and enter it in the table at the back of the book. After that, write your sentence to remember the **on-yomi** and **kun-yomi** readings in the box below.

LESS COMMON PRONUNCIATIONS
Less common **ON** reading: none
Less common **kun** reading: none

COMMON WORDS AND COMPOUNDS		
南	*south*	**minami** みなみ
南口	south + mouth = *south exit/entrance*	**minami**·guchi みなみ·ぐち
南米	south + rice (America) = *South America*	**NAN**·BEI ナン·ベイ
最南	most + south = *southernmost*	SAI·**NAN** サイ·ナン
南西	south + west = *southwest*	**NAN**·SEI ナン·セイ
南東	south + east = *southeast*	**NAN**·TŌ ナン·トウ

SAMPLE SENTENCE
バスターミナル の 南口 で 会いましょう。
basutāminaru no minami·guchi de a·imashō.
bus terminal south entrance let's meet
= *Let's meet at the south entrance of the bus terminal.*

WRITING PRACTICE

KANJI 47

工 CRAFT

一	丅	工						

MEANING

Have in mind the ideas of construction and manufacturing when you see this kanji; it's a versatile character that encompasses everything from handicrafts to industrial products. When found at the end of a compound (as in the final example below), this kanji can take on the meaning of "worker", and usually implies a person engaged in some type of manual labor.

REMEMBERING THIS KANJI

There's no better symbol for CRAFT than an anvil.

COMMON PRONUNCIATIONS

Common **ON** reading: **KŌ** (コウ)
Common **kun** reading: none

A final reminder about our major timesaving shortcut: your keyword for **KŌ** in this sentence will be the one you have entered in the **on-yomi** table, and that you have already applied to the kanji "口" (Entry 8). Create your **on-yomi** keyword and enter it in the table at the back of the book. After that, write your sentence to remember the **on-yomi** reading in the box below.

LESS COMMON PRONUNCIATIONS

Less common **ON** reading: **KU** (ク)
Less common **kun** reading: none

COMMON WORDS AND COMPOUNDS		
人工	person + craft = *artificial*	JIN·**KŌ** ジン·コウ
人工林	person + craft + grove = *planted forest*	JIN·**KŌ**·RIN ジン·コウ·リン
工学	craft + study = *engineering*	**KŌ**·GAKU コウ·ガク
工学士	craft + study + gentleman = *Bachelor of Engineering*	**KŌ**·GAKU·SHI コウ·ガク·シ
刀工	sword + craft = *swordmaker*	TŌ·**KŌ** トウ·コウ

SAMPLE SENTENCE

これ は 人工 の 島 です ね。
kore wa JIN·KŌ no shima desu ne.
this artificial island isn't it
= *This is an artificial island, isn't it?*

WRITING PRACTICE

KANJI 48

LEFT

一	ナ	左	左	左				

BUILDING THIS KANJI
Superhero ナ + **Craft** 工(47) = 左

MEANING

Left/Left-hand side. Take note: the writing order of the first two lines differs from that of Entries 35 and 36 ("右" and "有").

REMEMBERING THIS KANJI

Craft workers are traditionally LEFT wing, and when united can neutralize even a **superhero**, as the illustration makes clear.

COMMON PRONUNCIATIONS

Common **ON** reading: none
Common **kun** reading: **hidari** (ひだり)

kun-yomi suggestion: "**heed a reef**"

Create a sentence to remember the **kun-yomi** reading below.

LESS COMMON PRONUNCIATIONS

Less common **ON** reading: **SA** (サ)
Less common **kun** reading: none

COMMON WORDS AND COMPOUNDS		
左	*left*	**hidari** ひだり
左回り	left + rotate = *counter-clockwise*	**hidari** mawa·ri ひだり まわ·り
左上	left + upper = *upper left*	**hidari**·ue ひだり·うえ
左下	left + lower = *lower left*	**hidari**·shita ひだり·した
左手	left + hand = *left hand*	**hidari**·te ひだり·て
左足	left + leg = *left leg*	**hidari**·ashi ひだり·あし

SAMPLE SENTENCE

あの 人 の 左手 を見て 下さい。
ano hito no hidari·te o mi·te kuda·sai.
that person left hand see please
= *Please watch that person's left hand.*

WRITING PRACTICE

KANJI 49

TALL

'	一							高
高								

BUILDING THIS KANJI
Police 亠 **+ Mouth (vampire)** 口 (8) **+ Gorilla** 冂 **+ Mouth (vampire)** 口 (8) = 高

MEANING

Tall/High/Best. This kanji is also used to express the idea of "expensive".

REMEMBERING THIS KANJI

The story of King Kong the **gorilla** is well known. What most people don't realize, however, is that it is based on an obscure Transylvanian legend. In it, the angry **gorilla** kidnaps a baby **vampire** and climbs the TALLEST hut in the land. Unfortunately for him, the baby's father is none other than Dracula; the famous **vampire** dons his **police** hat (he is, for reasons yet to be understood, a part-time deputy in this legend) and flies to the rescue. Even today there are inhabitants in the region who hold this story to be true, although most people, to be sure, consider it a TALL tale.

COMMON PRONUNCIATIONS

Common **ON** reading: **KŌ** (コウ)
Common **kun** reading: **taka** (たか)

Note the intransitive/transitive verb pair below, and how the **kun-yomi** becomes voiced in the sixth example. This often occurs with 高 when it appears in the second or third position.

kun-yomi suggestion: "**tack a**pples"

Create your **on-yomi** keyword and enter it in the table at the back of the book. After that, write your sentence to remember the **on-yomi** and **kun-yomi** readings in the box below.

LESS COMMON PRONUNCIATIONS

Less common **ON** reading: none
Less common **kun** reading: none

COMMON WORDS AND COMPOUNDS		
高い	*tall; expensive*	**taka**·i たか·い
高まる (intr)	*to rise*	**taka**·maru たか·まる
高める (tr)	*to raise*	**taka**·meru たか·める
高山	tall + mountain = *alpine*	**KŌ**·ZAN コウ·ザン
高校	tall + school = *high school*	**KŌ**·KŌ コウ·コウ
円高	circle (yen) + tall = *strong yen*	EN·**daka** エン·だか
最高	most + tall = *highest; the best*	SAI·**KŌ** サイ·コウ

SAMPLE SENTENCE

あの 高い 山 は 美しい です ね。
ano taka·i yama wa utsuku·shii desu ne.
that tall mountain beautiful isn't it
= *That tall mountain is beautiful, isn't it?*

WRITING PRACTICE

COMPONENT 50

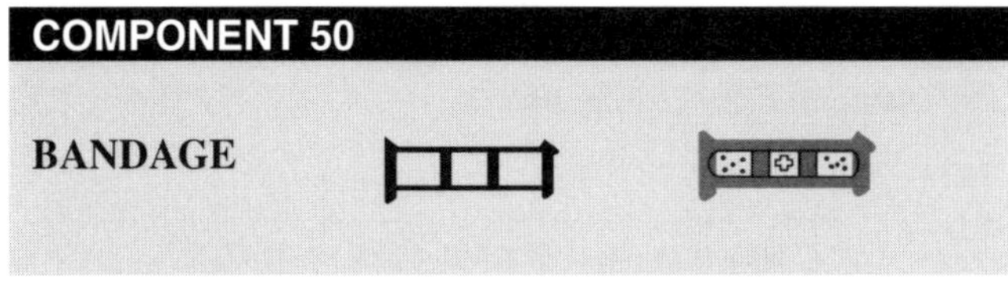

BANDAGE

KANJI 50

BUY

BUILDING THIS KANJI
Bandage 罒 **+ Shellfish** 貝(21) = 買

MEANING
Buy.

REMEMBERING THIS KANJI
As an animal rights activist, I regularly BUY **shellfish** in order to set them free. It's heartbreaking for me to go into a store and find them suffering in the tanks, their shells chipped and scarred. I BUY as many as possible, naturally, and do my best to help heal them by placing **bandages** on their wounds. But there are so many needing rescue… My only wish is for others to join the cause; after all, I can't BUY all the **shellfish** in the world.

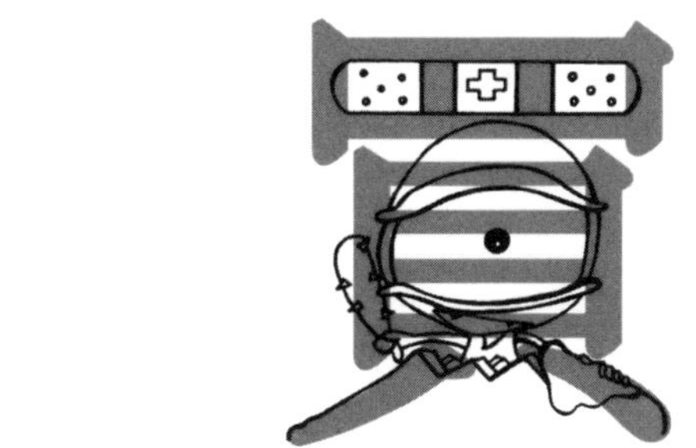

COMMON PRONUNCIATIONS
Common **ON** reading: none
Common **kun** reading: **ka** (か)

As nice as it is to have only one main reading to remember for this kanji, mention must be made of a particular quirk in written Japanese that occurs when certain verb stems are used to form nouns. The easiest way to understand this is by comparing the second and third examples below. As you can see, the noun in example 3 has "lost" the i (い) that would be present if the kanji were in its **-masu** verb form, **kaimasu** (買います). It is, in a sense, implied, based on the **hiragana** ending after 上. Unfortunately, there are no hard and fast rules for this aspect of the language, and it can be frustrating when such words are encountered. Our example, for instance, can be seen variously as "買い上げ", "買上げ", or even "買上" in different dictionaries!

It is worth keeping in mind, however, that not many kanji present such difficulties, and that once a "primary" word (usually the **-masu** form of a verb) has been learned, its related nouns will be easily recognized. Another consolation should be the following: by having reached the stage where you are dealing with such intricacies of the language, you are navigating among the deepest levels of written Japanese.

kun-yomi suggestion: "**ca**p"

Create your sentence to remember the **kun-yomi** reading in the box below.

LESS COMMON PRONUNCIATIONS
Less common **ON** reading: **BAI** (バイ)
Less common **kun** reading: none

COMMON WORDS AND COMPOUNDS		
買う	*to buy*	**ka**·u か・う
買い上げる	buy + upper = *to buy (up/out)*	**ka**·i a·geru か・い あ・げる
買上げ	buy + upper = *a purchase*	**kai** a·ge かい あ・げ
買い物	buy + thing = *shopping*	**ka**·i mono か・い もの
買い入れる	buy + enter = *to stock up on*	**ka**·i i·reru か・い い・れる
買い手	buy + hand = *buyer*	**ka**·i te か・い て

SAMPLE SENTENCE

山中さん は 高い 物 を 買う
Yama·naka-san wa taka·i mono o ka·u
Yamanaka-san expensive thing buy
つもり です。
tsumori desu.
plans
= *Yamanaka-san plans to buy something expensive.*

KANJI 51

HUNDRED

BUILDING THIS KANJI
One (top of a bun) 一(3) + **White** 白(7) = 百

MEANING

Hundred. In a few instances, the idea of "many" is conveyed.

REMEMBERING THIS KANJI

A recent survey found that ONE HUNDRED percent of **white bun tops** are **white**. ONE HUNDRED percent! Rarely is scientific research so conclusive.

COMMON PRONUNCIATIONS

Common **ON** reading: **HYAKU** (ヒャク)
Common **kun** reading: none

The thing to watch for here is how HYAKU changes phonetically with different numbers. Note also the **kun-yomi** in examples four and seven. Create your **on-yomi** keyword and enter it in the table at the back of the book. After that, write your sentence to remember the **on-yomi** reading in the box below.

LESS COMMON PRONUNCIATIONS

Less common **ON** reading: none
Less common **kun** reading: none

COMMON WORDS AND COMPOUNDS		
百	*one hundred*	**HYAKU** ヒャク
二百	two + hundred = *two hundred*	NI·**HYAKU** ニ·ヒャク
三百	three + hundred = *three hundred*	SAN·**BYAKU** サン·ビャク
四百	four + hundred = *four hundred*	yon·**HYAKU** よん·ヒャク
五百	five + hundred = *five hundred*	GO·**HYAKU** ゴ·ヒャク
六百	six + hundred = *six hundred*	ROP·**PYAKU** ロッ·ピャク
七百	seven + hundred = *seven hundred*	nana·**HYAKU** なな·ヒャク
八百	eight + hundred = *eight hundred*	HAP·**PYAKU** ハッ·ピャク
九百	nine + hundred = *nine hundred*	KYŪ·**HYAKU** キュウ·ヒャク

SAMPLE SENTENCE

肉 を 五百 グラム 買いました。
NIKU o GO·HYAKU guramu ka·imashita.
meat five hundred grams bought
= *(I) bought five hundred grams of meat.*

WRITING PRACTICE

KANJI 52

円 CIRCLE

丨	冂	𠘨	円					

BUILDING THIS KANJI
Gorilla 冂 + **Police** 一 = 円

MEANING

Circle/Round. This kanji is also used to denote the yen, Japan's currency. The connection originated from round one-yen coins.

REMEMBERING THIS KANJI

Every **gorilla** in the park hated the **ranger**, for his snide comments about their grooming habits were known to animals far and wide. It was not surprising, therefore, to hear that he had found himself surrounded by a CIRCLE of angry silverbacks on emerging from his tent one day. No one will know for certain what actually happened to the **ranger**, of course, because the **gorillas** CIRCLED their wagons and refused to cooperate with any investigation.

COMMON PRONUNCIATIONS

Common **ON** reading: **EN** (エン)
Common **kun** reading: **maru** (まる)

kun-yomi suggestion: "lla**ma ru**ins"

Create your **on-yomi** keyword and enter it in the table at the back of the book. After that, write your sentence to remember the **on-yomi** and **kun-yomi** readings in the box below.

LESS COMMON PRONUNCIATIONS

Less common **ON** reading: none
Less common **kun** reading: none

COMMON WORDS AND COMPOUNDS		
円い	*circular*	**maru**·i まる·い
円高	yen + tall = *strong yen*	**EN**·daka エン·だか
二円	two + yen = *two yen*	NI·**EN** ニ·エン
半円	half + circle = *semicircle*	HAN·**EN** ハン·エン
円安	yen + ease = *weak yen*	**EN**·yasu エン·やす
円周	circle + around = *circumference*	**EN**·SHŪ エン·シュウ

SAMPLE SENTENCE

あの 子 は 百円 をなくした。
ano ko wa HYAKU·EN o nakushita.
that child one hundred yen lost
= *That child lost a hundred yen.*

WRITING PRACTICE

KANJI 53

BASIS

一	二	テ	元					

BUILDING THIS KANJI
Two 二(4) + **Ballet** 儿 = 元

MEANING

This character expresses the idea of a basis or original state of something. When used with its **kun-yomi** before words such as "president", it can be translated as "ex-", or "former".

REMEMBERING THIS KANJI

Two ballet legs are the BASIS of any good performance of Swan Lake. I mean, no one likes to be rude, but every time I watch a one-legged swan take on the role of Princess Odette…well, the very BASIS of the play is called into question for me.

COMMON PRONUNCIATIONS

Common **ON** readings: **GEN** (ゲン); **GAN** (ガン)
Common **kun** reading: **moto** (もと)

GAN occurs only in the first position with a few common words.

kun-yomi suggestion: "**moto**cross"

Create your **on-yomi** keyword and enter it in the table at the back of the book. After that, write your sentence to remember the **on-yomi** and **kun-yomi** readings in the box below.

LESS COMMON PRONUNCIATIONS

Less common **ON** reading: none
Less common **kun** reading: none

COMMON WORDS AND COMPOUNDS		
元々	basis + basis = *from the first*	**moto·moto** もと·もと
元日	basis + sun (day) = *New Year's Day*	**GAN**·JITSU ガン·ジツ
手元	hand + basis = *at hand*	te·**moto** て·もと
元気	basis + spirit = *high spirits*	**GEN**·KI ゲン·キ
火元	fire + basis = *origin of a fire*	hi·**moto** ひ·もと
元来	basis + come = *by nature*	**GAN**·RAI ガン·ライ

SAMPLE SENTENCE

元日	な	ので	人	が	少ない。
GAN·JITSU	**na**	**no de**	**hito**	**ga**	**suku·nai.**
New Year's Day		because	person		few

= *It's New Year's Day, so there aren't many people.*

WRITING PRACTICE

KANJI 54

NECK

BUILDING THIS KANJI
Snowboard 䒑 + **Self** 自 (33) = 首

MEANING

Neck in its physical sense, as well as the ideas of leader or chief.

REMEMBERING THIS KANJI

His sense of **self** became so wrapped up in his **snowboard** that things started getting weird. After all, carrying a **snowboard** on your NECK at the ski slope is one thing, but wearing it around your NECK at work is another. When this started happening, even his colleagues in the office were concerned enough to seek advice.

"It all has to do with his sense of **self** worth," said the company psychologist. "What with the recent demotion, his **self** confidence is shaken. He'll get over it eventually."

COMMON PRONUNCIATIONS

Common **ON** reading: **SHU** (シュ)
Common **kun** reading: **kubi** (くび)

kun-yomi suggestion: "**Scooby** doo"

Create your **on-yomi** keyword and enter it in the table at the back of the book. After that, write your sentence to remember the **on-yomi** and **kun-yomi** readings in the box below.

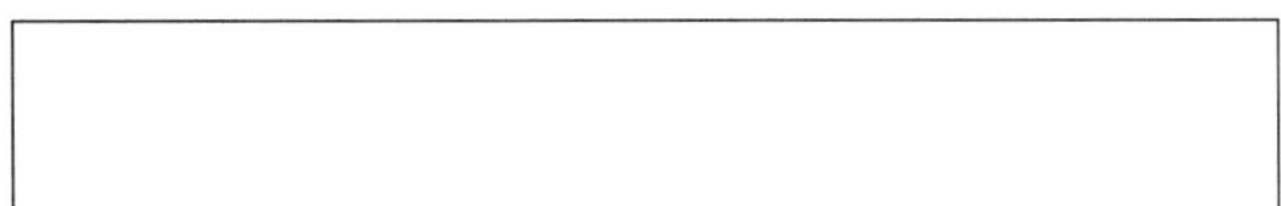

LESS COMMON PRONUNCIATIONS

Less common **ON** reading: none
Less common **kun** reading: none

COMMON WORDS AND COMPOUNDS		
首	*neck*	**kubi** くび
自首	self + neck = *surrender*	JI·**SHU** ジ·シュ
手首	hand + neck = *wrist*	te·**kubi** て·くび
足首	leg + neck = *ankle*	ashi·**kubi** あし·くび

SAMPLE SENTENCE

高木さん は 首 に 水 をかけました。
Taka·gi-san wa kubi ni mizu o kakemashita.
Takagi-san neck water put
= *Takagi-san put some water on his neck.*

WRITING PRACTICE

KANJI 55

WALK

丨	⺊	丨⺊	止	屮	歨	歩	歩	

BUILDING THIS KANJI
Stop 止(43) + **Few** 少(45) = 歩

MEANING

Walking/Step/Pace. A secondary meaning of "rate" (as used in a financial sense) is found only with **BU** (ブ), a less-common **on-yomi**.

REMEMBERING THIS KANJI

My WALKING style is a little unorthodox in that I'll **stop**, take a **few** steps, then **stop** once more. It can be frustrating for those WALKING with me, I suppose, for what with **stopping** every **few** steps, I rarely make it far beyond my front door.

COMMON PRONUNCIATIONS

Common **ON** reading: **HO** (ホ)
Common **kun** reading: **aru** (ある)

kun-yomi suggestion: "**a rou**te"

Create your **on-yomi** keyword and enter it in the table at the back of the book. After that, write your sentence to remember the **on-yomi** and **kun-yomi** readings in the box below.

LESS COMMON PRONUNCIATIONS

Less common **ON** readings: **BU** (ブ); **FU** (フ)
Less common **kun** reading: **ayu** (あゆ)

COMMON WORDS AND COMPOUNDS		
歩く	*to walk*	**aru**·ku ある·く
一歩	one + walk = *one step*	IP·**PO** イッ·ポ
歩き回る	walk + rotate = *to ramble about*	**aru**·ki mawa·ru ある·き まわ·る
歩道	walk + road = *sidewalk*	**HO**·DŌ ホ·ドウ
歩行	walk + go = *walking*	**HO**·KŌ ホ·コウ
歩行者	walk + go + individual = *pedestrian*	**HO**·KŌ·SHA ホ·コウ·シャ

SAMPLE SENTENCE

家 から 山 まで 歩きました。
ie kara yama made aru·kimashita.
house from mountain until walked
= *(We) walked from the house to the mountain.*

WRITING PRACTICE

KANJI 56

CHILD

㇇	了	子						

MEANING

Child. As seen in the final compound below, this character can also be used to suggest something small. No story required.

COMMON PRONUNCIATIONS

Common **ON** reading: **SHI** (シ)
Common **kun** reading: **ko** (こ)

Interestingly, both of these readings can at times become voiced (pronounced **JI** and **go**) in the second position, as seen in the third examples of this entry and that of Entry 167. Japanese parents often choose this kanji for a suffix when naming their children (eg. **Aki·*ko***); it is read "**SHI**" in the case of males, and "**ko**" when applied to females.

kun-yomi suggestion: "**co**at"

Create your **on-yomi** keyword and enter it in the table at the back of the book. After that, write your sentence to remember the **on-yomi** and **kun-yomi** readings in the box below.

LESS COMMON PRONUNCIATIONS

Less common **ON** reading: **SU** (ス)
Less common **kun** reading: none

COMMON WORDS AND COMPOUNDS		
子	*child*	**ko** こ
女子	woman + child = *women's*	JO·**SHI** ジョ·シ
王子	king + child = *prince*	Ō·**JI** オウ·ジ
男子	man + child = *men's*	DAN·**SHI** ダン·シ
子牛	child + cow = *calf*	**ko**·ushi こ·うし
電子	electric + child = *electron*	DEN·**SHI** デン·シ

SAMPLE SENTENCE

五月 に 女王 と 王子 が 米国 へ
GO·GATSU ni JO·Ō と **Ō·JI ga BEI·KOKU e**
May queen prince America
行きました。
i·kimashita.
went
= *In May, the queen and prince went to America.*

WRITING PRACTICE

KANJI 57

LIKE

く	女	女	女ᄀ	女了	好			

BUILDING THIS KANJI
Woman 女(16) + **Child** 子(56) = 好

MEANING
To like/Good/Favorable…nothing but positive feelings are associated with this gentle character!

REMEMBERING THIS KANJI
This is one of those kanji that is so logically constructed as to need no story at all.

COMMON PRONUNCIATIONS
Common **ON** reading: **KŌ** (コウ)
Common **kun** reading: **su** (す)

The **kun-yomi** is often voiced when in the second position (becoming "**zu**"), as below in examples three and four.

kun-yomi suggestion: "**soo**n"

Create your **on-yomi** keyword and enter it in the table at the back of the book. After that, write your sentence to remember the **on-yomi** and **kun-yomi** readings in the box below.

LESS COMMON PRONUNCIATIONS
Less common **ON** reading: none
Less common **kun** reading: **kono** (この)

COMMON WORDS AND COMPOUNDS		
好き	*like*	**su**·ki す·き
大好き	large + like = *to really like*	DAI **su**·ki ダイ す·き
人好き	person + like = *amiability*	hito **zu**·ki ひと ず·き
話し好き	speak + like = *talkative*	hana·shi **zu**·ki はな·し ず·き
友好	friend + like = *friendship*	YŪ·**KŌ** ユウ·コウ
同好	same + like = *same tastes*	DŌ·**KŌ** ドウ·コウ

SAMPLE SENTENCE
山口さん は あそこ の 女 の 人
Yama·guchi-san wa asoko no onna no hito
Yamaguchi-san over there woman person
が 大好き です。
ga DAI su·ki desu.
really likes
= *Yamaguchi-san really likes that woman over there.*

WRITING PRACTICE

KANJI 58

OLD

一	十	𠂇	古	古				

BUILDING THIS KANJI
Ten (scarecrow) 十(28) + **Mouth (vampire)** 口(8) = 古

MEANING
Old/Ancient/Antique.

REMEMBERING THIS KANJI
Even though **vampires** never die, they do grow OLD and suffer the same deterioration of mental faculties as the rest of us. The **scarecrow** can attest to this; as he lives in a field next to an OLD folks home, he'll often look down to find a elderly **vampire** bravely fastening its gums onto his ankle. It's more of a nuisance for him than anything, of course, but he's always nice enough to show respect for those OLDER by acting scared.

COMMON PRONUNCIATIONS
Common **ON** reading: **KO** (コ)
Common **kun** reading: **furu** (ふる)

Remember that your **on-yomi** keyword here will be different from that used in the preceding entry (for 好).

kun-yomi suggestion: "**who ru**es…"

Create your **on-yomi** keyword and enter it in the table at the back of the book. After that, write your sentence to remember the **on-yomi** and **kun-yomi** readings in the box below.

LESS COMMON PRONUNCIATIONS
Less common **ON** reading: none
Less common **kun** reading: none

COMMON WORDS AND COMPOUNDS		
古い	*old*	**furu**·i ふる·い
中古	middle + old = *secondhand*	CHŪ·**KO** チュウ·コ
最古	most + old = *oldest*	SAI·**KO** サイ·コ
古語	old + words = *archaic word*	**KO**·GO コ·ゴ
古来	old + come = *time honored*	**KO**·RAI コ·ライ
古里	old + hamlet = *the old hometown*	**furu**·sato ふる·さと

SAMPLE SENTENCE

山下さん は 中古 の 品 を よく
Yama·shita-san wa CHŪ·KO no shina o yoku
Yamashita-san secondhand goods often
買います。
ka·imasu.
buys
= *Yamashita-san often buys secondhand goods.*

WRITING PRACTICE

KANJI 59

FIRE

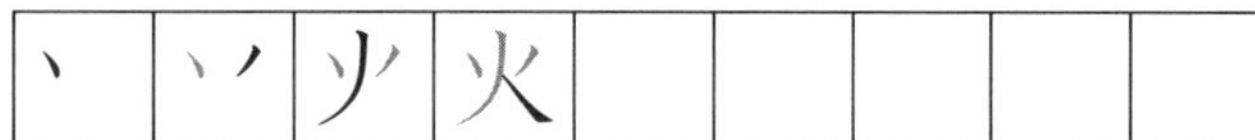

MEANING

This beautifully simple character encompasses all things to do with fire. No story required.

COMMON PRONUNCIATIONS

Common **ON** reading: **KA** (カ)
Common **kun** reading: **hi** (ひ)

The **kun-yomi** is always voiced (becomes **bi**) when in the second position, as seen here in example five.

kun-yomi suggestion: "**he**at"

Create your **on-yomi** keyword and enter it in the table at the back of the book. After that, write your sentence to remember the **on-yomi** and **kun-yomi** readings in the box below.

LESS COMMON PRONUNCIATIONS

Less common **ON** reading: none
Less common **kun** reading: **ho** (ほ)

COMMON WORDS AND COMPOUNDS		
火	*fire*	**hi** ひ
火元	fire + basis = *origin of a fire*	**hi**·moto ひ·もと
大火	large + fire = *conflagration*	TAI·**KA** タイ·カ
火山	fire + mountain = *volcano*	**KA**·ZAN カ·ザン
花火	flower + fire = *fireworks*	hana·**bi** はな·び
火曜日	fire + day of the week + sun (day) = *Tuesday*	**KA**·YŌ·bi カ·ヨウ·び
火星	fire + star = *Mars (planet)*	**KA**·SEI カ·セイ

SAMPLE SENTENCE

日本 には 火山 が あります。
NI·HON ni wa KA·ZAN ga arimasu.
Japan volcano are
= *There are volcanoes in Japan.*

WRITING PRACTICE

COMPONENT 60

RUNNING CHICKEN 夂 

KANJI 60

WINTER

ノ	ク	夂	冬	冬				

BUILDING THIS KANJI
Running Chicken 夂 **+ Jelly Bean** ヽ **+ Jelly Bean** ヽ
= 冬

MEANING
Winter.

REMEMBERING THIS KANJI
WINTER is such a drab time of year. To add a bit of color to the season, therefore, I enjoy strapping bags of **jelly beans** to **chickens running** in the yard, as the **beans** spill out and make everything more cheerful. It's a mystery to me why more people don't do this; even the grayest WINTER would be tolerable if everyone followed my lead.

COMMON PRONUNCIATIONS
Common **ON** reading: **TŌ** (トウ)
Common **kun** reading: **fuyu** (ふゆ)

kun-yomi suggestion: "**who u**ses…"

Create your **on-yomi** keyword and enter it in the table at the back of the book. After that, write your sentence to remember the **on-yomi** and **kun-yomi** readings in the box below.

LESS COMMON PRONUNCIATIONS
Less common **ON** reading: none
Less common **kun** reading: none

COMMON WORDS AND COMPOUNDS		
冬	*winter*	**fuyu** ふゆ
冬休み	winter + rest = *winter vacation*	**fuyu** yasu·mi ふゆ やす·み
立冬	stand + winter = *first day of winter*	RIT·**TŌ** リッ·トウ
冬物	winter + thing = *winter clothing*	**fuyu**·mono ふゆ·もの
冬空	winter + empty (sky) = *winter sky*	**fuyu**·zora ふゆ·ぞら

SAMPLE SENTENCE

冬 に なる と スイス の 山 は
fuyu ni naru to suisu no yama wa
winter becomes Switzerland mountain
美しい。
utsuku·shii.
beautiful
= *The mountains of Switzerland are beautiful in winter.*

WRITING PRACTICE

CHAPTER 3 REVIEW EXERCISES

A. Please match the following kanji to their meanings.

1.	高	a.	Few
2.	止	b.	Hundred
3.	古	c.	Basis
4.	百	d.	Tall
5.	南	e.	Winter
6.	京	f.	Left
7.	元	g.	Capital
8.	左	h.	Stop
9.	少	i.	South
10.	冬	j.	Old

B. Please match the following meanings to their kanji, and these to their **on** or **kun-yomi**.

1. Like (**kun-yomi**)	a. 歩	1.	**HO** (ホ)
2. Child	b. 火	2.	**ko** (こ)
3. Neck	c. 工	3.	**kubi** (くび)
4. Craft	d. 首	4.	**ka** (か)
5. Walk	e. 七	5.	**EN** (エン)
6. See	f. 子	6.	**SHICHI** (シチ)
7. Fire (**kun-yomi**)	g. 見	7.	**KŌ** (コウ)
8. Buy	h. 円	8.	**mi** (み)
9. Circle	i. 好	9.	**hi** (ひ)
10. Seven	j. 買	10.	**su** (す)

C. Please choose the best answer(s) to the following questions.

1. Which of the following readings apply to the kanji 南?
   a. **NAN** (ナン)
   b. **fuyu** (ふゆ)
   c. **HYAKU** (ヒャク)
   d. **minami** (みなみ)
   e. **hidari** (ひだり)

2. What is the worst thing you can hear someone say from behind while you're standing on a plank of a ship?
   a. 子
   b. 七
   c. 好
   d. 元
   e. 歩

3. Which of the following readings apply to the kanji 高?
   a. **hi** (ひ)
   b. **GETSU** (ゲツ)
   c. **KŌ** (コウ)
   d. **taka** (たか)
   e. **TAI** (タイ)

4. Which of the following readings apply to the kanji 元?
   a. **GEN** (ゲン)
   b. **moto** (もと)
   c. **furu** (ふる)
   d. **GAN** (ガン)
   e. **HAN** (ハン)

5. Which of the following readings apply to the kanji 少?
   a. **KŌ** (コウ)
   b. **SHŌ** (ショウ)
   c. **suko** (すこ)
   d. **suku** (すく)
   e. **to** (と)

D. Please choose the best answer to the following questions.

1. Which is the correct reading of 少し?
   a. **mawa·shi** (まわ·し)
   b. **suko·shi** (すこ·し)
   c. **de·shi** (で·し)
   d. **suku·shi** (すく·し)

2. Which kanji would precede 口 to form the compound for "volcanic crater"?
   a. 冬
   b. 火
   c. 左
   d. 首
   e. 止

3. Which is the correct reading of 古い?
   a. **furu·i** (ふる·い)
   b. **ka·i** (か·い)
   c. **yuru·i** (ゆる·い)
   d. **futo·i** (ふと·い)

4. Which of the following kanji has the most number of strokes?
   a. 見
   b. 好
   c. 南
   d. 歩
   e. 京

5. Which is the correct reading of 少ない?
   a. **aka·nai** (あか·ない)
   b. **to·nai** (と·ない)
   c. **aga·nai** (あが·ない)
   d. **suku·nai** (すく·ない)

E. Please match the following compounds and words to their meanings and pronunciations.

1. 南米	a. To really like	1. **CHŪ·SHI** (チュウ·シ)
2. 中古	b. Secondhand	2. **JŌ·KYŌ** (ジョウ·キョウ)
3. 上京	c. Semicircle	3. **JIN·KŌ** (ジン·コウ)
4. 大火	d. South America	4. **CHŪ·KO** (チュウ·コ)
5. 半円	e. Artificial	5. **IP·PO** (イッ·ポ)
6. 中止	f. Discontinue	6. **NAN·BEI** (ナン·ベイ)
7. 一歩	g. Seven hundred	7. **TAI·KA** (タイ·カ)
8. 七百	h. Come/ Go to Tokyo	8. **DAI su·ki** (ダイ す·き)
9. 人工	i. One step	9. **HAN·EN** (ハン·エン)
10. 大好き	j. Conflagration	10. **nana·HYAKU** (なな·ヒャク)

CHAPTER 4 (KANJI 61-80)

KANJI 61

水 WATER

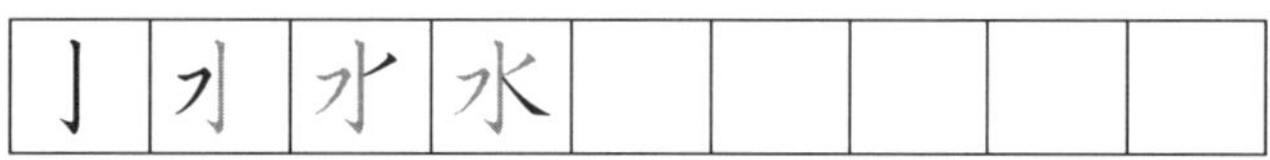

MEANING

Another gracefully balanced character, this one suggesting water. The "wavy" effect in the illustration will be easier to remember if you imagine the harpoon being pulled upward. No story required.

COMMON PRONUNCIATIONS

Common **ON** reading: **SUI** (スイ)
Common **kun** reading: **mizu** (みず)

kun-yomi suggestion: "make **me zoo**m"

Create your **on-yomi** keyword and enter it in the table at the back of the book. After that, write your sentence to remember the **on-yomi** and **kun-yomi** readings in the box below.

LESS COMMON PRONUNCIATIONS

Less common **ON** reading: none
Less common **kun** reading: none

COMMON WORDS AND COMPOUNDS		
水	*water*	**mizu** みず
水中	water + middle = *underwater; in the water*	**SUI**·CHŪ スイ·チュウ
下水	lower + water = *sewage*	GE·**SUI** ゲ·スイ
水玉	water + jewel = *drop of water*	**mizu**·tama みず·たま
水星	water + star = *Mercury (planet)*	**SUI**·SEI スイ·セイ
水曜日	water + day of the week + sun (day) = *Wednesday*	**SUI**·YŌ·bi スイ·ヨウ·び
水死	water + death = *drowning*	**SUI**·SHI スイ·シ

SAMPLE SENTENCE

あの　ダム　には　水　が　ありません。
ano DAMU ni wa mizu ga arimasen.
that dam water isn't
= *There is no water at that dam.*

WRITING PRACTICE

COMPONENT 62

PINCERS 

KANJI 62

安 EASE

丶	丿	宀	宀	安	安			

BUILDING THIS KANJI
Pincers 宀 + **Woman** 女(16) = 安

MEANING

The general sense is of "ease", "peacefulness", and "stability". An important secondary meaning is "inexpensive". In this regard, the kanji's opposite is "高" (Entry 49).

REMEMBERING THIS KANJI

Pincers have always allowed the legendary **women** of history to lead lives of EASE. Nefertiti and Cleopatra had **pincers** deposit them into cushiony boats on the Nile; Catherine the Great had **pincers** EASE her onto a bed strewn with sable… Even Joan of Arc, after a tiring day on the battlefield, would always have **pincers** set her gently into a bubble bath.

COMMON PRONUNCIATIONS

Common **ON** reading: **AN** (アン)
Common **kun** reading: **yasu** (やす)

kun-yomi suggestion: "**try a su**it"

Create your **on-yomi** keyword and enter it in the table at the back of the book. After that, write your sentence to remember the **on-yomi** and **kun-yomi** readings in the box below.

LESS COMMON PRONUNCIATIONS

Less common **ON** reading: none
Less common **kun** reading: none

COMMON WORDS AND COMPOUNDS		
安い	*easy; cheap*	**yasu**·i やす·い
円安	circle (yen) + ease = *weak yen*	EN·**yasu** エン·やす
安心	ease + heart = *peace of mind*	**AN**·SHIN アン·シン
安全	ease + complete = *safety*	**AN**·ZEN アン·ゼン
不安	not + ease = *uneasiness*	FU·**AN** フ·アン
公安	public + ease = *public peace*	KŌ·**AN** コウ·アン

SAMPLE SENTENCE

安心 して 下さい。
AN·SHIN shite kuda·sai.
peace of mind do please
= *Please don't worry.*

WRITING PRACTICE

KANJI 63

STRENGTH

フ	力							

MEANING

Strength/Power/Force. No story required.

COMMON PRONUNCIATIONS

Common **ON** readings: **RYOKU** (リョク); **RIKI** (リキ)
Common **kun** reading: **chikara** (ちから)

RYOKU will be encountered far more often than RIKI; the **kun-yomi** is a common word on its own.

kun-yomi suggestion: "in my **cheek a rat**..."

Create your **on-yomi** keyword and enter it in the table at the back of the book. After that, write your sentence to remember the **on-yomi** and **kun-yomi** readings in the box below.

LESS COMMON PRONUNCIATIONS

Less common **ON** reading: none
Less common **kun** reading: none

COMMON WORDS AND COMPOUNDS		
力	*strength*	**chikara** ちから
全力	complete + strength = *all one's power*	ZEN·**RYOKU** ゼン·リョク
有力	have + strength = *powerful*	YŪ·**RYOKU** ユウ·リョク
水力	water + strength = *hydro power*	SUI·**RYOKU** スイ·リョク
火力	fire + strength = *thermal power*	KA·**RYOKU** カ·リョク
電力	electric + strength = *electric power*	DEN·**RYOKU** デン·リョク
力士	strength + gentleman = *sumo wrestler*	**RIKI**·SHI リキ·シ

SAMPLE SENTENCE

中山さん は 車 のビジネス で
Naka·yama-san wa kuruma no bijinesu de
Nakayama-san car business
とても 有力 な 人 です。
totemo YŪ·RYOKU na hito desu.
very powerful person is
= *In the automotive business, Nakayama-san is a very powerful person.*

WRITING PRACTICE

KANJI 64

SUMMER

一	一	丆	丙	百	百	百	頁	夏
夏								

BUILDING THIS KANJI
One (top of a bun) 一 (3) + **Self** 自 (33) + **Running Chicken** 夂 = 夏

MEANING
Summer.

REMEMBERING THIS KANJI
When SUMMER rolls around I enjoy throwing parties, but like most farming folk, I don't stand on ceremony. After all, what with it being so darn hot in the SUMMER, the last thing I want to do is cook! So you'd better be prepared if you drop by. I'll give you the **top of a bun**, of course, but you'll be heading straight to the coop after that. "Go catch yourself a **running chicken**," I'll say. "This here's a **self**-serve party."

COMMON PRONUNCIATIONS
Common **ON** reading: **KA** (カ)
Common **kun** reading: **natsu** (なつ)

kun-yomi suggestion: "**gnat soup**"

Create your **on-yomi** keyword and enter it in the table at the back of the book. After that, write your sentence to remember the **on-yomi** and **kun-yomi** readings in the box below.

LESS COMMON PRONUNCIATIONS
Less common **ON** reading: **GE** (ゲ)
Less common **kun** reading: none

COMMON WORDS AND COMPOUNDS		
夏	*summer*	**natsu** なつ
夏休み	summer + rest = *summer vacation*	**natsu** yasu·mi なつ やす·み
夏物	summer + thing = *summer clothing*	**natsu**·mono なつ·もの
立夏	stand + summer = *first day of summer*	RIK·**KA** リッ·カ

SAMPLE SENTENCE

この 夏 には 東京 へ 行きます。
kono natsu ni wa TŌ·KYŌ e i·kimasu.
this summer Tokyo go
= *(We'll) be going to Tokyo this summer.*

WRITING PRACTICE

KANJI 65

THOUSAND

ノ	二	千						

BUILDING THIS KANJI
Comet 一 **+ Ten (scarecrow)** 十(28) = 千

MEANING
Thousand. Like the character for "hundred" (Entry 51), this kanji sometimes conveys a general idea of "many".

REMEMBERING THIS KANJI
My favorite story in the "THOUSAND and One Nights" is the tale in which a comet on a THOUSAND-year journey has a chat with a **scarecrow**.

"What's up?" he asks.

"Nothing much besides my getting sick of this view," answers the **scarecrow**. "I must say, I'd sure love to take a trip like yours."

"Well, why don't you go, then?" says the **comet**, smiling. "Remember: a journey of a THOUSAND miles starts with a single step."

"Gee, thanks for that pearl of wisdom," says the scarecrow sarcastically. "In case you haven't noticed, I'm tied to a couple of boards here."

COMMON PRONUNCIATIONS
Common **ON** reading: **SEN** (セン)
Common **kun** reading: none

As seen with the kanji "百", note how SEN changes phonetically with different numbers, and how **kun-yomi** are used in examples four and seven.

Create your **on-yomi** keyword and enter it in the table at the back of the book. After that, write your sentence to remember the **on-yomi** reading in the box below.

LESS COMMON PRONUNCIATIONS
Less common **ON** reading: none
Less common **kun** reading: **chi** (ち)

COMMON WORDS AND COMPOUNDS		
千	*one thousand*	**SEN** セン
二千	two + thousand = *two thousand*	NI·**SEN** ニ·セン
三千	three + thousand = *three thousand*	SAN·**ZEN** サン·ゼン
四千	four + thousand = *four thousand*	yon·**SEN** よん·セン
五千	five + thousand = *five thousand*	GO·**SEN** ゴ·セン
六千	six + thousand = *six thousand*	ROKU·**SEN** ロク·セン
七千	seven + thousand = *seven thousand*	nana·**SEN** なな·セン
八千	eight + thousand = *eight thousand*	HAS·**SEN** ハッ·セン
九千	nine + thousand = *nine thousand*	KYŪ·**SEN** キュウ·セン

SAMPLE SENTENCE

米 は 七千円 なので 安くない。
kome wa nana·SEN·EN na no de yasu·kunai.
rice seven thousand yen because not cheap
= *At seven thousand yen, rice isn't cheap.*

WRITING PRACTICE

COMPONENT 66

GIRAFFE 亻

You will notice this component used extensively in written Japanese, as it appears in almost one hundred kanji.

KANJI 66

休 **REST**

ノ	亻	亻一	什	休	休			

BUILDING THIS KANJI
Giraffe 亻 + **Tree** 木(13) = 休

MEANING
Rest.

REMEMBERING THIS KANJI
One of the surprises of my trip to Africa was learning that **giraffes** RESTED in trees. The safari leader mentioned that this was natural behavior. "They prefer baobabs," he said. "The branches are lower, so when the **giraffes** make a running leap at them they can jump higher into the **tree**. But this is not done simply for REST," he then added. "It also serves as an effective way for any **giraffe** to avoid its natural creditors."

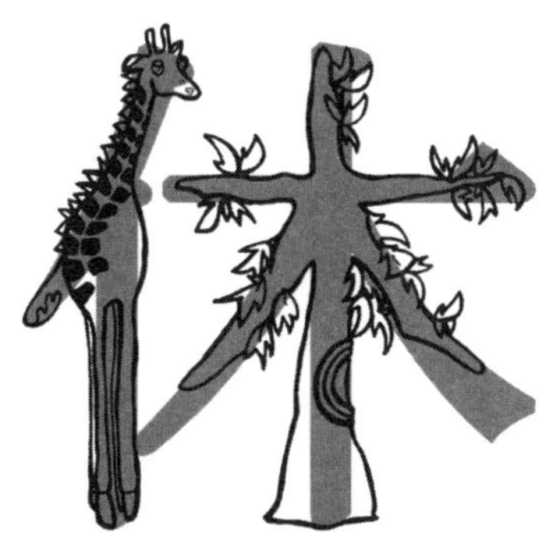

COMMON PRONUNCIATIONS
Common **ON** reading: **KYŪ** (キュウ)
Common **kun** reading: **yasu** (やす)

kun-yomi suggestion: "**try a sou**ffle"

Create your **on-yomi** keyword and enter it in the table at the back of the book. After that, write your sentence to remember the **on-yomi** and **kun-yomi** readings in the box below.

LESS COMMON PRONUNCIATIONS
Less common **ON** reading: none
Less common **kun** reading: none

COMMON WORDS AND COMPOUNDS		
休む	*to rest*	**yasu**·mu やす·む
お休み	*"Good night!"*	o·**yasu**·mi お·やす·み
休日	rest + sun (day) = *holiday*	**KYŪ**·JITSU キュウ·ジツ
夏休み	summer + rest = *summer vacation*	natsu **yasu**·mi なつ やす·み
冬休み	winter + rest = *winter vacation*	fuyu **yasu**·mi ふゆ やす·み
休火山	rest + fire + mountain = *dormant volcano*	**KYŪ**·KA·ZAN キュウ·カ·ザン

SAMPLE SENTENCE

山口さん は 半日 休みました。
Yama·guchi-san wa HAN·NICHI yasu·mimashita.
Yamaguchi-san half a day rested
= *Yamaguchi-san rested for half a day.*

WRITING PRACTICE

KANJI 67

手 HAND

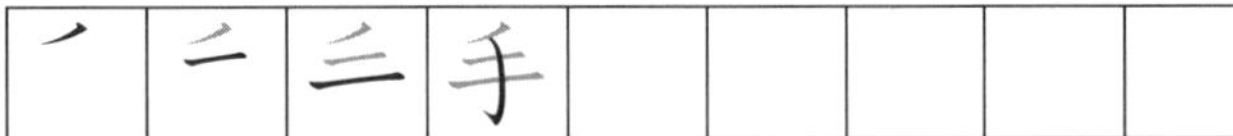

MEANING
Hand. No story required.

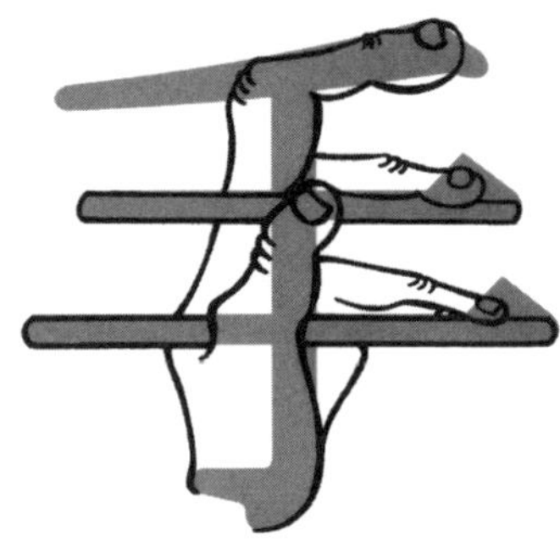

COMMON PRONUNCIATIONS
Common **ON** reading: **SHU** (シュ)
Common **kun** reading: **te** (て)

The **kun-yomi** is by far the most common reading.

kun-yomi suggestion: "**ta**ble"

Create your **on-yomi** keyword and enter it in the table at the back of the book. After that, write your sentence to remember the **on-yomi** and **kun-yomi** readings in the box below.

LESS COMMON PRONUNCIATIONS
Less common **ON** reading: none
Less common **kun** reading: **ta** (た)

ta (た) is an extremely rare reading, although it does show up in 下手, a common irregular reading we learned back in Chapter 2. It is presented again below following its companion; the two words are best learned as a pair.

IRREGULAR READINGS		
上手	upper + hand = *to be good at (something)*	JŌ·**zu** ジョウ·ず
下手	lower + hand = *to be poor at (something)*	he·**ta** へ·た

COMMON WORDS AND COMPOUNDS		
手	*hand*	**te** て
右手	right + hand = *right hand*	migi·**te** みぎ·て
左手	left + hand = *left hand*	hidari·**te** ひだり·て
手元	hand + basis = *at hand*	**te**·moto て·もと
手首	hand + neck = *wrist*	**te**·kubi て·くび
手話	hand + speak = *sign language*	**SHU**·WA シュ·ワ
空手	empty + hand = *karate*	kara·**te** から·て

SAMPLE SENTENCE
の ピアニスト の 手 は 美しい です ね。
ano pianisuto no te wa utsuku·shii desu ne.
that pianist hands beautiful aren't they
= *That pianist's hands are beautiful, aren't they?*

WRITING PRACTICE

KANJI 68

MAIN

BUILDING THIS KANJI
Tree 木(13) + One (hamburger patty) 一(3) = 本

MEANING

This intriguing character encompasses a range of meanings from "main" to "origin", and is also used to emphasize the idea of "this". When encountered alone, however, it often indicates a book. It is also one of the more common of an infamous group of kanji that Japanese uses for counting, being employed for long, cylindrical objects such as pencils and bottles. The sense of "origin", incidentally, is evident in the compound for Japan itself, the "Land of the Rising Sun".

REMEMBERING THIS KANJI

Despite cultural differences, there is a surprising amount of commonality in the world's MAIN myths. The people of Ur, for example, clearly tell Enkidu in the "Epic of Gilgamesh" that the MAIN race of people was conceived from a "union between **hamburger patty** and **tree**". Beowulf, too, quotes Norse mythology to explain the MAIN purpose of mankind: "Go forth, so that from **patties** will sprout mighty **trees**…" Coincidence? In the MAIN, it's unlikely.

COMMON PRONUNCIATIONS

Common **ON** reading: **HON** (ホン)
Common **kun** reading: **moto** (もと)

The **kun-yomi** is common in Japanese family and place names; the fifth compound below provides an example. Create your **on-yomi** keyword and enter it in the table at the back of the book. After that, write your sentence to remember the **on-yomi** and **kun-yomi** readings in the box below.

LESS COMMON PRONUNCIATIONS

Less common **ON** reading: none
Less common **kun** reading: none

COMMON WORDS AND COMPOUNDS		
本	*book*	**HON** ホン
日本	sun + main = *Japan*	NI·**HON** ニ·ホン NIP·**PON** ニッ·ポン
全日本	complete + sun + main = *all Japan*	ZEN·NI·**HON** ゼン·ニ·ホン
日本人	sun + main + person = *a Japanese (person)*	NI·**HON**·JIN ニ·ホン·ジン
山本さん	mountain + main = *Yamamoto-san*	yama·**moto**·san やま·もと·さん
日本語	sun + main + words = *Japanese (language)*	NI·**HON**·GO ニ·ホン·ゴ
本土	main + earth = *mainland*	**HON**·DO ホン·ド

SAMPLE SENTENCE

山下さん　は　高い　本　を買いました。
Yama·shita-san wa taka·i HON o ka·imashita.
Yamashita-san expensive book bought
= *Yamashita-san bought an expensive book.*

WRITING PRACTICE

COMPONENT 69

BEGGAR 匕 

KANJI 69

化 CHANGE

ノ	イ	イ丿	化				

BUILDING THIS KANJI
Giraffe 亻 + **Beggar** 匕 = 化

MEANING

Change/Transform. When used as a suffix (as in several of the compounds below), this character expresses a variety of English words ending in "-ification" or "-ization".

REMEMBERING THIS KANJI

Grandpa liked nothing more than to help those down on their luck. But he never gave money. I learned this when I saw him carrying a stuffed **giraffe** down to skid row one day.

"This is for you," he said to a **beggar**, passing him the toy. "A companion to share your woe."

The **beggar** nodded, and after taking his gift started immediately across the street.

"Where are you going?" Grandpa asked.

"This **giraffe** is so wonderful," said the **beggar**, "that I want to show it to all my friends in the pawn shop."

Grandpa smiled. "Now do you understand?" he said to me. "Giving money CHANGES nothing. It is only through stuffed **giraffes** that a **beggar's** life can truly be CHANGED."

COMMON PRONUNCIATIONS

Common **ON** reading: **KA** (カ)
Common **kun** reading: none

Create your **on-yomi** keyword and enter it in the table at the back of the book. After that, write your sentence to remember the **on-yomi** reading in the box below.

LESS COMMON PRONUNCIATIONS

Less common **ON** reading: **KE** (ケ)
Less common **kun** reading: **ba** (ば)

COMMON WORDS AND COMPOUNDS		
国有化	country + have + change = *nationalization*	KOKU·YŪ·**KA** コク·ユウ·カ
美化	beautiful + change = *beautification*	BI·**KA** ビ·カ
化学	change + study = *chemistry*	**KA**·GAKU カ·ガク
気化	spirit + change = *vaporize*	KI·**KA** キ·カ
電化	electric + change = *electrification*	DEN·**KA** デン·カ
同化	same + change = *assimilation*	DŌ·**KA** ドウ·カ

SAMPLE SENTENCE

山本さん は 化学 が 大好き です。
Yama·moto-san wa KA·GAKU ga DAI su·ki desu.
Yamamoto-san chemistry really likes
= *Yamamoto-san really likes chemistry.*

WRITING PRACTICE

KANJI 70

川 RIVER

ノ	川	川						

MEANING

River. No story required.

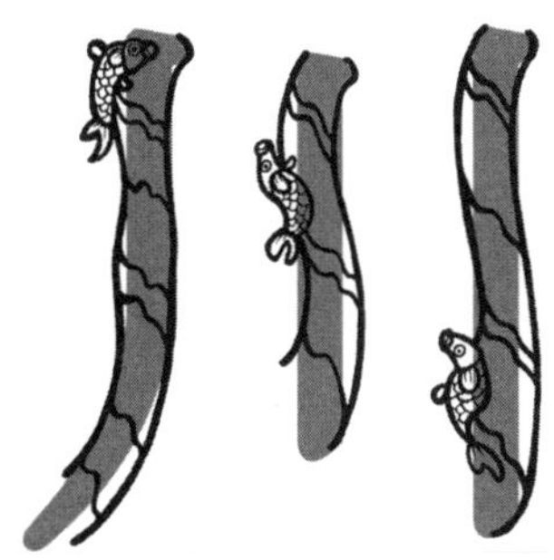

COMMON PRONUNCIATIONS

Common **ON** reading: none
Common **kun** reading: **kawa** (かわ)

When appearing as the final character in the names of rivers, this kanji is invariably voiced (becomes "**gawa**").

kun-yomi suggestion: "lac**k a wa**x"

Create your sentence to remember the **kun-yomi** reading in the box below.

LESS COMMON PRONUNCIATIONS

Less common **ON** reading: **SEN**
Less common **kun** reading: none

COMMON WORDS AND COMPOUNDS		
川	*river*	**kawa** かわ
川上	river + upper = *upstream*	**kawa**·kami かわ·かみ
川下	river + lower = *downstream*	**kawa**·shimo かわ·しも
川口	river + mouth = *river mouth*	**kawa**·guchi かわ·ぐち
川本さん	river + main = *Kawamoto-san*	**kawa**·moto·san かわ·もと·さん

SAMPLE SENTENCE

山 の 上 に 行くと 川 が 見えます か。
yama no ue ni i·ku to kawa ga mi·emasu ka.
mountain upper go river can see
= *Can you see the river if you go to the top of the mountain?*

WRITING PRACTICE

KANJI 71

BODY

ノ	イ	仁	什	付	休	体		

BUILDING THIS KANJI
Giraffe 亻 + **Main** 本(68) = 体

MEANING

The physical body (of a person or object), as well as secondary ideas of "substance" and "style". Make sure to keep this character distinct in your mind from "休" (Entry 66).

REMEMBERING THIS KANJI

As the **main** part of a **giraffe's** identity is tied to its statuesque BODY, all **giraffes** have a tendency to be vain. This naturally breeds conflict on the savanna. It is a rare wildebeest, for example, who hasn't been left with crippling BODY issues after watching a **giraffe** stride nobly along in the distance. As cats, however, it is the lions who are especially BODY conscious and apt to take a slight personally. Though the **main** part of their diet lies elsewhere, they will attack any **giraffe** who looks down on them.

COMMON PRONUNCIATIONS

Common **ON** reading: **TAI** (タイ)
Common **kun** reading: **karada** (からだ)

kun-yomi suggestion: "m**a**ke **a rad a**mbulance"

Create your **on-yomi** keyword and enter it in the table at the back of the book. After that, write your sentence to remember the **on-yomi** and **kun-yomi** readings in the box below.

LESS COMMON PRONUNCIATIONS

Less common **ON** reading: **TEI** (テイ)
Less common **kun** reading: none

COMMON WORDS AND COMPOUNDS		
体	*body*	**karada** からだ
大体	large + body = *in general*	DAI·**TAI** ダイ・タイ
全体	complete + body = *the whole*	ZEN·**TAI** ゼン・タイ
肉体	meat + body = *the body*	NIKU·**TAI** ニク・タイ
体力	body + strength = *physical strength*	**TAI**·RYOKU タイ・リョク
自体	self + body = *in itself*	JI·**TAI** ジ・タイ
団体	group + body = *organization*	**DAN**·TAI ダン・タイ

SAMPLE SENTENCE

あの 人	は	すごく	体力	が	有ります。
ano hito	**wa**	**sugoku**	**TAI·RYOKU**	**ga**	**a·rimasu.**
that person		incredible	physical strength		has

= *That person has incredible physical strength.*

WRITING PRACTICE

COMPONENT 72

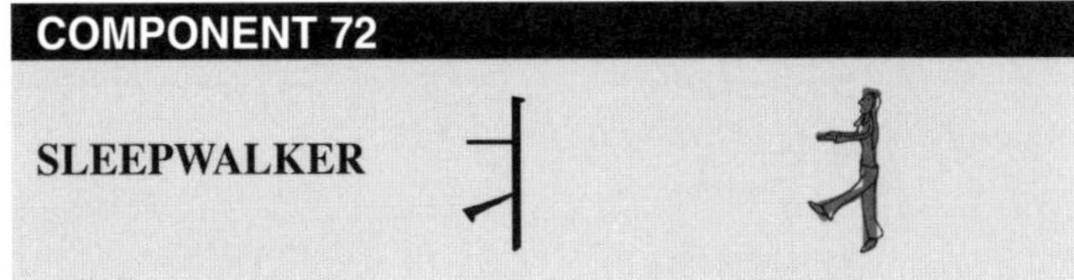

KANJI 72

NORTH

一	丨	丬	丬'	北				

BUILDING THIS KANJI
Sleepwalker 丬 + **Beggar** 匕 = 北

MEANING
North.

REMEMBERING THIS KANJI
Once upon a time, a **sleepwalker** heading NORTH passed a **beggar**. "I'd better follow," thought the **beggar**. "This **sleepwalker** might be on her way to Santa's workshop, and I hear that guy gives away lots of free stuff."

COMMON PRONUNCIATIONS
Common **ON** reading: **HOKU** (ホク)
Common **kun** reading: **kita** (きた)

As the final example shows, **HOKU** can double up with unvoiced consonant sounds.

kun-yomi suggestion: "**ski ta**x"

Create your **on-yomi** keyword and enter it in the table at the back of the book. After that, write your sentence to remember the **on-yomi** and **kun-yomi** readings in the box below.

LESS COMMON PRONUNCIATIONS
Less common **ON** reading: none
Less common **kun** reading: none

COMMON WORDS AND COMPOUNDS		
北	*north*	**kita** きた
北米	north + rice (America) = *North America*	**HOKU**·BEI ホク·ベイ
北口	north + mouth = *north exit/entrance*	**kita**·guchi きた·ぐち
北東	north + east = *northeast*	**HOKU**·TŌ ホク·トウ
北西	north + west = *northwest*	**HOKU**·SEI ホク·セイ
北海道	north + sea + road = *Hokkaido*	**HOK**·KAI·DŌ ホッ·カイ·ドウ

SAMPLE SENTENCE

北日本 の 冬 は とても 美しい。
kita·NI·HON no fuyu wa totemo utsuku·shii.
northern Japan winter very beautiful
= *Northern Japan's winter is very beautiful.*

WRITING PRACTICE

KANJI 73

田

RICE FIELD

MEANING

"Rice field", or a "field" in general. No story required.

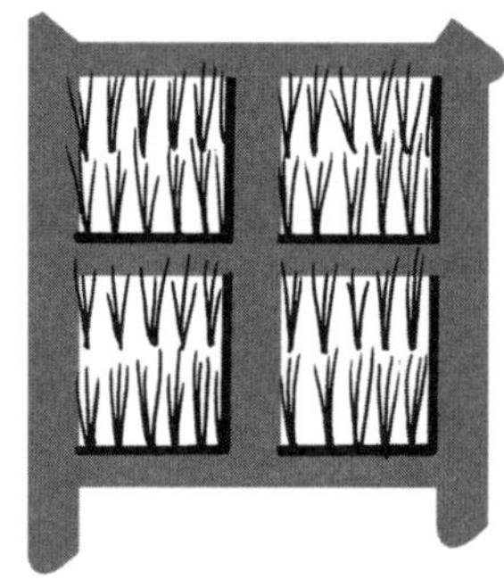

COMMON PRONUNCIATIONS

Common **ON** reading: **DEN** (デン)
Common **kun** reading: **ta** (た)

This kanji is commonly used in Japanese family names; it is often voiced, as in the fourth and fifth examples below, the latter of which has a mix of **on** and **kun-yomi**.

kun-yomi suggestion: "**ta**ck"

Create your **on-yomi** keyword and enter it in the table at the back of the book. After that, write your sentence to remember the **on-yomi** and **kun-yomi** readings in the box below.

LESS COMMON PRONUNCIATIONS

Less common **ON** reading: none
Less common **kun** reading: none

Here is a common irregular reading:

IRREGULAR READING		
田舎*	rice field + building = *the countryside*	**inaka** いなか

COMMON WORDS AND COMPOUNDS		
田	*rice field*	**ta** た
水田	water + rice field = *rice paddy*	SUI·**DEN** スイ·デン
田中さん	rice field + middle = *Tanaka-san*	**ta**·naka·san た·なか·さん
山田さん	mountain + rice field = *Yamada-san*	yama·**da**·san やま·だ·さん
本田さん	main + rice field = *Honda-san*	HON·**da**·san ホン·だ·さん

SAMPLE SENTENCE

水田　を　見　に　行きました。
SUI·DEN o mi ni i·kimashita.
rice paddy see went
= *(She) went to see the rice paddies.*

WRITING PRACTICE

KANJI 74

MAN

丨	冂	冂	田	田	男	男		

BUILDING THIS KANJI
Rice field 田(73) + **Strength** 力(63) = 男

MEANING
Man/Male.

REMEMBERING THIS KANJI
There is a story from feudal Japan in which a lord asks a group of MEN to demonstrate their **strength**. The task he sets them is simple: to lift up as much of a **rice field** as possible. Each MAN in the competition does his best, of course, but none save the last can pull up more than an armful of muck. What is this final MAN'S secret, you ask? It should be obvious: he was the only one with enough sense to use a bulldozer.

COMMON PRONUNCIATIONS
Common **ON** reading: **DAN** (ダン)
Common **kun** reading: **otoko** (おとこ)

kun-yomi suggestion: "**O! Toe co**ld"

Create your **on-yomi** keyword and enter it in the table at the back of the book. After that, write your sentence to remember the **on-yomi** and **kun-yomi** readings in the box below.

LESS COMMON PRONUNCIATIONS
Less common **ON** reading: **NAN** (ナン)
Less common **kun** reading: none

COMMON WORDS AND COMPOUNDS		
男	*man*	**otoko** おとこ
男女	man + woman = *men and women*	**DAN**·JO ダン·ジョ
男子	man + child = *men's*	**DAN**·SHI ダン·シ
大男	large + man = *large man*	ō·**otoko** おお·おとこ
雪男	snow + man = *the abominable snowman*	yuki·**otoko** ゆき·おとこ

SAMPLE SENTENCE

あの 男 の 人 は 五千円 をなくした。
ano otoko no hito wa GO·SEN·EN o nakushita.
that man person five thousand yen lost
= *That man lost five thousand yen.*

WRITING PRACTICE

COMPONENT 75

PIG 豕

KANJI 75

家 **HOUSE**

丶	丶丶	宀	宀	宀	宁	家	家	家
家								

BUILDING THIS KANJI
Pincers 宀 + **Pig** 豕 = 家

MEANING

This character generally imparts some sense of relation to a house or family. When used as a suffix, however, it denotes a person having some degree of skill or interest with respect to the kanji preceding it. The final compound below illustrates this aspect of its meaning.

REMEMBERING THIS KANJI

People told me I was crazy when they learned I was moving from my farm to the metropolis. 'The people are cold there, and you won't make any friends', they all said. Well, I went anyway, and to prove them I wrong got out my **pincers** and hung an enormous **pig** outside my HOUSE in order to welcome people as they walked by. And yet this is the strange thing: despite all the squealing for days on end, nobody visited, and when I told people my HOUSE was the one with the **pincers** and **pig**, they quit talking to me altogether! I guess everyone was right to say folks wouldn't be very friendly, 'cause they sure weren't when it came to my HOUSE.

COMMON PRONUNCIATIONS

Common **ON** reading: **KA** (カ)
Common **kun** reading: **ie** (いえ)

kun-yomi suggestion: "Canad**ia**n"

Create your **on-yomi** keyword and enter it in the table at the back of the book. After that, write your sentence to remember the **on-yomi** and **kun-yomi** readings in the box below.

LESS COMMON PRONUNCIATIONS

Less common **ON** reading: **KE** (ケ)
Less common **kun** reading: **ya** (や)

COMMON WORDS AND COMPOUNDS		
家	*house*	**ie** いえ
人家	person + house = *dwelling*	JIN·**KA** ジン·カ
売り家	sell + house = *"house for sale"*	u·ri **ie** う·り いえ
家具	house + tool = *furniture*	**KA**·GU カ·グ
愛鳥家	love + bird + house = *bird lover*	AI·CHŌ·**KA** アイ·チョウ·カ

SAMPLE SENTENCE

本田さん の 家 を 見ました か。
HON·da-san no ie o mi·mashita ka.
Honda-san house see
= *Did you see Honda-san's house?*

WRITING PRACTICE

KANJI 76

EAST

BUILDING THIS KANJI
Tree 木(13) + **Sun** 日(6) = 東

MEANING
East.

REMEMBERING THIS KANJI
Note that the writing order for this kanji does not follow that of the components as listed. This will happen only rarely; the image of a **sun** rising behind a **tree** in the EAST, however, is clearly the logical way to remember this character.

COMMON PRONUNCIATIONS
Common **ON** reading: **TŌ** (トウ)
Common **kun** reading: **higashi** (ひがし)

kun-yomi suggestion: "**he gash ea**sy…"

Create your **on-yomi** keyword and enter it in the table at the back of the book. After that, write your sentence to remember the **on-yomi** and **kun-yomi** readings in the box below.

LESS COMMON PRONUNCIATIONS
Less common **ON** reading: none
Less common **kun** reading: none

COMMON WORDS AND COMPOUNDS		
東	*east*	**higashi** ひがし
東口	east + mouth = *east exit/entrance*	**higashi**·guchi ひがし·ぐち
中東	middle + east = *the Middle East*	CHŪ·**TŌ** チュウ·トウ
東京	east + capital = *Tokyo*	**TŌ**·KYŌ トウ·キョウ
南東	south + east = *southeast*	NAN·**TŌ** ナン·トウ
北北東	north + north + east = *north-northeast*	HOKU·HOKU·**TŌ** ホク·ホク·トウ

SAMPLE SENTENCE
東口　のキオスクで　本　を買いました。
higashi·guchi no kiosuku de HON o ka·imashita.
east exit　kiosk　book　bought
= *(I) bought a book at the east exit kiosk.*

WRITING PRACTICE

KANJI 77

THINK

丨	冂	冂	冊	田	田	思	思	思

BUILDING THIS KANJI
Rice field 田(73) + **Heart** 心(25) = 思

MEANING
Think.

REMEMBERING THIS KANJI
And so I took the **heart** and buried it in a **rice field**. But soon I began to THINK: What if it rises to the surface? What if a thrifty animal digs it up for food? Horrors! All I could do was THINK…THINK of what I had done, until there was nothing in my head but the beating of that hideous **heart** in the **rice field**. But I know what you THINK: you either THINK I'm mad, or that this story sounds awfully familiar.

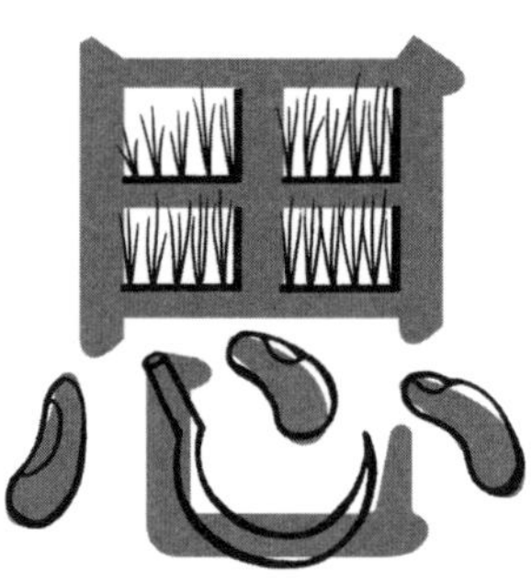

COMMON PRONUNCIATIONS
Common **ON** reading: **SHI** (シ)
Common **kun** reading: **omo** (おも)

kun-yomi suggestion: **"o, mow…"**

Create your **on-yomi** keyword and enter it in the table at the back of the book. After that, write your sentence to remember the **on-yomi** and **kun-yomi** readings in the box below.

LESS COMMON PRONUNCIATIONS
Less common **ON** reading: none
Less common **kun** reading: none

COMMON WORDS AND COMPOUNDS		
思う	*to think*	**omo**·u おも·う
思い出す	think + exit = *to remember*	**omo**·i da·su おも·い だ·す
物思い	thing + think = *pensiveness*	mono **omo**·i もの おも·い
思い切る	think + cut = *to make up one's mind*	**omo**·i ki·ru おも·い き·る
意思	mind + think = *(one's) intent*	**I·SHI** イ·シ

SAMPLE SENTENCE

テーブル の 上 に 四百円 ある と
tēburu no ue ni yon·HYAKU·EN aru to
table above four hundred yen is
思います。
omo·imasu.
think
= *(I) think there's four hundred yen on the table.*

WRITING PRACTICE

KANJI 78

EAR

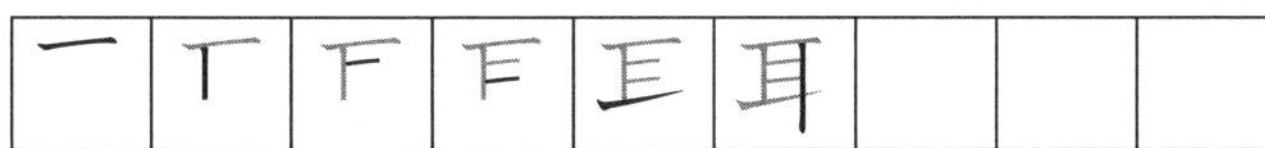

MEANING
Ear. No story required.

COMMON PRONUNCIATIONS
Common **ON** reading: none
Common **kun** reading: **mimi** (みみ)

kun-yomi suggestion: "**Me! Me!**"

Create your sentence to remember the **kun-yomi** reading in the box below.

LESS COMMON PRONUNCIATIONS
Less common **ON** reading: **JI** (ジ)
Less common **kun** reading: none

COMMON WORDS AND COMPOUNDS		
耳	*ear*	**mimi** みみ
耳元	ear + basis = *close to one's ear*	**mimi**·moto みみ·もと
空耳	empty + ear = *mishearing; feigned deafness*	sora·**mimi** そら·みみ

SAMPLE SENTENCE

田中さん　の　耳　が 赤い。
Ta·naka-san no mimi ga aka·i.
Tanaka-san ears red
= *Tanaka-san's ears are red.*

WRITING PRACTICE

COMPONENT 79

WISHBONES 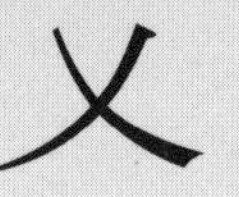 

KANJI 79

FATHER

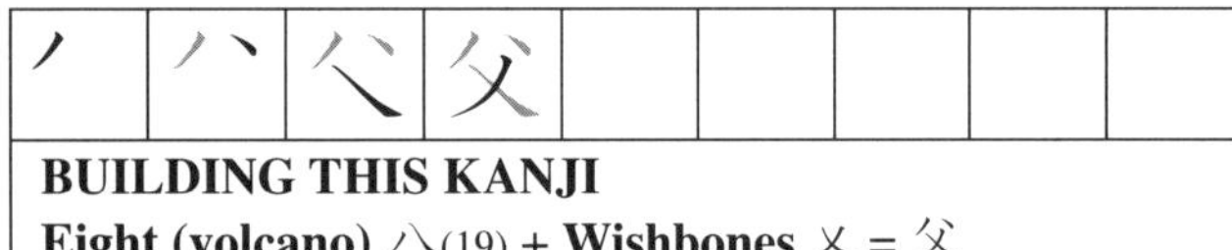

BUILDING THIS KANJI
Eight (volcano) 八(19) + **Wishbones** 乂 = 父

MEANING
Father.

REMEMBERING THIS KANJI
Jupiter, as FATHER of the gods, can do whatever he wants. Unfortunately, he's not as environmentally conscious as he should be, and often uses the nearest **volcano** to dump **wishbones** and other scraps from his plate. Jupiter's son Vulcan, the god of **volcanoes**, naturally takes exception to this behavior. "So help me, FATHER," he says, "if I wake up with any more **wishbones** on my rug, I might just erupt."

COMMON PRONUNCIATIONS
Common **ON** reading: **FU** (フ)
Common **kun** reading: **chichi** (ちち)

The various words for father shown below reflect differing levels of familiarity and politeness; most terms used for addressing people in Japan have multiple forms such as these.

kun-yomi suggestion: "**Chichi** Rodriguez"

Create your **on-yomi** keyword and enter it in the table at the back of the book. After that, write your sentence to remember the **on-yomi** and **kun-yomi** readings in the box below.

LESS COMMON PRONUNCIATIONS
Less common **ON** reading: none
Less common **kun** reading: none

These two irregular readings are extremely common.

IRREGULAR READINGS		
お父さん	father = *father*	otōsan おとうさん
伯父さん*	related + father = *uncle*	ojisan おじさん

COMMON WORDS AND COMPOUNDS		
父	*father*	**chichi** ちち
父の日	father + sun (day) = *Father's Day*	**chichi**·no·hi ちち·の·ひ
父母	father + mother = *father and mother*	**FU**·**BO** フ·ボ
父親	father + parent = *father*	**chichi**·oya ちち·おや

SAMPLE SENTENCE

父 は ビジネス で 東京 へ 行きました。
chichi wa bijinesu de TŌ·KYŌ e i·kimashita.
Father business Tokyo went
= *Father went to Tokyo on business.*

WRITING PRACTICE

KANJI 80

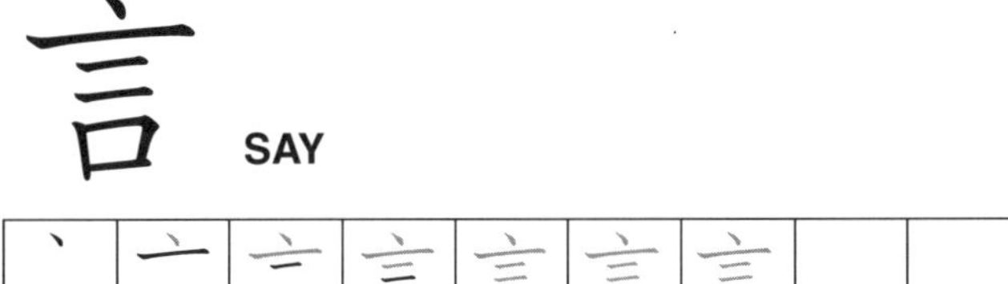

SAY

丶	亠	亠	言	言	言	言		

MEANING

"Saying", and things of a verbal nature. This character, incidentally, will become very familiar; it appears in more than sixty other kanji.

REMEMBERING THIS KANJI

"I vant…to drink…yours…blood". Isn't this what a **vampire** like Dracula always SAYS? Sure, you SAY, but what's with the bad grammar? Well, give Dracula a break; he's from Transylvania, and English isn't his first language. Notice, by the way, that the second stroke from the top is longer than those above or below it.

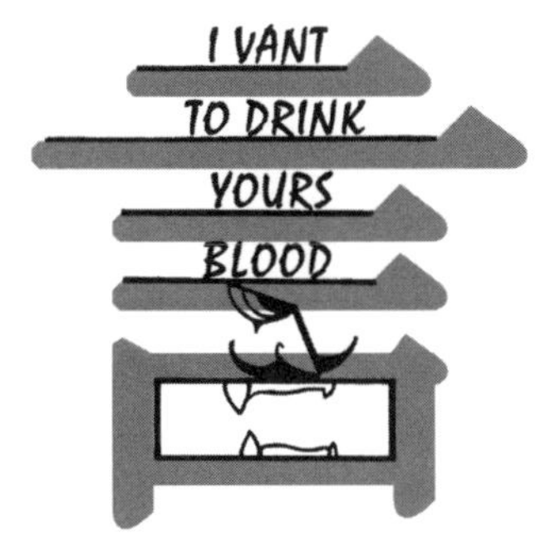

COMMON PRONUNCIATIONS

Common **ON** reading: **GEN** (ゲン)
Common **kun** reading: **i** (い)

kun-yomi suggestion: "**ea**ger"

Create your **on-yomi** keyword and enter it in the table at the back of the book. After that, write your sentence to remember the **on-yomi** and **kun-yomi** readings in the box below.

LESS COMMON PRONUNCIATIONS

Less common **ON** reading: **GON** (ゴン)
Less common **kun** reading: **koto** (こと)

The reading **koto** will be encountered primarily in the Japanese term for "word": **koto·ba** (こと·ば), composed of the kanji 言葉 (Say/Leaf *).

COMMON WORDS AND COMPOUNDS		
言う	*to say*	**i**·u い·う
言い回し	say + rotate = *(turn of) expression*	**i**·i mawa·shi い·い まわ·し
明言	bright + say = *declaration*	MEI·**GEN** メイ·ゲン
言語	say + words = *language*	**GEN**·GO ゲン·ゴ
言い出す	say + exit = *to begin to say*	**i**·i da·su い·い だ·す
言い切る	say + cut = *to say definitively*	**i**·i ki·ru い·い き·る

SAMPLE SENTENCE

川本さん　も　"はい"　と　言いました。
Kawa·moto-san mo "hai" to i·imashita.
Kawamoto-san also "yes" said
= Kawamoto-san also said "yes".

WRITING PRACTICE

CHAPTER 4 REVIEW EXERCISES

A. Please match the following kanji to their meanings.

1. 父	a. Body
2. 川	b. Hand
3. 安	c. Father
4. 東	d. Thousand
5. 手	e. Main
6. 男	f. Ease
7. 千	g. Man
8. 力	h. East
9. 体	i. Strength
10. 本	j. River

B. Please match the following meanings to their kanji, and these to their **on** or **kun-yomi**.

1. Rest	a. 田	1. **GEN** (ゲン)
2. Change	b. 耳	2. **HOKU** (ホク)
3. North	c. 化	3. **SHI** (シ)
4. House (**kun-yomi**)	d. 言	4. **yasu** (やす)
5. Rice field	e. 夏	5. **SUI** (スイ)
6. Think	f. 休	6. **ta** (た)
7. Summer (**kun-yomi**)	g. 家	7. **natsu** (なつ)
8. Say	h. 水	8. **ie** (いえ)
9. Water	i. 北	9. **KA** (カ)
10. Ear	j. 思	10. **mimi** (みみ)

C. Please choose the best answer(s) to the following questions.

1. Which of the following readings apply to the kanji 東?
   a. **TŌ** (トウ)
   b. **higashi** (ひがし)
   c. **KA** (カ)
   d. **kita** (きた)
   e. **minami** (みなみ)

2. Which of the following readings apply to the kanji 男?
   a. **onna** (おんな)
   b. **DAN** (ダン)
   c. **otoko** (おとこ)
   d. **KYŪ** (キュウ)
   e. **SUI** (スイ)

3. Which of the following kanji have an **on-yomi** of **KA** (カ)?
   a. 夏
   b. 北
   c. 思
   d. 家
   e. 化

4. What would make a nice gift for a pair of newlyweds?
   a. 手
   b. 体
   c. 耳
   d. 家
   e. 北

5. Which of the following readings apply to the kanji 体?
   a. **SHŌ** (ショウ)
   b. **TAI** (タイ)
   c. **omo** (おも)
   d. **DAI** (ダイ)
   e. **karada** (からだ)

D. Please choose the best answer to the following questions.

1. Which of the following kanji has the most number of strokes?
   a. 東
   b. 男
   c. 言
   d. 思
   e. 体

2. Which is the correct reading of 安い?
   a. **omo·i** (おも·い)
   b. **yasu·i** (やす·い)
   c. **taka·i** (たか·い)
   d. **ō·i** (おお·い)

3. Which is the correct reading of 思う?
   a. **ka·u** (か·う)
   b. **ko·u** (こ·う)
   c. **omo·u** (おも·う)
   d. **o·u** (お·う)

4. Which kanji would precede 力 to form the compound for "physical strength"?
   a. 休
   b. 本
   c. 東
   d. 体
   e. 耳

5. Which is the correct reading of 言う?
   a. **i·u** (い·う)
   b. **o·u** (お·う)
   c. **a·u** (あ·う)
   d. **omo·u** (おも·う)

E. Please match the following compounds and words to their meanings and pronunciations.

1. 大体	a. Close to one's ear	1. **SUI·CHŪ** (スイ·チュウ)
2. 全日本	b. Peace of mind	2. **te·kubi** (て·くび)
3. 北米	c. In general	3. **mimi·moto** (みみ·もと)
4. 耳元	d. Summer vacation	4. **i·i mawa·shi** (い·い まわ·し)
5. 水中	e. Powerful	5. **AN·SHIN** (アン·シン)
6. 有力	f. North America	6. **ZEN·NI·HON** (ゼン·ニ·ホン)
7. 言い回し	g. Wrist	7. **natsu yasu·mi** (なつ やす·み)
8. 夏休み	h. All Japan	8. **HOKU·BEI** (ホク·ベイ)
9. 手首	i. (Turn of) expression	9. **DAI·TAI** (ダイ·タイ)
10. 安心	j. Underwater/ In the water	10. **YŪ·RYOKU** (ユウ·リョク)

CHAPTER 5 (KANJI 81-100)

KANJI 81

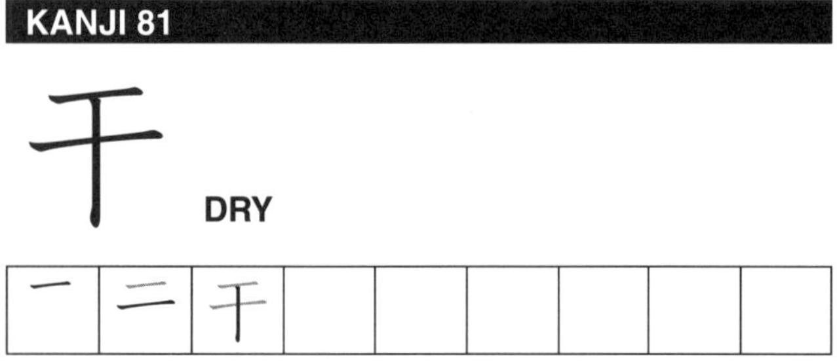

DRY

MEANING

Dry/Ebb. This character will not be encountered frequently. It does figure as a component in other more common kanji, however, and because of this is presented here. Take a moment to note the difference between this character and 千 (Entry 65). No story required.

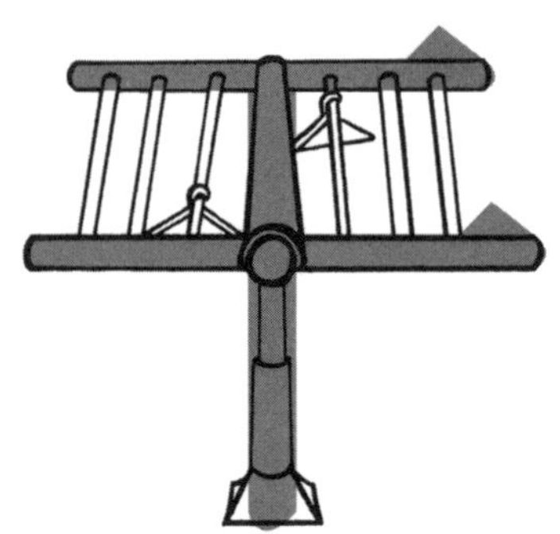

COMMON PRONUNCIATIONS

Common **ON** reading: none
Common **kun** readings: **hi** (ひ); **ho** (ほ)

As seen in the third example below, the **kun-yomi** "**ho**" can become voiced in the second position.

kun-yomi suggestions: "**he**at"; "**ho**se"

Create your sentence to remember the **kun-yomi** readings in the box below.

LESS COMMON PRONUNCIATIONS

Less common **ON** reading: **KAN** (カン)
Less common **kun** reading: none

COMMON WORDS AND COMPOUNDS		
干る (intr)	*to dry (on its own)*	**hi**·ru ひ·る
干す (tr)	*to dry (something)*	**ho**·su ほ·す
日干し	sun + dry = *sun-dried*	hi **bo**·shi ひ ぼ·し
干上がる	dry + upper = *to dry up*	**hi** a·garu ひ あ·がる
干物	dry + thing = *dried fish*	**hi**·mono ひ·もの

SAMPLE SENTENCE

干物 を買って 下さい。
hi·mono o kat·te kuda·sai.
dried fish buy please
= *Please buy dried fish.*

WRITING PRACTICE

KANJI 82

GOLD

BUILDING THIS KANJI
Umbrella 𠆢 + **Dry** 干(81) + **Snowboard** ⺍ = 金

MEANING

Depending on the context in which it appears, this common character signifies either "gold", "metal", or "money". It clearly means "gold", for instance, when referring to the status of an Olympic champion. When functioning as a component, however, it hints that the kanji involved has some connection to metal in general.

REMEMBERING THIS KANJI

Following a quick break with his buddies, the **snowboarder** had another vision. This time, however, the genie was very specific: "Dude, unless this GOLDEN snowboard is kept **dry** at all times, it will immediately turn back into fiberglass. You must, therefore, always use an **umbrella**, even on the gnarliest runs. Should you not keep it **dry**…well, it would still be a decent enough board, it just wouldn't be GOLD anymore. And GOLD is like, really valuable."

COMMON PRONUNCIATIONS

Common **ON** reading: **KIN** (キン)
Common **kun** reading: **kane** (かね)

kun-yomi suggestion: "**Khan a**te"

Create your **on-yomi** keyword and enter it in the table at the back of the book. After that, write your sentence to remember the **on-yomi** and **kun-yomi** readings in the box below.

LESS COMMON PRONUNCIATIONS

Less common **ON** reading: **KON** (コン)
Less common **kun** reading: **kana** (かな)

COMMON WORDS AND COMPOUNDS		
金	*gold; metal; money*	**KIN** キン
金	*metal; money*	**kane** かね
金山	gold + mountain = *gold mine*	**KIN**·ZAN キン·ザン
年金	year + gold (money) = *annuity/pension*	NEN·**KIN** ネン·キン
金曜日	gold + day of the week + sun (day) = *Friday*	**KIN**·YŌ·bi キン·ヨウ·び
金星	gold + star = *Venus (planet)*	**KIN**·SEI キン·セイ

SAMPLE SENTENCE

内田さん　は　あまり　お金　が　ない。
Uchi·da-san wa amari o·kane ga nai.
Uchida-san not much money not
= *Uchida-san doesn't have much money.*

WRITING PRACTICE

KANJI 83

WORDS

BUILDING THIS KANJI
Say 言(80)+ **Five** 五(14) + **Mouth (vampire)** 口(8) = 語

MEANING

Words. This kanji will become familiar as the character used to indicate languages; a pair of examples can be seen in the compounds below.

REMEMBERING THIS KANJI
Mark my WORDS: despite what **vampires** everywhere will **say**, you do not want to go to a pentagon party with **five** of them. Their reassuring WORDS of such events being "normal Transylvanian hospitality" are far from the truth.

COMMON PRONUNCIATIONS

Common **ON** reading: **GO** (ゴ)
Common **kun** reading: **kata** (かた)

Note the importance of long and short vowel sounds in Japanese by looking closely at the second and third examples below. Also note the presence of an irregular reading (上手) in the sample sentence.

kun-yomi suggestion: "**cat a**cne"

Create your **on-yomi** keyword and enter it in the table at the back of the book. After that, write your sentence to remember the **on-yomi** and **kun-yomi** readings in the box below.

LESS COMMON PRONUNCIATIONS

Less common **ON** reading: none
Less common **kun** reading: **katari** (かたり)

COMMON WORDS AND COMPOUNDS		
語る	*to talk*	**kata**·ru かた·る
口語	mouth + words = *colloquial language*	KŌ·**GO** コウ·ゴ
古語	old + words = *archaic word*	KO·**GO** コ·ゴ
日本語	sun + main + words = *Japanese (language)*	NI·HON·**GO** ニ·ホン·ゴ
言語	say + words = *language*	GEN·**GO** ゲン·ゴ
英語	English + words = *English (language)*	EI·**GO** エイ·ゴ
語学	words + study = *linguistics*	**GO**·GAKU ゴ·ガク

SAMPLE SENTENCE

あなた の 日本語 は 上手 です よ。
anata no NI·HON·GO wa JŌ·zu desu yo.
you Japanese good at
= *Your Japanese is good!*

WRITING PRACTICE

KANJI 84

士 GENTLEMAN

一	十	士						

MEANING

The sense is of a gentleman, or of a man who has attained status in a military or academic field. No story required.

COMMON PRONUNCIATIONS

Common **ON** reading: **SHI** (シ)

Common **kun** reading: none

Create your **on-yomi** keyword and enter it in the table at the back of the book. After that, write your sentence to remember the **on-yomi** reading in the box below.

LESS COMMON PRONUNCIATIONS

Less common **ON** reading: none

Less common **kun** reading: none

COMMON WORDS AND COMPOUNDS		
力士	strength + gentleman = *sumo wrestler*	RIKI·**SHI** リキ·シ
士気	gentleman + spirit = *morale*	**SHI**·KI シ·キ
工学士	craft + study + gentleman = *Bachelor of Engineering*	KŌ·GAKU·**SHI** コウ·ガク·シ

SAMPLE SENTENCE

あの 力士 は とても 大きい です よ。

ano RIKI·SHI wa totemo ōkii desu yo.

that sumo wrestler very large is

= *That sumo wrestler is really large!*

WRITING PRACTICE

KANJI 85

MORNING

一	十	十	古	古	古	直	卓	卓
朝	朝	朝						

BUILDING THIS KANJI
Ten (scarecrow) 十(28)+ **Early** 早(29) + **Moon** 月(11) = 朝

MEANING

Morning. A secondary meaning relates to royal dynasties.

REMEMBERING THIS KANJI

As always, each MORNING the **moon** gave a wink to the **scarecrow**. "You're up early," he said.

"For godsakes," said the **scarecrow**. "When are you going to get tired of that joke?"

COMMON PRONUNCIATIONS

Common **ON** reading: **CHŌ** (チョウ)
Common **kun** reading: **asa** (あさ)

Note the mix of **on** and **kun-yomi** in the final example below.

kun-yomi suggestion: "**Casa**nova"

Create your **on-yomi** keyword and enter it in the table at the back of the book. After that, write your sentence to remember the **on-yomi** and **kun-yomi** readings in the box below.

LESS COMMON PRONUNCIATIONS

Less common **ON** reading: none
Less common **kun** reading: none

IRREGULAR READING		
今朝*	now + morning = *this morning*	**kesa** けさ

COMMON WORDS AND COMPOUNDS		
朝	*morning*	**asa** あさ
朝日	morning + sun = *morning sun*	**asa**·hi あさ·ひ
王朝	king + morning = *dynasty*	Ō·**CHŌ** オウ·チョウ
早朝	early + morning = *early morning*	SŌ·**CHŌ** ソウ·チョウ
毎朝	every + morning = *every morning*	MAI·**asa** マイ·あさ

SAMPLE SENTENCE

上田さん は 朝 が 大好き です。
Ue·da-san wa asa ga DAI su·ki desu.
Ueda-san morning really likes
= *Ueda-san really likes mornings.*

WRITING PRACTICE

COMPONENT 86

CANDLESTICK HOLDER 𡗗

KANJI 86

青 BLUE

一	十	丰	丰	丰	青	青	青	

BUILDING THIS KANJI
Candlestick Holder 𡗗 + **Moon** 月 (11) = 青

MEANING

Blue. Interestingly, this character is also applied to a few objects that Westerners invariably consider green, so prepare yourself to be confronted with blue traffic lights and blue vegetables, amongst other things. As in English, the sense of youth and immaturity is tied up with this idea of "green"; the third compound below provides an example.

REMEMBERING THIS KANJI

Even the **moon** can get depressed, and on those occasions when he's feeling BLUE he doesn't give off his normal amount of light. To cover up for this he'll take out a **candlestick holder**, but as there's nothing in it, his ploy doesn't fool anyone. Luckily for us, he only feels this way once in a BLUE **moon**.

COMMON PRONUNCIATIONS

Common **ON** reading: **SEI** (セイ)
Common **kun** reading: **ao** (あお)

kun-yomi suggestion: "Laos"

Create your **on-yomi** keyword and enter it in the table at the back of the book. After that, write your sentence to remember the **on-yomi** and **kun-yomi** readings in the box below.

LESS COMMON PRONUNCIATIONS

Less common **ON** reading: **SHŌ** (ショウ)
Less common **kun** reading: none

COMMON WORDS AND COMPOUNDS		
青	*blue; green (noun)*	**ao** あお
青い	*blue; green (adjective)*	**ao**·i あお·い
青春	blue + spring = *youth*	**SEI**·SHUN セイ·シュン
青物	blue + thing = *green vegetables*	**ao**·mono あお·もの
青空	blue + empty (sky) = *blue sky*	**ao**·zora あお·ぞら

SAMPLE SENTENCE

山田さん　の　家　は　青い　です。
Yama·da-san no ie wa ao·i desu.
Yamada-san house blue
= *Yamada-san's house is blue.*

WRITING PRACTICE

KANJI 87

土 EARTH

MEANING

Think of earth here as in "dirt", not the planet on which we live. Take a moment to note the subtle difference between this kanji and "士" (Entry 84); you've developed a practiced eye if you're now able to take such variations into account! No story required.

COMMON PRONUNCIATIONS

Common **ON** reading: **DO** (ド)
Common **kun** reading: **tsuchi** (つ ち)

Note the mixture of **on-** and **kun-yomi** in the second example (and in the last, as expected).

kun-yomi suggestion: "go**t Sioux chee**tahs"

Create your **on-yomi** keyword and enter it in the table at the back of the book. After that, write your sentence to remember the **on-yomi** and **kun-yomi** readings in the box below.

LESS COMMON PRONUNCIATIONS

Less common **ON** reading: **TO** (ト)
Less common **kun** reading: none

IRREGULAR READING		
土産*	earth + produce = *souvenir*	**miyage** みやげ

COMMON WORDS AND COMPOUNDS		
土	*earth*	**tsuchi** つち
土手	earth + hand = *embankment*	**DO**·te ド·て
本土	main + earth = *mainland*	HON·**DO** ホン·ド
土木	earth + tree = *civil engineering*	**DO**·BOKU ド·ボク
土星	earth + star = *Saturn (planet)*	**DO**·SEI ド·セイ
土曜日	earth + day of the week + sun (day) = *Saturday*	**DO**·YŌ·bi ド·ヨウ·び

SAMPLE SENTENCE

川 の 土手 を 上がると 水田 が
kawa no DO·te o a·garu to SUI·DEN ga
river embankment go up rice paddies
見えます。
mi·emasu.
can see
= *If you go up the river embankment, you can see rice paddies.*

WRITING PRACTICE

COMPONENT 88

FINGER 扌 

A ring and a string for a finger. There will be little chance of forgetting this component, incidentally, as it is present in nearly a hundred kanji - most relating in some way to hands and arms.

KANJI 88

 **HANG**

一	亅	扌	扌	扌	扌	扌	扌	挂
掛	掛							

BUILDING THIS KANJI
Finger 扌 + **Earth** 土(87) + **Earth** 土(87) +
Poor Figure Skater 卜 = 掛

MEANING

Hang. Note how the last stroke of the bottom "earth" component leads into the next line by being drawn on an upward angle.

REMEMBERING THIS KANJI

Fingers can indicate harsh criticism, especially when it comes to bad figure skating. "HANG up your skates!" people will scream while pointing, making the **bad figure skater** want to hide behind a **couple piles of earth**. Some skaters, apparently, can do nothing but HANG their heads in shame.

COMMON PRONUNCIATIONS

Common **ON** reading: none
Common **kun** reading: **ka** (か)

As the final example below shows, this kanji can act similarly to 買う (Entry 50).

kun-yomi suggestion: "**ca**t"

There is no **on-yomi** reading for this character. Create your sentence to remember the **kun-yomi** reading in the box below.

LESS COMMON PRONUNCIATIONS

Less common **ON** reading: none
Less common **kun** reading: none

COMMON WORDS AND COMPOUNDS		
掛かる (intr)	*to hang (by oneself)*	**ka**·karu か·かる
掛ける (tr)	*to hang (something)*	**ka**·keru か·ける
掛金	hang + gold (money) = *installment*	**kake**·KIN かけ·キン

SAMPLE SENTENCE

シャツ を あそこ に 掛けて 下さい。
shatsu o asoko ni ka·kete kuda·sai.
shirts over there hang please
= *Please hang the shirts over there.*

WRITING PRACTICE

COMPONENT 89

CHAIR 力

KANJI 89

万 TEN THOUSAND

一	丂	万						

BUILDING THIS KANJI
One (top of a bun) 一(3) + **Chair** 力 = 万

MEANING

Ten thousand. More so than "百" and "千" (Entries 51 and 65), this character can express the general idea of a "countless amount" of something.

REMEMBERING THIS KANJI

The ancient writer Xenophon tells the story of TEN THOUSAND Greek mercenaries marching against Persia in 401 B.C. What is interesting is that each of the TEN THOUSAND carries a lawn **chair**, together with a shield shaped like the **top of a bun**.

COMMON PRONUNCIATIONS

Common **ON** reading: **MAN** (マン)
Common **kun** reading: none

As we saw for the kanji "百" and "千", note how the numbers four and seven appear with their **kun-yomi**.

Create your **on-yomi** keyword and enter it in the table at the back of the book. After that, write your sentence to remember the **on-yomi** and **kun-yomi** readings in the box below.

LESS COMMON PRONUNCIATIONS

Less common **ON** reading: **BAN** (バン)
Less common **kun** reading: none

BAN shows up in Japan's famous word for "hurrah!", 万歳 (Ten thousand/Annual *): **BAN·ZAI** (バン·ザイ)

COMMON WORDS AND COMPOUNDS		
一万	one + ten thousand = *ten thousand*	ICHI·**MAN** イチ·マン
二万	two + ten thousand = *twenty thousand*	NI·**MAN** ニ·マン
三万	three + ten thousand = *thirty thousand*	SAN·**MAN** サン·マン
四万	four + ten thousand = *forty thousand*	yon·**MAN** よん·マン
五万	five + ten thousand = *fifty thousand*	GO·**MAN** ゴ·マン
六万	six + ten thousand = *sixty thousand*	ROKU·**MAN** ロク·マン
七万	seven + ten thousand = *seventy thousand*	nana·**MAN** なな·マン
八万	eight + ten thousand = *eighty thousand*	HACHI·**MAN** ハチ·マン
九万	nine + ten thousand = *ninety thousand*	KYŪ·**MAN** キュウ·マン

SAMPLE SENTENCE

あの 国 の 人口 は 八万人
ano kuni no JIN·KŌ wa HACHI·MAN·NIN
that country population eighty thousand people
です。
desu.
is
= *That country's population is eighty thousand.*

WRITING PRACTICE

KANJI 90

RAIN

MEANING

Rain. This wonderfully distinctive character is more easily learned without being broken into components. Because of this, no story is required.

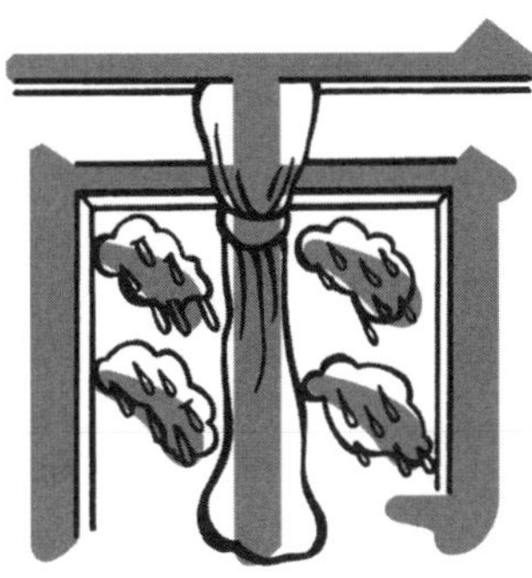

COMMON PRONUNCIATIONS

Common **ON** reading: none
Common **kun** readings: **ame** (あめ); **ama** (あま)

The **kun-yomi** "**ama**" only appears in the first position.

kun-yomi suggestions: "sc**am a**ge"; "**ama**retto"

Create your sentence to remember the **kun-yomi** readings in the box below.

LESS COMMON PRONUNCIATIONS

Less common **ON** reading: **U** (ウ)
Less common **kun** reading: none

The following word can be read with its normal **on-yomi**, but is often heard with the irregular reading pronunciation below.

IRREGULAR READING		
梅雨*	plum tree + rain = *the rainy season*	**tsuyu** つゆ

COMMON WORDS AND COMPOUNDS		
雨	*rain*	**ame** あめ
雨上がり	rain + upper = *after the rain*	**ame** a·gari あめ あ·がり
大雨	large + rain = *heavy rain*	ō·**ame** おお·あめ
雨空	rain + empty (sky) = *a rainy sky*	**ama**·zora あま·ぞら
雨雲	rain + cloud = *rain cloud*	**ama**·gumo あま·ぐも

SAMPLE SENTENCE

九月 には 日本 で 大雨 の
KU·GATSU ni wa NI·HON de ō·ame no
September Japan heavy rain
日 が 多い です。
hi ga ō·i desu.
day many
= *In September, Japan has many days with heavy rain.*

WRITING PRACTICE

KANJI 91

ELECTRIC

BUILDING THIS KANJI
Rain 雨(90) + **Sun** 日(6) + **Hook** L = 電

MEANING
Electric/Electricity.

REMEMBERING THIS KANJI
The atmosphere was ELECTRIC: **rain** and **sun** were on a collision course! At the last moment, however, a **hook** was used to hold the **sun** back, saving either it from being extinguished or the **rain** from being evaporated. As the kanji shows, the elements remain in this state even now, so close than an ELECTRIC current would have difficulty passing between them.

COMMON PRONUNCIATIONS
Common **ON** reading: **DEN** (デン)
Common **kun** reading: none

Create your **on-yomi** keyword and enter it in the table at the back of the book. After that, write your sentence to remember the **on-yomi** reading in the box below.

LESS COMMON PRONUNCIATIONS
Less common **ON** reading: none
Less common **kun** reading: none

COMMON WORDS AND COMPOUNDS		
電化	electric + change = *electrification*	**DEN**·KA デン·カ
電力	electric + strength = *electric power*	**DEN**·RYOKU デン·リョク
電子	electric + child = *electron*	**DEN**·SHI デン·シ
電気	electric + spirit = *electricity*	**DEN**·KI デン·キ
電話	electric + speak = *telephone*	**DEN**·WA デン·ワ
電車	electric + car = *(electric) train*	**DEN**·SHA デン·シャ

SAMPLE SENTENCE
田中さん　は　電車　を　下りました。
Ta·naka-san wa DEN·SHA o o·rimashita.
Tanaka-san train descended
= *Tanaka-san got off the train.*

WRITING PRACTICE

COMPONENT 92

UFO 

Make sure you clearly see the difference between this component and the "pincers" 𠂊.

KANJI 92

 **SELL**

一	十	士	声	声	壳	売		

BUILDING THIS KANJI
Gentleman 士(84) + **UFO** 冖 + **Ballet** 儿 = 売

MEANING
Sell.

REMEMBERING THIS KANJI
It is common knowledge that the statues of Easter Island relate to the visit of a UFO. What is less well known is that the **gentleman** piloting this UFO chose to SELL **ballet** gear to the locals. What was the purpose of this? Were the natives to put tutus on the monoliths? Wear the slippers themselves? Given the lack of **ballet** dancers or practice facilities on Easter Island at the time, anthropologists wonder why this **gentleman** didn't SELL the locals something more useful.

COMMON PRONUNCIATIONS
Common **ON** reading: **BAI** (バイ)
Common **kun** reading: **u** (う)

As the final example below shows, this is another kanji that can function similarly to "買" (Entry 50).

kun-yomi suggestion: "**oo**dles"

Create your **on-yomi** keyword and enter it in the table at the back of the book. After that, write your sentence to remember the **on-yomi** and **kun-yomi** readings in the box below.

LESS COMMON PRONUNCIATIONS
Less common **ON** reading: none
Less common **kun** reading: none

COMMON WORDS AND COMPOUNDS		
売る	*to sell*	**u**·ru う·る
売り歩く	sell + walk = *to peddle*	**u**·ri aru·ku う·り ある·く
売春	sell + spring = *prostitution*	**BAI**·SHUN バイ·シュン
売り家	sell + house = *"house for sale"*	**u**·ri ie う·り いえ
売り切れる	sell + cut = *to be sold out*	**u**·ri ki·reru う·り き·れる
売切れ	sell + cut = *"sold out"*	**uri** ki·re うり き·れ

SAMPLE SENTENCE

田口さん　は　日本語　の　本　を　売って
Ta·guchi-san wa NI·HON·GO no HON o u·tte
Taguchi-san　Japanese　books　sells
います。
imasu.
= *Taguchi-san sells Japanese books.*

WRITING PRACTICE

KANJI 93

INDIVIDUAL

一	十	土	耂	耂	者	者	者	

BUILDING THIS KANJI
Earth 土(87) + **Comet** 一 + **Sun** 日(6) = 者

MEANING
Think of individual in the sense of a human being. The characters in a compound that precede this kanji (it never comes first) define the person.

REMEMBERING THIS KANJI
It's never a good idea to generalize, but let's face it: you can tell a lot about an INDIVIDUAL by the way they look. A heap of **earth**, for example, tends to be dirty; it clearly doesn't care about appearances and is thus down to **earth**. **Suns**, on the other hand, are obviously outgoing INDIVIDUALS with blazing style. **Comets**, however, have personalities that lie between these extremes (as the kanji shows); with qualities of **earth** and **sun**, each must be considered a separate INDIVIDUAL.

COMMON PRONUNCIATIONS
Common **ON** reading: **SHA** (シャ)
Common **kun** reading: none

Create your **on-yomi** keyword and enter it in the table at the back of the book. After that, write your sentence to remember the **on-yomi** reading in the box below.

LESS COMMON PRONUNCIATIONS
Less common **ON** reading: none
Less common **kun** reading: **mono** (もの)

COMMON WORDS AND COMPOUNDS		
有力者	have + strength + individual = *powerful person*	YŪ·RYOKU·**SHA** ユウ·リョク·シャ
前者	before + individual = *the former*	ZEN·**SHA** ゼン·シャ
後者	after + individual = *the latter*	KŌ·**SHA** コウ·シャ
学者	study + individual = *scholar*	GAKU·**SHA** ガク·シャ

SAMPLE SENTENCE
あの 国 で 王子 は 有力者 です。
ano kuni de Ō·JI wa YŪ·RYOKU·SHA desu.
that country prince powerful person
= *The prince is a powerful person in that country.*

WRITING PRACTICE

KANJI 94

ENTER

ノ	入							

MEANING

Entering/Putting in. Make sure that you clearly see the difference between this kanji and those for "人" (Entry 2), and "八" (Entry 19). No story required.

COMMON PRONUNCIATIONS

Common **ON** reading: **NYŪ** (ニュウ)
Common **kun** readings: **hai** (はい); **i** (い)

It is worth looking carefully at the first three entries below. The word "**hai·ru**" expresses the **intransitive** meaning of the verb "enter" (that is, to enter some type of place); it is rarely used in compounds. "**i·ru**", on the other hand, is most commonly found in compounds, primarily when the other kanji is read with **kun-yomi** (**NYŪ** performs this function when the other kanji is read with **on-yomi**). The word **i·reru** is simply the transitive companion of **hai·ru**.

One last twist is that the kanji can behave on rare occasions like 買; this can be seen in the fourth example.

kun-yomi suggestions: "**high**way"; "**e**ther"

Create your **on-yomi** keyword and enter it in the table at the back of the book. After that, write your sentence to remember the **on-yomi** and **kun-yomi** readings in the box below.

LESS COMMON PRONUNCIATIONS

Less common **ON** reading: none
Less common **kun** reading: none

COMMON WORDS AND COMPOUNDS		
入る (intr)	*to enter*	**hai**·ru はい·る
入る (intr)	*to enter*	**i**·ru い·る
入れる (tr)	*to put (something) into*	**i**·reru い·れる
入口	enter + mouth = *entrance*	**iri**·guchi いり·ぐち
入国	enter + country = *to enter a country*	**NYŪ**·KOKU ニュウ·コク
入金	enter + gold (money) = *payment*	**NYŪ**·KIN ニュウ·キン
買い入れる	buy + enter = *to stock up on*	ka·i **i**·reru か·い い·れる

SAMPLE SENTENCE

お金 を 入れて 下さい。
o·kane o i·rete kuda·sai.
money put in please
= *Please insert the money.*

WRITING PRACTICE

COMPONENT 95

COMB ⺕

KANJI 95

SNOW

BUILDING THIS KANJI
Rain 雨(90) + **Comb** ⺕ = 雪

MEANING
Snow.

REMEMBERING THIS KANJI
I've come in from the **rain** and need to straighten my hair for a date. I do this, of course, but looking down moments later I tremble like a kitten: my **comb** is now covered with dandruff! I start to panic…until realizing that the **rain** had at some point become SNOW.

COMMON PRONUNCIATIONS
Common **ON** reading: none
Common **kun** reading: **yuki** (ゆき)

Note that the sample sentence contains an irregular reading (明日).

kun-yomi suggestion: "**you kee**p"

Create your sentence to remember the **kun-yomi** reading in the box below.

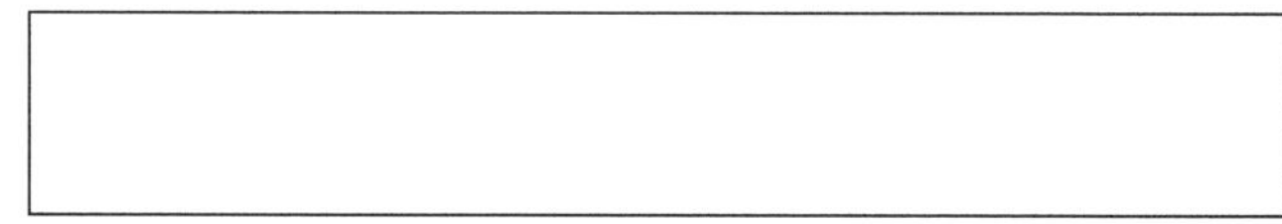

LESS COMMON PRONUNCIATIONS
Less common **ON** reading: **SETSU** (セツ)
Less common **kun** reading: none

Here are two irregular readings that make use of this character.

IRREGULAR READINGS		
吹雪*	blow + snow = *blizzard*	**fubuki** ふぶき
雪崩*	snow + crumble = *avalanche*	**nadare** なだれ

COMMON WORDS AND COMPOUNDS		
雪	*snow*	**yuki** ゆき
雪玉	snow + jewel = *snowball*	**yuki**·dama ゆき·だま
雪女	snow + woman = *snow fairy*	**yuki**·onna ゆき·おんな
雪男	snow + man = *the Abominable Snowman*	**yuki**·otoko ゆき·おとこ
大雪	large + snow = *heavy snow*	ō·**yuki** おお·ゆき
小雪	small + snow = *light snow*	ko·**yuki** こ·ゆき

SAMPLE SENTENCE

テレビ の ニュース に よる と 明日 から
terebi no nyūsu ni yoru to ashita kara
television news according to tomorrow from
大雪 です。
ōyuki desu.
heavy snow
= *According to the TV news, heavy snow will be starting tomorrow.*

WRITING PRACTICE

KANJI 96

門 GATE

丨	⺆	𠃜	𠃜	門	門	門	門	

MEANING
Gate. No story required.

COMMON PRONUNCIATIONS
Common **ON** reading: **MON** (モン)
Common **kun** reading: **kado** (かど)

Note that this kanji is usually read with its **on-yomi** when appearing alone.

kun-yomi suggestion: "**cod o**ver"

Create your **on-yomi** keyword and enter it in the table at the back of the book. After that, write your sentence to remember the **on-yomi** and **kun-yomi** readings in the box below.

LESS COMMON PRONUNCIATIONS
Less common **ON** reading: none
Less common **kun** reading: none

COMMON WORDS AND COMPOUNDS		
門	*gate*	**MON** モン
門口	gate + mouth *= front door*	**kado**·guchi かど·ぐち
水門	water + gate *= sluice gate*	SUI·**MON** スイ·モン
校門	school + gate *= school gate*	KŌ·**MON** コウ·モン

SAMPLE SENTENCE

あそこ の 高い 門 は とても 古い です ね。
asoko no taka·i MON wa totemo furu·i desu ne.
over there tall gate very old
= That tall gate over there is very old, isn't it?

WRITING PRACTICE

KANJI 97

INTERVAL

BUILDING THIS KANJI
Gate 門(96) + **Sun** 日(6) = 間

MEANING

This character indicates an interval in time or space, and thus incorporates the ideas of "during", "between" and "among". When used with the **kun-yomi** "**ma**", it can also mean a room.

REMEMBERING THIS KANJI

If the **sun** in this kanji is rising (as every fiber in my being leads me to believe), it will pass, after a short INTERVAL, through that INTERVAL between the **gates**.

COMMON PRONUNCIATIONS

Common **ON** reading: **KAN** (カン)
Common **kun** readings: **aida** (あいだ); **ma** (ま)

kun-yomi suggestions: "**Ida**ho"; "**ma**p"

Create your **on-yomi** keyword and enter it in the table at the back of the book. After that, write your sentence to remember the **on-yomi** and **kun-yomi** readings in the box below.

LESS COMMON PRONUNCIATIONS

Less common **ON** reading: **KEN** (ケン)
Less common **kun** reading: none

COMMON WORDS AND COMPOUNDS		
間	*interval*	**aida** あいだ
手間	hand + interval = *labor; trouble*	te·**ma** て·ま
中間	middle + interval = *midway*	CHŪ·**KAN** チュウ·カン
時間	time + interval = *time*	JI·**KAN** ジ·カン
空間	empty + interval = *space*	KŪ·**KAN** クウ·カン

SAMPLE SENTENCE

アメリカ に いる 間 英語 を 話します。
Amerika ni iru aida EI·GO o hana·shimasu.
America be interval English speak
= *I'll speak English while I'm in America.*

WRITING PRACTICE

COMPONENT 98

GARBAGE CAN ⊔ 

KANJI 98

出 EXIT

丨	屮	屮	出	出				

BUILDING THIS KANJI
Pole 丨 + **Garbage Can** ⊔ + **Garbage Can** ⊔ = 出

MEANING

Leave/Let out. Take care with the stroke order of this character.

REMEMBERING THIS KANJI

All right, so maybe I misunderstood my boss: putting a couple of **garbage cans** on a **pole** and standing at the EXIT of the voting station wasn't the right thing to do. But asking people to put "yes" votes in one **can** and "no" votes in the other...wouldn't anyone have thought that's what she meant by an EXIT poll?

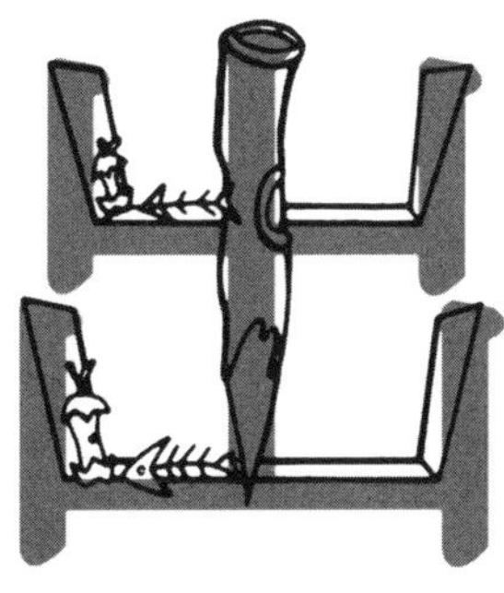

COMMON PRONUNCIATIONS

Common **ON** reading: **SHUTSU** (シュツ)
Common **kun** readings: **de** (で); **da** (だ)

Note how the **on-yomi** "doubles up" with an unvoiced consonant sound in the last example below.

kun-yomi suggestions: "**da**te"; "**da**sh"

Create your **on-yomi** keyword and enter it in the table at the back of the book. After that, write your sentence to remember the **on-yomi** and **kun-yomi** readings in the box below.

LESS COMMON PRONUNCIATIONS

Less common **ON** reading: **SUI** (スイ)
Less common **kun** reading: none

COMMON WORDS AND COMPOUNDS		
出る (intr)	*to leave*	**de**·ru で·る
出す (tr)	*to let out*	**da**·su だ·す
出かける	*to leave (for somewhere)*	**de**·kakeru で·かける
思い出す	think + exit = *to remember*	omo·i **da**·su おも·い だ·す
出口	exit + mouth = *exit*	**de**·guchi で·ぐち
出国	exit + country = *to leave a country*	**SHUK**·KOKU シュッ·コク

SAMPLE SENTENCE

すみません、 出口 は どこ です か。
sumimasen de·guchi wa doko desu ka.
excuse me exit where
= *Excuse me, where's the exit?*

WRITING PRACTICE

KANJI 99

LIFE

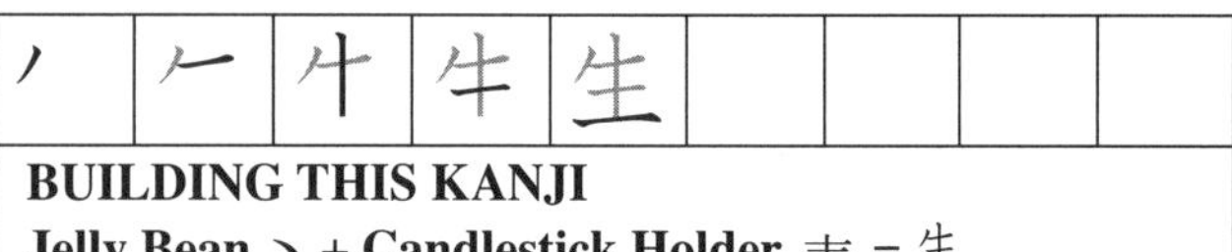

BUILDING THIS KANJI
Jelly Bean ㇏ + Candlestick Holder 龶 = 生

MEANING

One of the most fascinating characters in the language, this kanji deals with life in all its guises. Along with the ideas of "birth", "production", and "growing", it also incorporates the notions of "pure", "raw", and "fresh", in everything from beer to silk. When used as a suffix, it will often indicate "student".

REMEMBERING THIS KANJI

"Is there a better symbol of LIFE," asked Sartre, "than a **jelly bean** stuck to the side of a **candlestick holder**, one that sits there alone and grows brittle with each passing year?"

It's an interesting question. From what I've heard, though, **jelly beans** hold their flavor quite well, even when stuck to **candlestick holders**. So who knows, maybe LIFE isn't so bad after all.

COMMON PRONUNCIATIONS

Common **ON** reading: **SEI** (セイ)
Common **kun** readings: **i** (い); **u** (う); **nama** (なま)

In terms of its variety of pronunciations, kanji do not come any more complicated than this. Perhaps it's appropriate, though: life itself can be complicated, so shouldn't the character representing it be as well? Fortunately, the two initial **kun-yomi** are verb stems (as are "**o**" and "**ha**" of the less common **kun-yomi** below), and **nama** appears only in the first position. This will always belong to the ranks of the toughest kanji, however, so allow yourself time to learn it, while not forgetting to enjoy a few of the fifth example below along the way.

kun-yomi suggestions: "**eagle**"; "**oo**dles"; "Viet**nam a**pple"

Create your **on-yomi** keyword and enter it in the table at the back of the book. After that, write your sentence to remember the **on-yomi** and **kun-yomi** readings in the box below.

LESS COMMON PRONUNCIATIONS

Less common **ON** reading: **SHŌ** (ショウ)
Less common **kun** readings: **o** (お); **ha** (は); **ki** (き)

IRREGULAR READING		
芝生*	lawn + life = *lawn*	**shiba·fu** しば·ふ

COMMON WORDS AND COMPOUNDS		
生きる (intr)	*to live*	**i**·kiru い·きる
生かす (tr)	*to give life to*	**i**·kasu い·かす
生まれる (intr)	*to be born*	**u**·mareru う·まれる
生む (tr)	*to give birth to*	**u**·mu う·む
生ビール	life + beer = *draft beer*	**nama**·bīru なま·ビール
人生	person + life = *(human) life*	JIN·**SEI** ジン·セイ
学生	study + life = *student*	GAKU·**SEI** ガク·セイ
先生	precede + life = *teacher*	SEN·**SEI** セン·セイ

SAMPLE SENTENCE

生ビール は 好き です か。
nama bīru wa su·ki desu ka.
draft beer like
= *Do you like draft beer?*

WRITING PRACTICE

KANJI 100

COW

ノ	𠂉	𠂉	牛					

MEANING

Cow/Ox/Bull. Note the difference in stroke order between this character and that of "生" (Entry 99). No story required.

COMMON PRONUNCIATIONS

Common **ON** reading: **GYŪ** (ギュウ)
Common **kun** reading: **ushi** (うし)

kun-yomi suggestion: "tr**ue sheen**"

Create your **on-yomi** keyword and enter it in the table at the back of the book. After that, write your sentence to remember the **on-yomi** and **kun-yomi** readings in the box below.

LESS COMMON PRONUNCIATIONS

Less common **ON** reading: none
Less common **kun** reading: none

COMMON WORDS AND COMPOUNDS		
牛	*cow*	**ushi** うし
子牛	child + cow = *calf*	ko·**ushi** こ·うし
水牛	water + cow = *water buffalo*	SUI·**GYŪ** スイ·ギュウ
牛肉	cow + meat = *beef*	**GYŪ**·NIKU ギュウ·ニク
牛馬	cow + horse = *cattle and horses*	**GYŪ**·BA ギュウ·バ

SAMPLE SENTENCE

アフリカ で 水牛 と キリン を 見ました。
Afurika de SUI·GYŪ to kirin o mi·mashita.
Africa water buffalo giraffe saw
= *(I) saw a water buffalo and a giraffe in Africa.*

WRITING PRACTICE

CHAPTER 5 REVIEW EXERCISES

A. Please match the following kanji to their meanings.

1. 土	a. Words
2. 士	b. Gentleman
3. 雨	c. Sell
4. 間	d. Exit
5. 売	e. Rain
6. 千	f. Life
7. 生	g. Interval
8. 電	h. Earth
9. 出	i. Electric
10. 語	j. Dry

B. Please match the following meanings to their kanji, and these to their **on** or **kun-yomi**.

1. Hang	a. 者	1. **SHA** (シャ)
2. Snow	b. 牛	2. **MAN** (マン)
3. Individual	c. 青	3. **asa** (あさ)
4. Morning	d. 掛	4. **GYŪ** (ギュウ)
5. Gold	e. 雪	5. **yuki** (ゆき)
6. Gate	f. 入	6. **MON** (モン)
7. Cow	g. 金	7. **ao** (あお)
8. Enter	h. 万	8. **KIN** (キン)
9. Ten thousand	i. 門	9. **NYŪ** (ニュウ)
10. Blue	j. 朝	10. **ka** (か)

C. Please choose the best answer(s) to the following questions.

1. Which of the following kanji have an **on-yomi** of **SEI** (セイ)?
   a. 士
   b. 者
   c. 生
   d. 朝
   e. 青

2. Which of the following readings apply to the kanji 出?
   a. **da** (だ)
   b. **SHUTSU** (シュツ)
   c. **MON** (モン)
   d. **de** (で)
   e. **u** (う)

3. I went to the Himalayas and saw the Abominable ___ Man.
   a. 牛
   b. 雨
   c. 青
   d. 土
   e. 雪

4. Which of the following kanji have an **on-yomi** of **KAN** (カン)?
   a. 士
   b. 金
   c. 語
   d. 間
   e. 電

5. Which of the following readings apply to the kanji 生?
   a. **de** (で)
   b. **i** (い)
   c. **kado** (かど)
   d. **nama** (なま)
   e. **u** (う)

D. Please choose the best answer to the following questions.

1. Which of the following kanji has the most number of strokes?
   a. 間
   b. 語
   c. 掛
   d. 朝
   e. 電

2. Which is the correct reading of 売る?
   a. **de·ru** (で·る)
   b. **i·ru** (い·る)
   c. **u·ru** (う·る)
   d. **kata·ru** (かた·る)

3. Which is the correct reading of 入れる?
   a. **ka·reru** (か·れる)
   b. **omo·reru** (おも·れる)
   c. **kama·reru** (かま·れる)
   d. **i·reru** (い·れる)

4. Which answer best captures the meaning of the compound 電化?
   a. Toast
   b. Electrification
   c. Cactus
   d. Lawnmower
   e. Yogurt

5. Which is the most common reading of 入る when it appears alone (is not part of a compound)?
   a. **i·ru** (い·る)
   b. **kata·ru** (かた·る)
   c. **u·ru** (う·る)
   d. **hai·ru** (はい·る)
   e. **hai·ru** (ひ·る)

E. Please match the following compounds and words to their meanings and pronunciations.

1. 朝日	a. Entrance	1. **DEN·RYOKU** (デン·リョク)
2. 掛金	b. Snow fairy	2. **DO·te** (ド·て)
3. 口語	c. Midway	3. **KŌ·GO** (コウ·ゴ)
4. 入口	d. Installment	4. **asa·hi** (あさ·ひ)
5. 中間	e. Youth	5. **yuki·onna** (ゆき·おんな)
6. 大雨	f. Morning sun	6. **CHŪ·KAN** (チュウ·カン)
7. 青春	g. Electric power	7. **kake·KIN** (かけ·キン)
8. 電力	h. Colloquial language	8. **ō·ame** (おお·あめ)
9. 雪女	i. Embankment	9. **iri·guchi** (いり·ぐち)
10. 土手	j. Heavy rain	10. **SEI·SHUN** (セイ·シュン)

CUMULATIVE REVIEW EXERCISES FOR CHAPTERS 1 - 5

A. Please match the following kanji to their meanings.

1.	京	a. Self
2.	北	b. Summer
3.	玉	c. Half
4.	自	d. North
5.	化	e. Spring
6.	半	f. Capital
7.	朝	g. Like
8.	春	h. Change
9.	好	i. Jewel
10.	夏	j. Morning

B. Which kanji does not belong in the group?

1. a. 耳 b. 目 c. 北 d. 手 e. 首
2. a. 土 b. 女 c. 王 d. 男 e. 子
3. a. 川 b. 回 c. 山 d. 木 e. 田
4. a. 木 b. 牛 c. 米 d. 貝 e. 玉
5. a. 子 b. 上 c. 左 d. 右 e. 下
6. a. 二 b. 九 c. 七 d. 工 e. 三
7. a. 万 b. 干 c. 十 d. 千 e. 百
8. a. 川 b. 雪 c. 全 d. 水 e. 雨
9. a. 肉 b. 出 c. 歩 d. 回 e. 入
10. a. 日 b. 月 c. 火 d. 水 e. 木 f. 金 g. 土 h. 夏

C. Identify the kanji having the most number of strokes.

1. a. 山 b. 日 c. 工 d. 万 e. 女
2. a. 男 b. 貝 c. 回 d. 金 e. 体
3. a. 冬 b. 木 c. 子 d. 五 e. 元
4. a. 言 b. 者 c. 東 d. 南 e. 売
5. a. 早 b. 出 c. 耳 d. 全 e. 見
6. a. 家 b. 雪 c. 買 d. 掛 e. 高
7. a. 夏 b. 歩 c. 首 d. 雨 e. 思
8. a. 家 b. 掛 c. 明 d. 国 e. 青
9. a. 生 b. 本 c. 白 d. 古 e. 肉
10. a. 電 b. 朝 c. 語 d. 間 e. 雪

D. Please list the following kanji in the order indicated (alphabetical).

1. Body / Main / Rest / Rice / Tree
   a. 休 d. 体
   b. 木 e. 米
   c. 本

2. Dry / Earth / Gentleman / Ten thousand / Thousand
   a. 士 d. 土
   b. 干 e. 万
   c. 千

3. Cow / Half / Jewel / King / Life
   a. 王 d. 玉
   b. 生 e. 半
   c. 牛

4. Buy / Eye / See / Self / Shellfish
   a. 自 d. 貝
   b. 目 e. 見
   c. 買

5. Early / Hundred / Individual / Sun / White
a. 早
b. 白
c. 日
d. 者
e. 百

6. Capital / Early / Morning / Old / Tall
a. 高
b. 京
c. 早
d. 朝
e. 古

7. Eight / Enter / Gentleman / Large / Person
a. 士
b. 人
c. 入
d. 大
e. 八

8. Basis / Hand / Ten thousand / Thousand / Three
a. 元
b. 万
c. 三
d. 手
e. 千

9. Circle / Ear / Inside / Meat / Moon
a. 肉
b. 耳
c. 円
d. 内
e. 月

10. Change / Lower / North / Stop / Upper
a. 下
b. 化
c. 上
d. 北
e. 止

E. Please choose the best answer to the following questions.

1. I went on a nice vacation to the ____.
a. 日
b. 火
c. 耳
d. 牛
e. 南

2. What is the best thing to take on a desert crossing?
a. 木
b. 水
c. 火
d. 門
e. 掛

3. I bought some boots and took up ____ climbing.
a. 米
b. 肉
c. 雨
d. 山
e. 口

4. A country would be run most poorly by a ____.
a. 王
b. 男
c. 女
d. 牛
e. All of the preceding

5. The vampire bat flew in and went straight for my ___.
a. 目
b. 貝
c. 首
d. 手
e. Wallet

F. Please choose the best answer(s) to the following questions.

1. Which of the following are readings for the kanji 木?
a. **BOKU** (ボク)
b. **ki** (き)
c. **SETSU** (セツ)
d. **haru** (はる)
e. **MOKU** (モク)

2. Which of the following are readings for the kanji 下?
a. **shita** (した)
b. **o** (お)
c. **kado** (かど)
d. **kuda** (くだ)
e. **KA** (カ)
f. **sa** (さ)
g. **GE** (ゲ)

3. Which of the following are readings for the kanji 米?
a. **MAI** (マイ)
b. **kome** (こめ)
c. **BEI** (ベイ)
d. **HOKU** (ホク)
e. **yuki** (ゆき)

4. Which of the following are readings for the kanji 上?
a. **kami** (かみ)
b. **ue** (うえ)
c. **JŌ** (ジョウ)
d. **nobo** (のぼ)
e. **a** (あ)
f. **ie** (いえ)
g. **uwa** (うわ)

5. Which of the following are readings for the kanji 生?
a. **i** (い)
b. **nama** (なま)
c. **SEI** (セイ)
d. **haru** (はる)
e. **u** (う)

G. Please choose the best answer to the following questions.

1. Which is the correct reading of 歩く?
a. **haba·ku** (はば·く)
b. **aru·ku** (ある·く)
c. **fu·ku** (ふ·く)
d. **kata·ku** (かた·く)

2. Which is the correct reading of 高い?
   a. **taka·i** (たか·い)
   b. **kata·i** (かた·い)
   c. **ara·i** (あら·い)
   d. **usu·i** (うす·い)

3. Which is the correct reading of 休む?
   a. **kara·mu** (から·む)
   b. **i·mu** (い·む)
   c. **u·mu** (う·む)
   d. **yasu·mu** (やす·む)

4. Which is the correct reading of 入れる?
   a. **de·reru** (で·れる)
   b. **u·reru** (う·れる)
   c. **kata·reru** (かた·れる)
   d. **i·reru** (い·れる)

5. Which is the correct reading of 二つ?
   a. **mi·tsu** (み·つ)
   b. **futa·tsu** (ふた·つ)
   c. **hito·tsu** (ひと·つ)
   d. **u·tsu** (う·つ)

6. Which is the correct reading of 古い?
   a. **taka·i** (たか·い)
   b. **omo·i** (おも·い)
   c. **furu·i** (ふる·い)
   d. **haya·i** (はや·い)

7. Which is the correct reading of 早い?
   a. **haya·i** (はや·い)
   b. **yasu·i** (やす·い)
   c. **ao·i** (あお·い)
   d. **furu·i** (ふる·い)

8. Which is the correct reading of 小さい?
   a. **ka·sai** (か·さい)
   b. **ko·sai** (こ·さい)
   c. **chii·sai** (ちい·さい)
   d. **uru·sai** (うる·さい)

9. Which is the correct reading of 少ない?
   a. **de·nai** (で·ない)
   b. **suku·nai** (すく·ない)
   c. **taka·nai** (たか·ない)
   d. **kata·nai** (かた·ない)

10. Which is the correct reading of 少し?
    a. **ma·shi** (ま·し)
    b. **saga·shi** (さが·し)
    c. **u·shi** (う·し)
    d. **suko·shi** (すこ·し)

H. Please match the following compounds and words to their meanings and pronunciations.

1. 東京	a. To stock up on	1. **HON·DO** (ホン·ド)
2. 見上げる	b. To remember	2. **AN·ZEN** (アン·ゼン)
3. 休日	c. Five hundred	3. **TŌ·KYŌ** (トウ·キョウ)
4. 人生	d. Mainland	4. **JŪ·ICHI·GATSU** (ジュウ·イチ·ガツ)
5. 思い出す	e. To look up (to/at)	5. **ka·i i·reru** (か·い い·れる)
6. 十一月	f. November	6. **JIN·SEI** (ジン·セイ)
7. 五百	g. To enter a country	7. **ko·haru** (こ·はる)
8. 下水	h. Holiday	8. **GYŪ·NIKU** (ギュウ·ニク)
9. 小春	i. Safety	9. **GO·HYAKU** (ゴ·ヒャク)
10. 入国	j. One time	10. **mi a·geru** (み あ·げる)
11. 安全	k. Tokyo	11. **IK·KAI** (イッ·カイ)
12. 牛肉	l. Indian summer	12. **omo·i da·su** (おも·い だ·す)
13. 買い入れる	m. (Human) Life	13. **NYŪ·KOKU** (ニュウ·コク)
14. 一回	n. Sewage	14. **KYŪ·JITSU** (キュウ·ジツ)
15. 本土	o. Beef	15. **GE·SUI** (ゲ·スイ)

CHAPTER 6 (KANJI 101-120)

KANJI 101

BEAUTIFUL

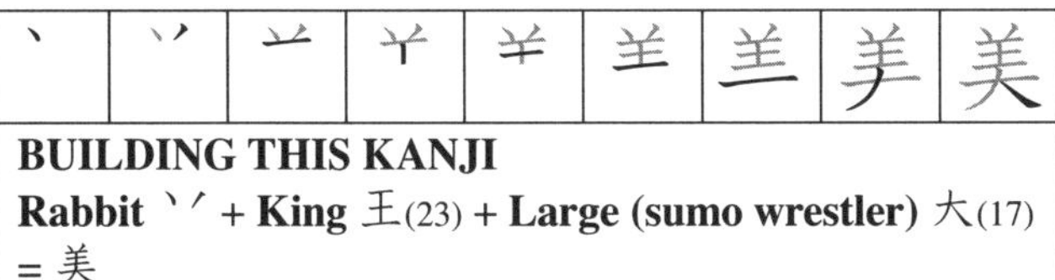

BUILDING THIS KANJI
Rabbit 丷 + **King** 王(23) + **Large (sumo wrestler)** 大(17) = 美

MEANING

Used for all things beautiful, this character lives up to its name in a visual sense as well. Take care with the stroke order by writing the components as listed.

REMEMBERING THIS KANJI

The Zulu, along with several other tribes in southern Africa, equate **large** size with being BEAUTIFUL. A **king**, therefore, will make good use of the region's **rabbit** population to grow as **large** as possible, through eating incredible amounts of a filling **rabbit** stew. Read from the top down, the kanji shows this process clearly: rabbit goes into **king**…**king** becomes as **large** a sumo wrestler… **large** is BEAUTIFUL.

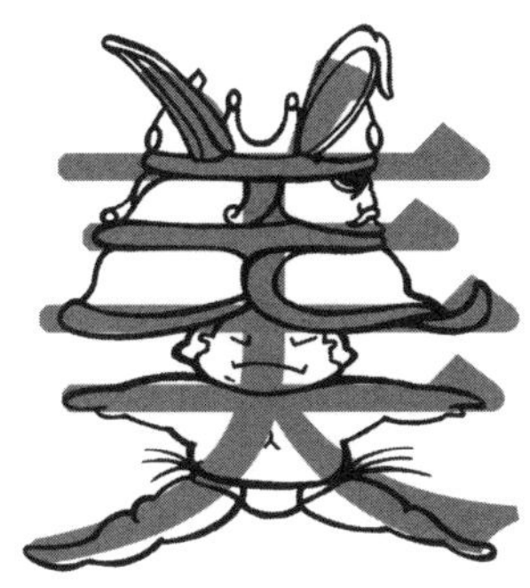

COMMON PRONUNCIATIONS

Common **ON** reading: **BI** (ビ)
Common **kun** reading: **utsuku** (うつく)

kun-yomi suggestion: "**fruits cool**ing"

Create your **on-yomi** keyword and enter it in the table at the back of the book. After that, write your sentence to remember the **on-yomi** and **kun-yomi** readings in the box below.

LESS COMMON PRONUNCIATIONS

Less common **ON** reading: none
Less common **kun** reading: none

The following is a very common irregular reading.

IRREGULAR READING		
美味しい*	beautiful + taste = *delicious*	**oi·shii** おい·しい

COMMON WORDS AND COMPOUNDS		
美しい	*beautiful*	**utsuku**·shii うつく·しい
美人	beautiful + person = *beautiful woman*	**BI**·JIN ビ·ジン
美化	beautiful + change = *beautification*	**BI**·KA ビ·カ
美学	beautiful + study = *aesthetics*	**BI**·GAKU ビ·ガク

SAMPLE SENTENCE

山 の 木 が 美しい です。
yama no ki ga utsuku·shii desu.
mountain trees beautiful
= *The trees on the mountain are beautiful.*

WRITING PRACTICE

COMPONENT 102

DINOSAUR  

KANJI 102

 **ISLAND**

ノ	丆	力	户	白	自	阜	阜	阜
島								

BUILDING THIS KANJI
Dinosaur 鳥 **+ Mountain** 山(1) = 島

MEANING
Island.

REMEMBERING THIS KANJI
OK, so I have this great idea for a movie. It's set on an ISLAND, but what makes this ISLAND interesting is that some **dinosaurs** are still living on one of its **mountains**! It's a blockbuster concept, and though I'm still working out the details, I've already decided on a title: "Jurassic ISLAND".

COMMON PRONUNCIATIONS
Common **ON** reading: **TŌ** (トウ)
Common **kun** reading: **shima** (しま)

The **kun-yomi** for this kanji is often voiced when in the final position, as in the second compound below. Note also the voiced reading for 国 in the third example.

kun-yomi suggestion: "**she ma**ps"

Create your **on-yomi** keyword and enter it in the table at the back of the book. After that, write your sentence to remember the **on-yomi** and **kun-yomi** readings in the box below.

LESS COMMON PRONUNCIATIONS
Less common **ON** reading: none
Less common **kun** reading: none

COMMON WORDS AND COMPOUNDS		
島	*island*	**shima** しま
小島	small + island = *small island*	ko·**jima** こ·じま
島国	island + country = *island nation*	**shima**·guni しま·ぐに
半島	half + island = *peninsula*	HAN·**TŌ** ハン·トウ
本島	main + island = *main island*	HON·**TŌ** ホン·トウ

SAMPLE SENTENCE

オーストラリア と 日本 は 島国 です。
Ōsutoraria to NI·HON wa shima·guni desu.
Australia Japan island nation
= *Australia and Japan are island nations.*

WRITING PRACTICE

KANJI 103

寸 TINY

一	寸	寸						

MEANING
Tiny.

REMEMBERING THIS KANJI
How TINY, you ask? Well, given that the soccer player in this illustration is life-size…pretty TINY. This kanji, as the lack of compounds below makes clear, will be much more important for us as a component than a character on its own; the tiny soccer player will be used to suggest it in all future stories.

COMMON PRONUNCIATIONS
Common **ON** reading: **SUN** (スン)
Common **kun** reading: none

Create your **on-yomi** keyword and enter it in the table at the back of the book. After that, write your sentence to remember the **on-yomi** reading in the box below.

LESS COMMON PRONUNCIATIONS
Less common **ON** reading: none
Less common **kun** reading: none

COMMON WORDS AND COMPOUNDS		
一寸	one + tiny = *a tiny bit*	IS·**SUN** イッ·スン
寸前	tiny + before = *immediately before*	**SUN**·ZEN スン·ゼン

SAMPLE SENTENCE

出かける 寸前 に 高木さん を
de·kakeru SUN·ZEN ni Taka·gi-san o
leave immediately before Takagi-san
見ました。
mi·mashita.
saw
= *I saw Takagi-san just before I left.*

WRITING PRACTICE

KANJI 104

TEMPLE

一	十	土	丰	寺	寺			

BUILDING THIS KANJI
Earth 土(87) + **Tiny (soccer player)** 寸(103) = 寺

MEANING
(Buddhist) temple.

REMEMBERING THIS KANJI
Tiny soccer players are always in danger of being pushed around by their opponents. As a result of this, they usually become known as fearless defenders who protect their positions at all costs — treating even the **tiniest** piece of **earth** they occupy like a TEMPLE that must not be defiled. A TEMPLE in which it is permitted to wear cleats, of course.

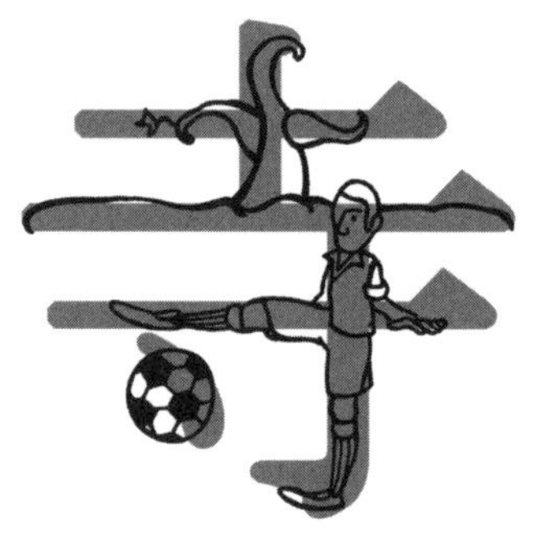

COMMON PRONUNCIATIONS
Common **ON** reading: **JI** (ジ)
Common **kun** reading: **tera** (てら)

The **kun-yomi** becomes voiced when not in the first position, as it does below in the third example. The final compound can also be read by the respective **kun-yomi**: **furu·dera** (ふる·でら).

kun-yomi suggestion: "**tear a**pples"

Create your **on-yomi** keyword and enter it in the table at the back of the book. After that, write your sentence to remember the **on-yomi** and **kun-yomi** readings in the box below.

LESS COMMON PRONUNCIATIONS
Less common **ON** reading: none
Less common **kun** reading: none

COMMON WORDS AND COMPOUNDS		
寺	*temple*	**tera** てら
寺田さん	temple + rice field = *Terada-san*	**tera·da·san** てら·だ·さん
山寺	mountain + temple = *mountain temple*	**yama·dera** やま·でら
古寺	old + temple = *old temple*	**KO·JI** コ·ジ

SAMPLE SENTENCE

山寺	の	古い	門	の	下	で
yama·dera	**no**	**furu·i**	**MON**	**no**	**shita**	**de**
mountain temple		old	gate		under	

休みました。
yasu·mimashita.
rested

= *(We) rested under the old gate of the mountain temple.*

WRITING PRACTICE

KANJI 105

PRECEDE

ノ	㇐	𠂉	生	先	先			

BUILDING THIS KANJI
Jelly Bean ヽ + **Earth** 土(87) + **Ballet** 儿 = 先

MEANING
This character has a multitude of meanings, all of them derived from the general sense of "preceding", or the idea of an object "ahead" in a literal or figurative way. Depending on the context in which it appears, this kanji can signify the "tip" or "point" of something, the general future (or the specific past, when used as in the third compound), or a destination. It can also refer to people in the sense of "the other party".

REMEMBERING THIS KANJI
Most people are unaware that Tchaikovsky deleted a **jelly bean** character from his **ballet** "The Nutcracker". This **jelly bean** was to always PRECEDE the Sugar Plum Fairy onstage, then be pinned to the **earth** and devoured by her at the end of the work (she by this time having been driven wild with sugar cravings). It was an edgy scene, but fortunately for **ballet** lovers everywhere, Tchaikovsky concluded it was incompatible with what PRECEDED, and decided to remove the **jelly bean** character altogether.

COMMON PRONUNCIATIONS
Common **ON** reading: **SEN** (セン)
Common **kun** reading: **saki** (さき)

kun-yomi suggestion: "**sack eel**s". If using your own idea for this **kun-yomi**, keep in mind that Japan's famous rice wine is pronounced **sake** (さけ), and should not be confused with the reading of this character.

Create your **on-yomi** keyword and enter it in the table at the back of the book. After that, write your sentence to remember the **on-yomi** and **kun-yomi** readings in the box below.

LESS COMMON PRONUNCIATIONS
Less common **ON** reading: none
Less common **kun** reading: none

COMMON WORDS AND COMPOUNDS		
先	*precede; point; tip*	**saki** さき
先生	precede + life = *teacher*	**SEN**·SEI セン·セイ
先月	precede + moon (month) = *last month*	**SEN**·GETSU セン·ゲツ
口先	mouth + precede = *lip service*	kuchi·**saki** くち·さき

SAMPLE SENTENCE

先生 は 冬休み に 日本アルプス
SEN·SEI wa fuyu yasu·mi ni NI·HON arupusu
teacher winter vacation Japanese Alps
へ 行きました。
e i·kimashita.
went
= *(Our) teacher went to the Japanese Alps for winter vacation.*

WRITING PRACTICE

COMPONENT 106

PICNIC TABLE 开 

Admittedly, this is not the most comfortable-looking picnic table.

KANJI 106

 **OPEN**

BUILDING THIS KANJI
Gate 門(96) + **Picnic Table** 开 = 開

MEANING

Open. Secondary meanings include "starting", and the idea of "developing" things (in the sense of opening or reclaiming land, for example).

REMEMBERING THIS KANJI

Their picnic thrown into chaos by the sight of Visigoths on the horizon, the partiers ran desperately back to the castle. "OPEN the **gates**!", "OPEN the **gates**!" they yelled to no avail, for nobody on the other side could hear them. It was only when the **picnic table** was used as a battering ram (thus breaking it) that the **gates** finally flew OPEN to let them in.

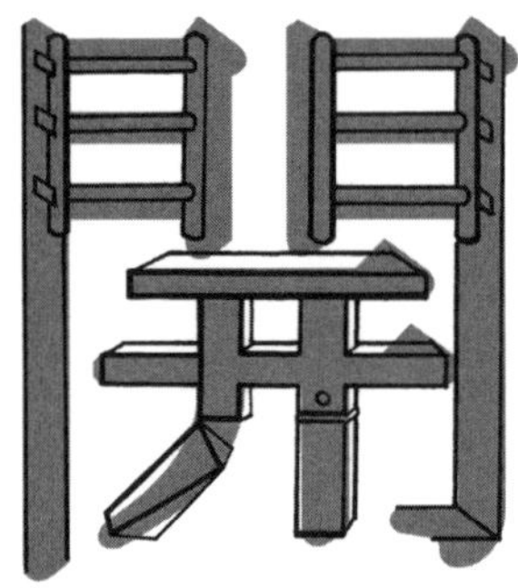

COMMON PRONUNCIATIONS

Common **ON** reading: **KAI** (カイ)
Common **kun** readings: **a** (あ); **hira** (ひら)

As a glance at the first three examples below suggests, this character can be a little tricky. In the general physical sense of "to open", however, **a·ku** (あ·く) and **a·keru** (あ·ける) function as a normal intransitive/transitive verb pair. The word **hira·ku**, on the other hand, is more concerned with a metaphorical or non-physical sense of "opening", and appears primarily in certain expressions (in the "opening", for example, of a conference, of new lands, or of cherry blossoms). Expressing the sense of a shop's front door being open would thus call for the verb **a·ku**, while conveying the idea of opening a business would require **hira·ku**.

In the first position, this kanji invariably takes the **on-yomi**.

kun-yomi suggestions: "**a**ppetite"; "**he ra**pidly"

Create your **on-yomi** keyword and enter it in the table at the back of the book. After that, write your sentence to remember the **on-yomi** and **kun-yomi** readings in the box below.

LESS COMMON PRONUNCIATIONS

Less common **ON** reading: none
Less common **kun** reading: none

COMMON WORDS AND COMPOUNDS		
開く (intr)	*to be open*	**a**·ku あ·く
開ける (tr)	*to open (something)*	**a**·keru あ·ける
開く (intr/tr)	*to open; to develop*	**hira**·ku ひら·く
開化	open + change = *becoming civilized*	**KAI**·KA カイ·カ
開国	open + country = *to open up a country*	**KAI**·KOKU カイ·コク
開会	open + meet = *to open a meeting*	**KAI**·KAI カイ·カイ
公開	public + open = *open to the public*	KŌ·**KAI** コウ·カイ

SAMPLE SENTENCE

水門 を 開けて 下さい。
SUI·MON o a·kete kuda·sai.
sluice gate open please
= *Please open the sluice gate.*

COMPONENT 107

GAS STOVE ノ丶丶丶

KANJI 107

鳥 BIRD

ノ	丫	户	户	白	皀	鳥	鳥	鳥
鳥	鳥							

BUILDING THIS KANJI
Dinosaur 鳥 + **Gas Stove** 灬 = 鳥

MEANING
Bird.

REMEMBERING THIS KANJI
As recent archaeological evidence has shown, BIRDS were an important part of a **dinosaur's** diet. Numerous cave drawings, in fact, show **dinosaurs** cooking BIRDS over **gas stoves**. This is interesting, for it has led some scholars to theorize that it was the **dinosaurs'** clumsy use of **gas stoves** that led to their extinction. If this is true, it explains nicely how BIRDS have managed to survive to the present day.

COMMON PRONUNCIATIONS
Common **ON** reading: **CHŌ** (チョウ)
Common **kun** reading: **tori** (とり)

kun-yomi suggestion: "lava**tory**"

Create your **on-yomi** keyword and enter it in the table at the back of the book. After that, write your sentence to remember the **on-yomi** and **kun-yomi** readings in the box below.

LESS COMMON PRONUNCIATIONS
Less common **ON** reading: none
Less common **kun** reading: none

COMMON WORDS AND COMPOUNDS		
鳥	*bird*	**tori** とり
白鳥	white + bird = *swan*	HAKU·**CHŌ** ハク·チョウ
小鳥	small + bird = *small bird*	ko·**tori** こ·とり
夜鳥	night + bird = *nocturnal bird*	YA·**CHŌ** ヤ·チョウ
愛鳥家	love + bird + house = *bird lover*	AI·**CHŌ**·KA アイ·チョウ·カ

SAMPLE SENTENCE

あの 青い 小鳥 の 名前 が 分かります か。
ano ao·i ko·tori no na·mae ga wa·karimasu ka.
that blue little bird name understand
= *Do you know the name of that little blue bird?*

WRITING PRACTICE

KANJI 108

EVENING

ノ	ク	タ						

MEANING

Evening. At this time of day, our friend the moon is not yet entirely visible through the evening mist. No story required.

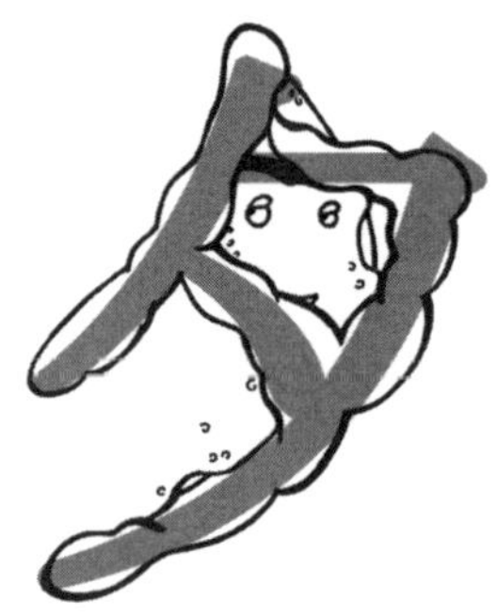

COMMON PRONUNCIATIONS

Common **ON** reading: none
Common **kun** reading: **yū** (ゆう)

kun-yomi suggestion: "**u**kulele"

Create your sentence to remember the **kun-yomi** reading in the box below.

LESS COMMON PRONUNCIATIONS

Less common **ON** reading: **SEKI** (セキ)
Less common **kun** reading: none

COMMON WORDS AND COMPOUNDS		
夕べ	*evening*	**yū**·be ゆう·べ
夕日	evening + sun = *setting sun*	**yū**·hi ゆう·ひ
夕立	evening + stand = *late afternoon (rain) shower*	**yū**·dachi ゆう·だち

SAMPLE SENTENCE

山 から 見る 夕日 が 美しい。
yama kara mi·ru yū·hi ga utsuku·shii.
river from see setting sun beautiful
= *The setting sun is beautiful when seen from the mountain.*

WRITING PRACTICE

KANJI 109

OUTSIDE

ノ	ク	タ	タ|	外				

BUILDING THIS KANJI
Evening タ (108) + **Poor Figure Skater** ト = 外

MEANING

Outside. The idea of "foreign" or "other" is also present, as the third example below makes clear. The less common readings convey some secondary meanings of removal and disconnection.

REMEMBERING THIS KANJI

There is a very rigid hierarchy in the world of figure skating. When **evening** arrives, for instance, the arenas are often so full that the **poor figure skaters** are forced OUTSIDE. Unfortunately, the frozen puddles on the OUTSIDE parking lot do not provide nearly enough room for jumps.

COMMON PRONUNCIATIONS

Common **ON** reading: **GAI** (ガイ)
Common **kun** reading: **soto** (そと)

kun-yomi suggestion: "**so to**asty"

Create your **on-yomi** keyword and enter it in the table at the back of the book. After that, write your sentence to remember the **on-yomi** and **kun-yomi** readings in the box below.

LESS COMMON PRONUNCIATIONS

Less common **ON** reading: **GE** (ゲ)
Less common **kun** readings: **hoka** (ほか); **hazu** (はず)

COMMON WORDS AND COMPOUNDS		
外	*outside*	**soto** そと
外見	outside + see = *external appearance*	**GAI**·KEN ガイ·ケン
外国人	outside + country + person = *foreigner*	**GAI**·KOKU·JIN ガイ·コク·ジン
外出	outside + exit = *going out*	**GAI**·SHUTSU ガイ·シュツ
海外	sea + outside = *overseas*	KAI·**GAI** カイ·ガイ

SAMPLE SENTENCE

日本 には 外国人 が 多い。
NI·HON ni wa GAI·KOKU·JIN ga ō·i.
Japan foreigners many
= *There are many foreigners in Japan.*

WRITING PRACTICE

KANJI 110

TONGUE

ノ	二	千	千	舌	舌			

BUILDING THIS KANJI
Thousand 千(65) + **Mouth (vampire)** 口(8) = 外

MEANING

Tongue.

REMEMBERING THIS KANJI

Interesting fact: a survey showed that **Thousand** Island dressing was a favorite amongst **vampires**. "It's very pleasing to the TONGUE," said one, "and it doesn't have any…unfortunate ingredients." Manufacturers of garlic-based dressings, it seems, need to take the TONGUES of **vampires** more into account if they want access to this market segment.

COMMON PRONUNCIATIONS

Common **ON** reading: none
Common **kun** reading: **shita** (した)

kun-yomi suggestion: "**she ta**ps"

Create your sentence to remember the **kun-yomi** reading in the box below.

LESS COMMON PRONUNCIATIONS

Less common **ON** reading: **ZETSU** (ゼツ)
Less common **kun** reading: none

COMMON WORDS AND COMPOUND		
舌	*tongue*	**shita** した

SAMPLE SENTENCE

内田さん は 舌 に ピアス を しました。
Uchi·da-san wa shita ni piasu o shimashita.
Uchida-san tongue piercing did
= *Uchida-san got her tongue pierced.*

WRITING PRACTICE

COMPONENT 111

BANANA PEELS  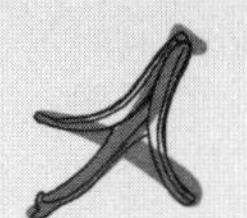

KANJI 111

 **DIAGRAM**

丨	冂	冂	冂	㓁	図	図		

BUILDING THIS KANJI
Prison 囗 + **Jelly Bean** 丶 + **Jelly Bean** 丶 + **Banana Peels** 乂 + = 図

MEANING
Diagram/Drawing. By extension comes the idea of "planning".

REMEMBERING THIS KANJI
"You have to be sly if you're going to break out of this **prison**," my cellmate told me as I settled in. "The guards won't allow us any pens so there's no way to draw up an escape DIAGRAM. That's why I have these." He placed a couple of moldy **jelly beans** and some rotting **banana peels** on my bunk. "These **jelly beans** will be us," he whispered, "and the **banana peels** will represent the guards. It's not much, but we can plan our break using these as a DIAGRAM."

I nodded. My time in **prison**, it seemed, was not only going to be long, but more boring than I could have possibly imagined.

COMMON PRONUNCIATIONS
Common **ON** readings: **ZU** (ズ); **TO** (ト)
Common **kun** reading: none

ZU is the more common reading. Note in the second example below how effectively Japanese can express complex English words.

Create your **on-yomi** keywords and enter them in the table at the back of the book. After that, write your sentence to remember the **on-yomi** readings in the box below.

LESS COMMON PRONUNCIATIONS
Less common **ON** reading: none
Less common **kun** reading: **haka** (はか)

COMMON WORDS AND COMPOUNDS		
図工	diagram + craft = *drawing and manual arts*	**ZU**·KŌ ズ·コウ
心電図	heart + electric + diagram = *electrocardiogram*	SHIN·DEN·**ZU** シン·デン·ズ
海図	sea + diagram = *nautical chart*	KAI·**ZU** カイ·ズ
意図	mind + diagram = *(one's) aim*	I·**TO** イ·ト

SAMPLE SENTENCE

心電図 モニター を 見せて 下さい。
SHIN·DEN·ZU monitā o mi·sete kuda·sai.
electrocardiogram monitor show please
= *Please show me the electrocardiogram monitor.*

WRITING PRACTICE

KANJI 112

STAND

MEANING
Stand/Rise. No story required.

COMMON PRONUNCIATIONS
Common **ON** reading: **RITSU** (リツ)
Common **kun** reading: **ta** (た)

Consistent with other **on-yomi** ending in **TSU** (ツ), **RITSU** "doubles up" with unvoiced consonant sounds that follow it, as the fifth example below demonstrates. It can also act like 買 (Entry 50) and become voiced in the second position. The final compound shows these aspects of its meaning.

kun-yomi suggestion: "**ta**x"

Create your **on-yomi** keyword and enter it in the table at the back of the book. After that, write your sentence to remember the **on-yomi** and **kun-yomi** readings in the box below.

LESS COMMON PRONUNCIATIONS
Less common **ON** reading: **RYŪ** (リュウ)
Less common **kun** reading: none

COMMON WORDS AND COMPOUNDS		
立つ (intr)	*to stand*	**ta**·tsu た·つ
立てる (tr)	*to set up*	**ta**·teru た·てる
自立	self + stand = *independence*	JI·**RITSU** ジ·リツ
中立	middle + stand = *neutrality*	CHŪ·**RITSU** チュウ·リツ
立春	stand + spring = *first day of spring*	**RIS**·SHUN リッ·シュン
立ち入る	stand + enter = *to go into*	**ta**·chi i·ru た·ち い·る
夕立	evening + stand = *late afternoon (rain) shower*	yū·**dachi** ゆう·だち

SAMPLE SENTENCE

女 の 人 が 美しい 月 の 下
onna no hito ga utsuku·shii tsuki no shita
woman person beautiful moon under
に 立っています。
ni tat·te imasu.
is standing
= *The woman is standing under a beautiful moon.*

WRITING PRACTICE

KANJI 113

PARENT

亠	亠	亠	亠	立	立	辛	亲	亲
亲	新	新	親	親	親	親		

BUILDING THIS KANJI
Stand 立(112) + **Tree** 木(13) + **See** 見(42) = 親

MEANING
"Parent", together with the senses of intimacy and closeness.

REMEMBERING THIS KANJI
When she was young, her PARENTS would often sing the following ditty:

"**Stand** on a **tree**,
And what do you **see**?
Your PARENTS! Your PARENTS!"

It was cute, of course, but they really should have stopped at some point. After all, it wasn't easy for her as a university student having to answer the question "What's up with your PARENTS and that dumb song?"

COMMON PRONUNCIATIONS
Common **ON** reading: **SHIN** (シン)
Common **kun** reading: **oya** (おや)

kun-yomi suggestion: "**coy a**bout"

Create your **on-yomi** keyword and enter it in the table at the back of the book. After that, write your sentence to remember the **on-yomi** and **kun-yomi** readings in the box below.

LESS COMMON PRONUNCIATIONS
Less common **ON** reading: none
Less common **kun** reading: **shita** (した)

COMMON WORDS AND COMPOUNDS		
親	*parent*	**oya** おや
父親	father + parent = *father*	chichi·**oya** ちち·おや
親子	parent + child = *parent and child*	**oya**·ko おや·こ
肉親	meat + parent = *blood relative*	NIKU·**SHIN** ニク·シン
母親	mother + parent = *mother*	haha·**oya** はは·おや
親切	parent + cut = *kindhearted*	**SHIN**·SETSU シン·セツ

SAMPLE SENTENCE

中川さん の 父親 は 山 が
Naka·gawa-san no chichi·oya wa yama ga
Nakagawa-san father mountain
大好き です。
DAI su·ki desu.
really likes
= *Nakagawa-san's father really likes the mountains.*

WRITING PRACTICE

KANJI 114

STAR

丨	冂	冃	日	戸	旦	早	星	星

BUILDING THIS KANJI
Sun 日(6) + **Life** 生(99) = 星

MEANING
Star.

REMEMBERING THIS KANJI
When the **sun** is shining over your **life**, it's impossible not to feel like a STAR. A famous STAR like Sirius, mind you, not one of those dim ones nobody cares about.

COMMON PRONUNCIATIONS
Common **ON** reading: **SEI** (セイ)
Common **kun** reading: **hoshi** (ほし)

kun-yomi suggestion: "tally **ho, Shee**ba!"

Create your **on-yomi** keyword and enter it in the table at the back of the book. After that, write your sentence to remember the **on-yomi** and **kun-yomi** readings in the box below.

LESS COMMON PRONUNCIATIONS
Less common **ON** reading: **SHŌ** (ショウ)
Less common **kun** reading: none

COMMON WORDS AND COMPOUNDS		
星	*star*	**hoshi** ほし
水星	water + star = *Mercury (planet)*	SUI·**SEI** スイ·セイ
金星	gold + star = *Venus (planet)*	KIN·**SEI** キン·セイ
火星	fire + star = *Mars (planet)*	KA·**SEI** カ·セイ
木星	tree + star = *Jupiter (planet)*	MOKU·**SEI** モク·セイ
土星	earth + star = *Saturn (planet)*	DO·**SEI** ド·セイ

SAMPLE SENTENCE

あの 明るい 星 は 金星 だ と 思います か。
ano aka·rui hoshi wa KIN·SEI da to omo·imasu ka.
that bright star Venus think
= *Do you think that bright "star" is Venus?*

WRITING PRACTICE

COMPONENT 115

CROPS  

When this component appears it usually indicates a kanji with some connection to crops and harvesting.

KANJI 115

 **AUTUMN**

BUILDING THIS KANJI
Crops 禾 + **Fire** 火(59) = 秋

MEANING
Autumn.

REMEMBERING THIS KANJI
No need for a long story here, given that the origin of this graceful character is clearly apparent, AUTUMN being the time when **fire** was set to the stubble of **crops** left after harvesting.

COMMON PRONUNCIATIONS
Common **ON** reading: **SHŪ** (シュウ)
Common **kun** reading: **aki** (あき)

Note the great four-kanji compound in the third example below.

kun-yomi suggestion: "**stack ea**sily"

Create your **on-yomi** keyword and enter it in the table at the back of the book. After that, write your sentence to remember the **on-yomi** and **kun-yomi** readings in the box below.

LESS COMMON PRONUNCIATIONS
Less common **ON** reading: none
Less common **kun** reading: none

COMMON WORDS AND COMPOUNDS		
秋	*autumn*	**aki** あき
立秋	stand + autumn = *first day of autumn*	RIS·**SHŪ** リッ·シュウ
春夏秋冬	spring + summer + autumn + winter = *the four seasons; year round*	SHUN·KA·**SHŪ**·TŌ シュン·カ·シュウ·トウ
秋空	autumn + empty (sky) = *autumn sky*	**aki**·zora あき·ぞら
秋分	autumn + part = *autumnal equinox*	**SHŪ**·BUN シュウ·ブン

SAMPLE SENTENCE

秋 には 日本 の 山 が 美しい。
aki ni wa NI·HON no yama ga utsuku·shii.
autumn Japan mountain beautiful
= *Japan's mountains are beautiful in autumn.*

WRITING PRACTICE

COMPONENT 116

WHISKEY JUG  

It's hard to imagine many whiskey drinkers being happy about the stopper for this jug taking up so much room!

KANJI 116

 **WEST**

MEANING
West.

REMEMBERING THIS KANJI
Everyone knows there were a lot of alcohol problems in the wild WEST. Fittingly, a drained **whiskey jug** is used to show this.

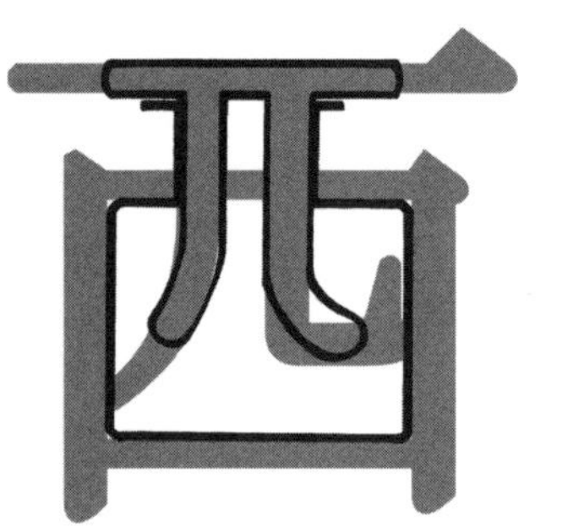

COMMON PRONUNCIATIONS
Common **ON** reading: **SEI** (セイ)
Common **kun** reading: **nishi** (にし)

kun-yomi suggestion: "ho**ney shi**eld"

Create your **on-yomi** keyword and enter it in the table at the back of the book. After that, write your sentence to remember the **on-yomi** and **kun-yomi** readings in the box below.

LESS COMMON PRONUNCIATIONS
Less common **ON** reading: **SAI** (サイ)
Less common **kun** reading: none

COMMON WORDS AND COMPOUNDS		
西	*west*	**nishi** にし
西口	west + mouth = *west exit/entrance*	**nishi**·guchi にし·ぐち
北西	north + west = *northwest*	HOKU·**SEI** ホク·セイ
北北西	north + north + west = *north-northwest*	HOKU·HOKU·**SEI** ホク·ホク·セイ
南西	south + west = *southwest*	NAN·**SEI** ナン·セイ
南南西	south + south + west = *south-southwest*	NAN·NAN·**SEI** ナン·ナン·セイ

SAMPLE SENTENCE

西口 から 出て 父 に 会いました。
nishi·guchi kara de·te chichi ni a·imashita.
west exit — exit father — met
= *(She) left by the west exit and met her father.*

WRITING PRACTICE

KANJI 117

刀 SWORD

フ	刀							

MEANING
Sword. No story required.

COMMON PRONUNCIATIONS
Common **ON** reading: **TŌ** (トウ)
Common **kun** reading: **katana** (かたな)

kun-yomi suggestion: "ma**k**e **a tan a**pple"

Create your **on-yomi** keyword and enter it in the table at the back of the book. After that, write your sentence to remember the **on-yomi** and **kun-yomi** readings in the box below.

LESS COMMON PRONUNCIATIONS
Less common **ON** reading: none
Less common **kun** reading: none

COMMON WORDS AND COMPOUNDS		
刀	*sword*	**katana** かたな
刀工	sword + craft = *sword maker*	**TŌ**·KŌ トウ·コウ
日本刀	sun + main + sword = *Japanese sword*	NI·HON·**TŌ** ニ·ホン·トウ

SAMPLE SENTENCE

先月 東京 で 日本刀 を買いました。
SEN·GETSU TŌ·KYŌ de NI·HON·TŌ o ka·imashita.
last month Tokyo Japanese sword bought
= *Last month I bought a Japanese sword in Tokyo.*

WRITING PRACTICE

KANJI 118

切 CUT

一	七	切	切					

BUILDING THIS KANJI
Seven 七(44) + **Sword** 刀(117) = 切

MEANING

Cut. When the **kun-yomi** is used as a suffix it can impart a sense of completely finishing something, or acting in a decisive manner. The final compound provides an example.

REMEMBERING THIS KANJI

Seven samurai means **seven swords**, and **seven swords** can mean trouble on the set:

"For the last time," said the director, exasperated, "when I yell "CUT", it does *not* mean to CUT each other."

COMMON PRONUNCIATIONS

Common **ON** reading: **SETSU** (セツ)
Common **kun** reading: **ki** (き)

As can be seen in the fourth example, this is another kanji that behaves like 買.

kun-yomi suggestion: "**qui**che"

Create your **on-yomi** keyword and enter it in the table at the back of the book. After that, write your sentence to remember the **on-yomi** and **kun-yomi** readings in the box below.

LESS COMMON PRONUNCIATIONS

Less common **ON** reading: **SAI** (サイ)
Less common **kun** reading: none

As the **kun-yomi** of 切 "doubles up" with the kanji following it in this next pair of words, these compounds are best learned as irregular readings.

IRREGULAR READINGS		
切手	cut + hand = *postage stamp*	**kit·te** きっ·て
切符*	cut + symbol = *ticket*	**kip·pu** きっ·ぷ

COMMON WORDS AND COMPOUNDS		
切れる (intr)	*to break (by itself)*	**ki**·reru き·れる
切る (tr)	*to cut (something)*	**ki**·ru き·る
切り下げる	cut + lower = *to devalue*	**ki**·ri sa·geru き·り さ·げる
切下げ	cut + lower = *devaluation*	**kiri** sa·ge きり さ·げ
親切	parent + cut = *kindhearted*	SHIN·**SETSU** シン·セツ
大切	large + cut = *important*	TAI·**SETSU** タイ·セツ
思い切る	think + cut = *to make up one's mind*	omo·i **ki**·ru おも·い き·る

SAMPLE SENTENCE

水力 と 火力 は 大切 ですね。
SUI·RYOKU to KA·RYOKU wa TAI·SETSU desu ne.
hydro power thermal power important
= *Hydro and thermal power are important, aren't they?*

WRITING PRACTICE

COMPONENT 119

SQUIRRELS (ON A BRICK WALL)  

Why are they hanging out on a brick wall? 'Cause they're tough, that's why.

KANJI 119

DAY OF THE WEEK

BUILDING THIS KANJI
Sun 日 (6) + **Comb** ⺕ + **Comb** ⺕ + **Squirrels** 隹 = 曜

MEANING
Day of the week.

REMEMBERING THIS KANJI
Every DAY OF THE WEEK the **squirrels** sit on their brick wall and wait for the **sun** to come up. Once it does, it becomes light enough for each to grab a **comb** and start slicking back his fur in order to look tough. This is always necessary. After all, every DAY OF THE WEEK is a struggle if you're a **squirrel**.

COMMON PRONUNCIATIONS
Common **ON** reading: **YŌ** (ヨウ)
Common **kun** reading: none

Remember that the final kanji in each compound below is read with its **kun-yomi** (in voiced form). Create your **on-yomi** keyword and enter it in the table at the back of the book. After that, write your sentence to remember the **on-yomi** reading in the box below.

LESS COMMON PRONUNCIATIONS
Less common **ON** reading: none
Less common **kun** reading: none

COMMON WORDS AND COMPOUNDS		
日曜日	sun + day of the week + sun (day) = *Sunday*	NICHI·**YŌ**·bi ニチ·ヨウ·び
月曜日	moon + day of the week + sun (day) = *Monday*	GETSU·**YŌ**·bi ゲツ·ヨウ·び
火曜日	fire + day of the week + sun (day) = *Tuesday*	KA·**YŌ**·bi カ·ヨウ·び
水曜日	water + day of the week + sun (day) = *Wednesday*	SUI·**YŌ**·bi スイ·ヨウ·び
木曜日	tree + day of the week + sun (day) = *Thursday*	MOKU·**YŌ**·bi モク·ヨウ·び
金曜日	gold + day of the week + sun (day) = *Friday*	KIN·**YŌ**·bi キン·ヨウ·び
土曜日	earth + day of the week + sun (day) = *Saturday*	DO·**YŌ**·bi ド·ヨウ·び

SAMPLE SENTENCE

土曜日 に パーティー が あります。
DO·YŌ·bi ni pātī ga arimasu.
Saturday party is
= *There's a party on Saturday.*

WRITING PRACTICE

KANJI 120

AROUND

丿	冂	冂	冂	円	周	周	周	

BUILDING THIS KANJI
Gorilla 冂 + **Earth** 土(87) + **Mouth (vampire)** 口(8) = 周

MEANING
"Around", as in the sense of a lap or circuit.

REMEMBERING THIS KANJI
If a **gorilla** and **vampire** show up at your local square dance, you'd best be gettin' outta their way. Reason being that they'll spin AROUND and AROUND, tramplin' the **earth** and anything else that gets between 'em. Yup, there's no gettin' AROUND it: they ain't exactly graceful.

COMMON PRONUNCIATIONS
Common **ON** reading: **SHŪ** (シュウ)
Common **kun** reading: none

Create your **on-yomi** keyword and enter it in the table at the back of the book. After that, write your sentence to remember the **on-yomi** reading in the box below.

LESS COMMON PRONUNCIATIONS
Less common **ON** reading: none
Less common **kun** reading: none

COMMON WORDS AND COMPOUNDS		
円周	circle + around = *circumference*	EN·**SHŪ** エン·シュウ
周回	around + rotate = *going around*	**SHŪ**·KAI シュウ·カイ
一周	one + around = *once around*	IS·**SHŪ** イッ·シュウ

SAMPLE SENTENCE

寺田さん は ニュージーランド を 一周
Tera·da-san wa Nyūjīrando o IS·SHŪ
Terada-san New Zealand once around
しました。
shimashita.
did
= *Terada-san did a circuit of New Zealand.*

WRITING PRACTICE

CHAPTER 6 REVIEW EXERCISES

A. Please match the following kanji to their meanings.

1. 立	a. Bird
2. 星	b. Autumn
3. 切	c. Star
4. 鳥	d. Temple
5. 秋	e. Outside
6. 外	f. Stand
7. 美	g. Cut
8. 先	h. West
9. 寺	i. Beautiful
10. 西	j. Precede

B. Please match the following meanings to their kanji, and these to their **on** or **kun-yomi**.

1. Island	a. 刀	1. **ZU** (ズ)
2. Parent	b. 図	2. **oya** (おや)
3. Day of the week	c. 寸	3. **SHŪ** (シュウ)
4. Tiny	d. 夕	4. **shita** (した)
5. Sword	e. 開	5. **katana** (かたな)
6. Around	f. 親	6. **YŌ** (ヨウ)
7. Evening	g. 舌	7. **shima** (しま)
8. Open	h. 曜	8. **yū** (ゆう)
9. Tongue	i. 島	9. **a** (あ)
10. Diagram	j. 周	10. **SUN** (スン)

C. Please choose the best answer(s) to the following questions.

1. Which of the following readings apply to the kanji 鳥?
   a. **AI** (アイ)
   b. **tori** (とり)
   c. **hoshi** (ほし)
   d. **SHŪ** (シュウ)
   e. **CHŌ** (チョウ)

2. Which of the following readings apply to the kanji 星?
   a. **SEI** (セイ)
   b. **soto** (そと)
   c. **BUN** (ブン)
   d. **hoshi** (ほし)
   e. **ZU** (ズ)

3. Which of the following presents the greatest danger to a newly-washed car?
   a. 夕
   b. 星
   c. 鳥
   d. 外
   e. 舌

4. Which of the following readings apply to the kanji 秋?
   a. **BI** (ビ)
   b. **a** (あ)
   c. **tera** (てら)
   d. **SHŪ** (シュウ)
   e. **aki** (あき)

5. Which of the following readings apply to the kanji 先?
   a. **saki** (さき)
   b. **YŌ** (ヨウ)
   c. **SEN** (セン)
   d. **yū** (ゆう)
   e. **JI** (ジ)

D. Please choose the best answer(s) to the following questions.

1. Which is the correct reading of 美しい?
   a. **ara·shii** (あら·しい)
   b. **tama·shii** (たま·しい)
   c. **mawa·shii** (まわ·しい)
   d. **utsuku·shii** (うつく·しい)

2. Which answer best captures the meaning of the compound 月曜日?
   a. Sunday
   b. Thursday
   c. Monday
   d. Saturday
   e. All of the preceding

3. Which of the following kanji has the most number of strokes?
   a. 開
   b. 鳥
   c. 美
   d. 秋
   e. 星

4. Which is the correct reading of 立つ?
   a. **ta·tsu** (た·つ)
   b. **u·tsu** (う·つ)
   c. **ma·tsu** (ま·つ)
   d. **ka·tsu** (か·つ)

5. Which are the correct readings of 開く? (There are two possible answers.)
   a. **o·ku** (お·く)
   b. **a·ku** (あ·く)
   c. **ama·ku** (あま·く)
   d. **hira·ku** (ひら·く)

E. Please match the following compounds and words to their meanings and pronunciations.

1. 木曜日	a. Setting sun	1. **SHIN·SETSU** (シン·セツ)
2. 自立	b. Mars (planet)	2. **HAN·TŌ** (ハン·トウ)
3. 親切	c. Beautiful woman	3. **MOKU·YŌ·bi** (モク·ヨウ·び)
4. 先生	d. Independence	4. **yū·hi** (ゆう·ひ)
5. 西口	e. Foreigner	5. **nishi·guchi** (にし·ぐち)
6. 火星	f. Peninsula	6. **KA·SEI** (カ·セイ)
7. 夕日	g. Thursday	7. **SEN·SEI** (セン·セイ)
8. 外国人	h. Kindhearted	8. **GAI·KOKU·JIN** (ガイ·コク·ジン)
9. 半島	i. West exit/ entrance	9. **BI·JIN** (ビ·ジン)
10. 美人	j. Teacher	10. **JI·RITSU** (ジ·リツ)

CHAPTER 7 (KANJI 121-140)

KANJI 121

 READ

丶	亠	亡	言	言	言	言	言一	言十
言土	言土	言声	読	読				

BUILDING THIS KANJI
Say 言(80) + **Sell** 売(92) = 読

MEANING
Read.

REMEMBERING THIS KANJI
The sales manager rose to address her staff. It was time for the READING.
"And lo, I **say** unto you who **sell**," she intoned. "READ carefully the customer's face. READ their gestures and clothes. But READ not, I **say**, our price protection guarantee; this let them READ for themselves."

COMMON PRONUNCIATIONS
Common **ON** reading: **DOKU** (ドク)
Common **kun** reading: **yo** (よ)

kun-yomi suggestion: "**yo**ga"

Create your **on-yomi** keyword and enter it in the table at the back of the book. After that, write your sentence to remember the **on-yomi** and **kun-yomi** readings in the box below.

LESS COMMON PRONUNCIATIONS
Less common **ON** readings: **TOKU** (トク); **TŌ** (トウ)
Less common **kun** reading: none

COMMON WORDS AND COMPOUNDS		
読む	*to read*	**yo**·mu よ·む
読み切る	read + cut = *to finish reading*	**yo**·mi ki·ru よ·み き·る
読者	read + individual = *reader*	**DOKU**·SHA ドク·シャ
読み物	read + thing = *reading matter*	**yo**·mi mono よ·み もの
多読家	many + read + house = *well-read person*	TA·**DOKU**·KA タ·ドク·カ

SAMPLE SENTENCE

この 古い 本 を 読んでいます か。
kono furu·i HON o yo·nde imasu ka.
this old book are reading
= *Are you reading this old book?*

WRITING PRACTICE

COMPONENT 122

SEAL ⻌ 

KANJI 122

道 ROAD

丶	丷	䒑	䒑	产	产	首	首	首
首	道	道						

BUILDING THIS KANJI
Neck 首(51) + **Seal** ⻌ = 道

MEANING

Road/Way. This interesting kanji can signify both a physical road and a spiritual "path". In this latter sense it is often translated as "the way".

REMEMBERING THIS KANJI

Being so poor growing up, we had to use our imaginations when it came time for fun. That's why it was so lucky for us when the **seal** washed up on the beach that day; once some yellow lines were painted down the back of its **neck**, we had ourselves a nice ROAD on which to race our toys. And did we ever get good mileage out of that ROAD! We played on it for ages, and only quit using it when our wheels started getting stuck.

COMMON PRONUNCIATIONS

Common **ON** reading: **DŌ** (ドウ)
Common **kun** reading: **michi** (みち)

kun-yomi suggestion: "give **me chee**se"

Create your **on-yomi** keyword and enter it in the table at the back of the book. After that, write your sentence to remember the **on-yomi** and **kun-yomi** readings in the box below.

LESS COMMON PRONUNCIATIONS

Less common **ON** reading: **TŌ** (トウ)
Less common **kun** reading: none

TŌ is extremely rare, although it is found in a common word formed by the characters "God" and "Road" to indicate the Japanese religion Shinto (神道*): **SHIN·TŌ** (シン·トウ).

COMMON WORDS AND COMPOUNDS		
道	*road; way*	**michi** みち
小道	small + road = *path*	ko·**michi** こ·みち
水道	water + road = *water supply system*	SUI·**DŌ** スイ·ドウ
下水道	lower + water + road = *sewer system*	GE·SUI·**DŌ** ゲ·スイ·ドウ
歩道	walk + road = *sidewalk*	HO·**DŌ** ホ·ドウ
国道	country + road = *national highway*	KOKU·**DŌ** コク·ドウ

SAMPLE SENTENCE

あの 国 に は 安全 な 水道水 が
ano kuni ni wa AN·ZEN na SUI·DŌ·SUI ga
that country safe tap water
ありません。
arimasen.
isn't
= *There is no safe tap water in that country.*

WRITING PRACTICE

KANJI 123

HEAVEN

一	二	于	天					

BUILDING THIS KANJI

One (top of a bun) 一(3) + **Large (sumo wrestler)** 大(17) = 天

MEANING

Heaven/The heavens. This character can indicate both the spiritual sense of heaven as well as the more down to earth notions of sky and air.

REMEMBERING THIS KANJI

The Japanese believe that **sumo wrestlers** in HEAVEN live in mansions built of food. The ceilings of these are made from the **tops of buns** that exude various types of mustards and sauces when they leak. Such living conditions must truly be HEAVEN for a **sumo wrestler**.

COMMON PRONUNCIATIONS

Common **ON** reading: **TEN** (テン)

Common **kun** reading: none

Note how the **on-yomi** for "country" (国) is voiced in the first example below. One more curiosity occurs in the fourth compound; in this word, note how 天 changes the **on-yomi** of "king" from **Ō** (オウ) to **NŌ** (ノウ) in order to make the pronunciation smoother. This type of phonetic change is extremely rare. Note that the sample sentence contains an irregular reading (明日).

Create your **on-yomi** keyword and enter it in the table at the back of the book. After that, write your sentence to remember the **on-yomi** reading in the box below.

LESS COMMON PRONUNCIATIONS

Less common **ON** reading: none

Less common **kun** readings: **ame** (あめ); **ama** (あま)

COMMON WORDS AND COMPOUNDS		
天国	heaven + country = *heaven*	**TEN**·GOKU テン·ゴク
天下	heaven + lower = *the whole land*	**TEN**·KA テン·カ
天体	heaven + body = *heavenly body*	**TEN**·TAI テン·タイ
天王星	heaven + king + star = *Uranus (planet)*	**TEN**·NŌ·SEI テン·ノウ·セイ
天気	heaven + spirit = *the weather*	**TEN**·KI テン·キ

SAMPLE SENTENCE

明日 の 天気 は 雨 だ そう です。

ashita no TEN·KI wa ame da sō desu.

tomorrow weather rain seems

= *It seems the weather will be rainy tomorrow.*

WRITING PRACTICE

KANJI 124

PART

ノ	八	分	分					

BUILDING THIS KANJI
Eight (volcano) 八(19) + **Sword** 刀(117) = 分

MEANING
This important character suggests the ideas of "dividing" and "portion". It appears in a wide range of words, but the sense of division is always present in some way; the first example below, for instance, can be thought of as "parting" the unknown to arrive at understanding.

REMEMBERING THIS KANJI
Modern scientists may scoff at the notion, but a lot of people still believe that **volcanoes** show how the underground dwellers made their way to the surface. By PARTING the rock and magma with **swords** on the way up, it is thought, they created the **volcanoes** we have today. Though the kanji clearly shows a **sword** beneath the missing PART of a **volcano**, it is impossible to verify this theory until the underground dwellers themselves shed more light on their past.

COMMON PRONUNCIATIONS
Common **ON** reading: **BUN** (ブン)
Common **kun** reading: **wa** (わ)

kun-yomi suggestion: "**wa**cky"

Create your **on-yomi** keyword and enter it in the table at the back of the book. After that, write your sentence to remember the **on-yomi** and **kun-yomi** readings in the box below.

LESS COMMON PRONUNCIATIONS
Less common **ON** readings: **FUN** (フン); **BU** (ブ)
Less common **kun** reading: none

As these readings are both used following numbers, is important to know the context in which each is employed. **FUN** relates to minutes (of time or arc), as in the example 五分 **GO·FUN** (ゴ·フン): five minutes. **BU** deals with percentages and rates; 五分 in this sense would be pronounced **GO·BU** (ゴ·ブ), and mean either five (or fifty) percent. It merits learning the words for minutes as irregular readings, as they will be needed for telling time.

Note also that 大分 **DAI·BUN** (ダイ·ブン), one of many Japanese words expressing the idea of "much" or "very", is often pronounced **DAI·BU** (ダイ·ブ).

COMMON WORDS AND COMPOUNDS		
分かる (intr)	*to understand*	**wa**·karu わ·かる
分ける (tr)	*to part; to divide*	**wa**·keru わ·ける
自分	self + part = *oneself*	JI·**BUN** ジ·ブン
半分	half + part = *half*	HAN·**BUN** ハン·ブン
春分	spring + part = *vernal equinox*	SHUN·**BUN** シュン·ブン
秋分	autumn + part = *autumnal equinox*	SHŪ·**BUN** シュウ·ブン

SAMPLE SENTENCE

日本語　が 分かります か。
NI·HON·GO ga wa·karimasu ka.
Japanese　understand
= *Do you understand Japanese?*

WRITING PRACTICE

COMPONENT 125

STOOPING 勿 

Labor Code regulations require the following disclaimer be inserted: "This is not an appropriate method of lifting heavy objects."

KANJI 125

 **THING**

丿	𠂉	牛	牛	牜	牞	物	物	

BUILDING THIS KANJI
Cow 牛(100) + **Stooping** 勿 = 物

MEANING
Thing/Object. Note that the writing order for "cow" differs when it is used as a component; slanting the final stroke upward makes for a smoother transition to the next part of the character.

REMEMBERING THIS KANJI
"What's that THING?" asked a guy **stooping** next to a **cow**.

"That's my tail," said the **cow**, irritated.

"And what's that THING?"

"It's a hoof, OK?" Everyone knows it's a hoof."

"And what about those THINGS?"

"What?! How dare you **stoop** so low as to question me about my udder!"

Though THINGS had started out well, relations between **cows** and tourists had slowly become strained.

COMMON PRONUNCIATIONS
Common **ON** reading: **BUTSU** (ブツ)
Common **kun** reading: **mono** (もの)

Pronunciation-wise, this is a tough kanji to pin down; both readings are found extensively, and there are no easy rules to fall back on as to when each is used in compounds. This is a character that has to be taken on a word-for-word basis.

kun-yomi suggestion: "**moan o**ver"

Create your **on-yomi** keyword and enter it in the table at the back of the book. After that, write your sentence to remember the **on-yomi** and **kun-yomi** readings in the box below.

LESS COMMON PRONUNCIATIONS
Less common **ON** reading: **MOTSU** (モツ)
Less common **kun** reading: none

COMMON WORDS AND COMPOUNDS		
物	*thing*	**mono** もの
買い物	buy + thing = *shopping*	ka·i **mono** か·い もの
読み物	read + thing = *reading matter*	yo·mi **mono** よ·み もの
人物	person + thing = *one's character*	JIN·**BUTSU** ジン·ブツ
見物	see + thing = *sightseeing*	KEN·**BUTSU** ケン·ブツ
物体	thing + body = *an object*	**BUT**·TAI ブッ·タイ

SAMPLE SENTENCE

本田さん は どんな 人物 ですか。
Hon·da-san wa donna JIN·BUTSU desu ka.
Honda-san what kind of character
= *What kind of person is Honda-san?*

WRITING PRACTICE

KANJI 126

斤 AXE

ノ	厂	斤	斤					

MEANING

Axe. Though rarely encountered on its own, this character serves as a component in several important kanji (an example being Entry 127). No story required.

COMMON PRONUNCIATIONS

Common **ON** reading: **KIN** (キン)
Common **kun** reading: none

Create your **on-yomi** keyword and enter it in the table at the back of the book. After that, write your sentence to remember the **on-yomi** reading in the box below.

LESS COMMON PRONUNCIATIONS

Less common **ON** reading: none
Less common **kun** reading: none

COMMON WORDS AND COMPOUND		
斤	axe = *axe*	**KIN** キン

SAMPLE SENTENCE

"斤" が 読めます か。
"KIN" ga yo·memasu ka.
KIN can read
= *Can you read "斤"?*

WRITING PRACTICE

KANJI 127

NEW

丶	亠	亠	立	立	立	辛	辛	亲
亲	新	新	新					

BUILDING THIS KANJI
Stand 立(112) + **Tree** 木(13) + **Axe** 斤(126) = 新

MEANING
New.

REMEMBERING THIS KANJI
Standing in the **tree**, I felt safe from the **axe**-wielding maniac.

"Come on down," he said. "I'll give you my **axe**."

I thought about this for a moment and realized I needed to split some wood behind the barn. "Is it NEW?" I asked warily.

"Brand NEW," he said. "I just got it."

"What's that stuff on the blade, then?"

"Oh, that? That's from the wrapper. Trust me, it's totally NEW."

"Well, OK then," I said, climbing down from the **tree**. I suppose you can't hurt me if you don't have your **axe**."

COMMON PRONUNCIATIONS
Common **ON** reading: **SHIN** (シン)
Common **kun** reading: **atara** (あたら)

kun-yomi suggestion: "**at a ra**ffle"

Create your **on-yomi** keyword and enter it in the table at the back of the book. After that, write your sentence to remember the **on-yomi** and **kun-yomi** readings in the box below.

LESS COMMON PRONUNCIATIONS
Less common **ON** reading: none
Less common **kun** readings: **arata** (あらた); **nii** (にい)

COMMON WORDS AND COMPOUNDS		
新しい	*new*	**atara**·shii あたら·しい
一新	one + new = *complete renewal*	IS·**SHIN** イッ·シン
新月	new + moon = *new moon*	**SHIN**·GETSU シン·ゲツ
新星	new + star = *nova*	**SHIN**·SEI シン·セイ
最新	most + new = *newest*	SAI·**SHIN** サイ·シン

SAMPLE SENTENCE
新しい　日本刀　を 買いました。
atara·shii NI·HON·TŌ o ka·imashita.
new　Japanese sword　bought
= (I) bought a new Japanese sword.

WRITING PRACTICE

COMPONENT 128

WREATH  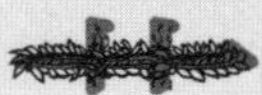

This component figures prominently in characters related to grasses and plants.

KANJI 128

 **FLOWER**

BUILDING THIS KANJI
Wreath 艹 + **Change** 化(69) = 花

MEANING

Flower.

REMEMBERING THIS KANJI

Crowned with a **wreath**, Caesar strode into Rome.

"Everything has **changed**," whispered a senator. "Look how the masses throw FLOWERS! It bodes ill."

"Perhaps," said another, slowly "But the FLOWERS in that **wreath** – be they sweet smelling roses – will also **change**, and become as these that are now trampled underfoot."

COMMON PRONUNCIATIONS

Common **ON** reading: **KA** (カ)
Common **kun** reading: **hana** (はな)

As the second example below shows, **hana** can become voiced when not in the first position. Also note the interesting juxtaposition of characters in the fourth and fifth examples as well as the irregular reading (上手) used in the sample sentence.

kun-yomi suggestion: "**Han a**mulet"

Create your **on-yomi** keyword and enter it in the table at the back of the book. After that, write your sentence to remember the **on-yomi** and **kun-yomi** readings in the box below.

LESS COMMON PRONUNCIATIONS

Less common **ON** reading: none
Less common **kun** reading: none

COMMON WORDS AND COMPOUNDS		
花	*flower*	**hana** はな
生け花	life + flower = *flower arrangement*	i·ke **bana** い·け ばな
花見	flower + see = *cherry blossom viewing*	**hana**·mi はな·み
花火	flower + fire = *fireworks*	**hana**·bi はな·び
火花	fire + flower = *sparks*	hi·**bana** ひ·ばな
開花	open + flower = *bloom*	KAI·**KA** カイ·カ

SAMPLE SENTENCE

西田さん　は　生け花　が　上手　です　ね。
Nishi·da san wa i·ke bana ga JŌ·zu desu ne.
Nishida-san ikebana good at
= *Nishida-san is good at ikebana isn't (she)?*

WRITING PRACTICE

KANJI 129

NAME

ノ	ク	タ	タ	名	名			

BUILDING THIS KANJI
Evening タ (108) + **"Mouth (vampire)** ロ (8) = 名

MEANING

Name. By extension, this kanji also includes the ideas of "reputation" and "fame".

REMEMBERING THIS KANJI

Dracula, of course, is a **vampire** whose NAME is synonymous with **evening**. This is the real reason he comes out only then; his NAME and reputation would suffer, after all, if someone were to spot him at a coffee shop in broad daylight.

COMMON PRONUNCIATIONS

Common **ON** reading: **MEI** (メイ)
Common **kun** reading: **na** (な)

kun-yomi suggestion: "**na**pkin"

Create your **on-yomi** keyword and enter it in the table at the back of the book. After that, write your sentence to remember the **on-yomi** and **kun-yomi** readings in the box below.

LESS COMMON PRONUNCIATIONS

Less common **ON** reading: **MYŌ** (ミョウ)
Less common **kun** reading: none

COMMON WORDS AND COMPOUNDS		
名高い	name + tall = *renowned*	**na** daka·i な だか·い
有名	have + name = *famous*	YŪ·**MEI** ユウ·メイ
名山	name + mountain = *famous mountain*	**MEI**·ZAN メイ·ザン
名物	name + thing = *famous regional product*	**MEI**·BUTSU メイ·ブツ
名前	name + before = *name*	**na**·mae な·まえ

SAMPLE SENTENCE

日本 の 名山 の 一つ を
NI·HON no MEI·ZAN no hito·tsu o
Japan famous mountains one
見ました か。
mi·mashita ka.
seen
= *Have you seen one of Japan's famous mountains?*

WRITING PRACTICE

KANJI 130

MOTHER

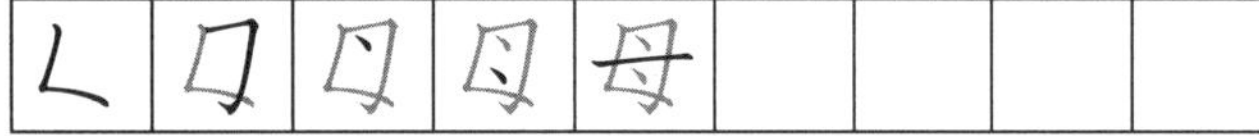

MEANING
Mother. No story required.

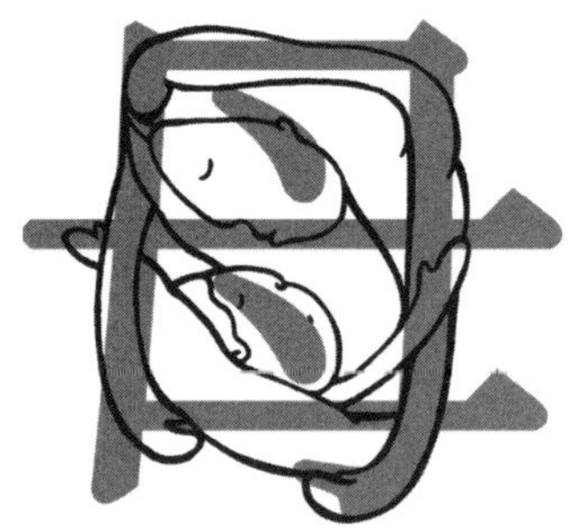

COMMON PRONUNCIATIONS
Common **ON** reading: **BO** (ボ)
Common **kun** reading: **haha** (はは)

As with the kanji for father (Entry 79), the variety of words for mother shown below reflect different levels of familiarity and politeness.

kun-yomi suggestion: "**Ha! Ha!**"

Create your **on-yomi** keyword and enter it in the table at the back of the book. After that, write your sentence to remember the **on-yomi** and **kun-yomi** readings in the box below.

LESS COMMON PRONUNCIATIONS
Less common **ON** reading: none
Less common **kun** reading: none

These two irregular readings correspond to those we learned earlier for "father".

IRREGULAR READINGS		
お母さん	*mother*	**okāsan** おかあさん
伯母さん*	related + mother = *aunt*	**obasan** おばさん

COMMON WORDS AND COMPOUNDS		
母	*mother*	**haha** はは
母親	mother + parent = *mother*	**haha**·oya はは·おや
母国語	mother + country + words = *mother tongue*	**BO**·KOKU·GO ボ·コク·ゴ
母の日	mother + sun (day) = *Mother's Day*	**haha**·no·hi はは·の·ひ
父母	father + mother = *father and mother*	FU·**BO** フ·ボ

SAMPLE SENTENCE

新しい 先生 の 母国語 は 英語 です。
atara·shii SEN·SEI no BO·KOKU·GO wa EI·GO desu.
new teacher mother tongue English
= *The new teacher's mother tongue is English.*

WRITING PRACTICE

COMPONENT 131

BROKEN CRUTCH  

Although this component appears to have three strokes, it is actually written with two; this is shown in the following kanji.

KANJI 131

 **PRIVATE**

BUILDING THIS KANJI
Crops 禾 + **Broken Crutch** 厶 = 私

MEANING

Private. This character is also used for the first person singular, "I".

REMEMBERING THIS KANJI

Nobody could figure out what was going on with the **crops**. The oats were acting wilder than ever, and rumor had it that gangs of wheat were causing trouble amongst the barley. PRIVATELY we began to worry about the harvest, especially when stalks of rye began showing up with bruises and **broken crutches**. Several of us tried to ask the **crops** what was going on, but nobody got very far. "What happens between us **crops** is none of your business," they always replied. "It's PRIVATE, you got that? PRIVATE!"

COMMON PRONUNCIATIONS

Common **ON** reading: **SHI** (シ)
Common **kun** reading: **watashi** (わたし)

kun-yomi suggestion: "**what a shee**r"

Create your **on-yomi** keyword and enter it in the table at the back of the book. After that, write your sentence to remember the **on-yomi** and **kun-yomi** readings in the box below.

LESS COMMON PRONUNCIATIONS

Less common **ON** reading: none
Less common **kun** reading: **watakushi** (わたくし)

COMMON WORDS AND COMPOUNDS		
私	*I*	**watashi** わたし
私有	private + have = *privately owned*	**SHI**·YŪ シ·ユウ
私道	private + road = *private road*	**SHI**·DŌ シ·ドウ
私物	private + thing = *private property*	**SHI**·BUTSU シ·ブツ
私学	private + study = *private school*	**SHI**·GAKU シ·ガク

SAMPLE SENTENCE

私　は　本　を 読んでいます。
watashi wa HON o yo·nde imasu.
I book reading
= *I'm reading a book.*

WRITING PRACTICE

KANJI 132

NIGHT

丶	亠	广	亣	疒	夜	夜	夜	

BUILDING THIS KANJI
Police 亠 + **Giraffe** 亻 + **Evening** タ (108) + **Comet** 一 = 夜

MEANING
Night. Make sure to write this character in the order given.

REMEMBERING THIS KANJI
After a long day policing the savanna, the **ranger** went to her local watering hole for a drink. Surprisingly, the **giraffes** were already there, and seemed well on the way to making a NIGHT of it.

"It's safe to come here the moment a **comet** is visible in the **evening**," said one, slurring over a gin and tonic. "That means it's NIGHT, and dark enough so that nothing can hunt."

"I wouldn't be so sure about that," said the **ranger**. "The leopards I just passed on the way over didn't look like they were coming here for a NIGHTCAP."

COMMON PRONUNCIATIONS
Common **ON** reading: **YA** (ヤ)
Common **kun** reading: **yoru** (よる); **yo** (よ)

yoru is only used when this kanji appears alone; **yo** and **YA** are distributed evenly through compounds.

kun-yomi suggestions: "**you're oo**zing"; "**yo**gurt"

Create your **on-yomi** keyword and enter it in the table at the back of the book. After that, write your sentence to remember the **on-yomi** and **kun-yomi** readings in the box below.

LESS COMMON PRONUNCIATIONS
Less common **ON** reading: none
Less common **kun** reading: none

COMMON WORDS AND COMPOUNDS		
夜	*night*	**yoru** よる
夜中	night + middle = *middle of the night*	**yo**·naka よ·なか
夜明け	night + bright = *dawn*	**yo** a·ke よ あ·け
月夜	moon + night = *moonlit night*	tsuki·**yo** つき·よ
夜間	night + interval = *night time*	**YA**·KAN ヤ·カン

SAMPLE SENTENCE

夜明けに 家 を 出ました。
yo a·ke ni ie o de·mashita.
dawn house exit
= *I left the house at dawn.*

WRITING PRACTICE

COMPONENT 133

CHISEL 刂 

KANJI 133

前 BEFORE

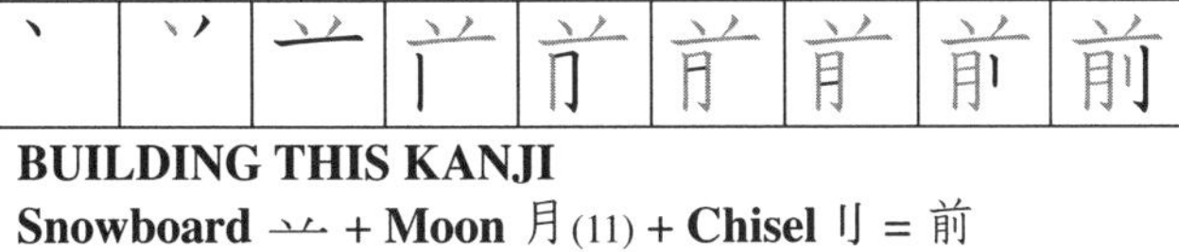

BUILDING THIS KANJI
Snowboard 䒑 + **Moon** 月 (11) + **Chisel** 刂 = 前

MEANING

Before/Front. It is worth comparing the compounds below to those for "先" (Entry 105) to get a sense of the subtle differences between these two characters.

REMEMBERING THIS KANJI

We all know that a waxing **moon** comes BEFORE a full **moon**, but how many know where the expression "waxing **moon**" originated? It's an interesting story, in that the **moon** used to work at a **snowboard** shop long BEFORE he took his place in the sky. Using a **chisel**, he would wax the **snowboards** as carefully as possible, trying not to let the **chisel** slip and add yet another crater to his face. He was, by all accounts, a conscientious worker, one who always reminded customers to prep their boards BEFORE they hit the slopes.

COMMON PRONUNCIATIONS

Common **ON** reading: **ZEN** (ゼン)
Common **kun** reading: **mae** (まえ)

kun-yomi suggestion: "ll**ama a**te"

Create your **on-yomi** keyword and enter it in the table at the back of the book. After that, write your sentence to remember the **on-yomi** and **kun-yomi** readings in the box below.

LESS COMMON PRONUNCIATIONS

Less common **ON** reading: none
Less common **kun** reading: none

COMMON WORDS AND COMPOUNDS		
前	*before*	**mae** まえ
名前	name + before = *name*	na·**mae** な·まえ
手前	hand + before = *this side of*	te·**mae** て·まえ
前半	before + half = *first half*	**ZEN**·HAN ゼン·ハン
前者	before + individual = *the former*	**ZEN**·SHA ゼン·シャ
午前	noon + before = *A.M.; morning*	GO·**ZEN** ゴ·ゼン

SAMPLE SENTENCE

門 の 前 に 美しい 花 が あります。
MON no mae ni utsuku·shii hana ga arimasu.
gate before beautiful flower are
= *There are beautiful flowers in front of the gate.*

WRITING PRACTICE

KANJI 134

MANY

ノ	ク	タ	夛	多	多			

BUILDING THIS KANJI
Evening 夕 (108) + **Evening** 夕 (108) = 多

MEANING
Many/Much.

REMEMBERING THIS KANJI
Evening after **evening**, MANY **evenings** ago, something happened…to MANY.

COMMON PRONUNCIATIONS
Common **ON** reading: **TA** (タ)
Common **kun** reading: **ō** (おお)

kun-yomi suggestion: "**o**boe"

Create your **on-yomi** keyword and enter it in the table at the back of the book. After that, write your sentence to remember the **on-yomi** and **kun-yomi** readings in the box below.

LESS COMMON PRONUNCIATIONS
Less common **ON** reading: none
Less common **kun** reading: none

COMMON WORDS AND COMPOUNDS		
多い	*many*	**ō**·i おお·い
多少	many + few = *more or less*	**TA**·SHŌ タ·ショウ
多分	many + part = *perhaps*	**TA**·BUN タ·ブン
多大	many + large = *great quantity*	**TA**·DAI タ·ダイ
多読家	many + read + house = *well-read person*	**TA**·DOKU·KA タ·ドク·カ

SAMPLE SENTENCE

この 国 には お金 が 大好き な 人
kono kuni ni wa o kane ga DAI su·ki na hito
this country money really like person
が 多い。
ga ō·i.
many
= *In this country, there are a lot of people who really like money.*

WRITING PRACTICE

KANJI 135

HOLD

一	亅	扌	扌一	扌十	扌土	扌土一	持	持

BUILDING THIS KANJI
Finger 扌 + **Temple** 寺 (104) = 多

MEANING
Hold/Possess.

REMEMBERING THIS KANJI
I saw a **finger** emerge from a **temple** I was passing one day. "HOLD me," came a shaky voice from behind a curtain. For some reason, I decided not to.

COMMON PRONUNCIATIONS
Common **ON** reading: none
Common **kun** reading: **mo** (も)

As the fourth example below shows, this kanji can act like 買.

kun-yomi suggestion: "**mo**cha"

Create your sentence to remember the **kun-yomi** reading in the box below.

LESS COMMON PRONUNCIATIONS
Less common **ON** reading: **JI** (ジ)
Less common **kun** reading: none

COMMON WORDS AND COMPOUNDS		
持つ	*to hold*	**mo**·tsu も·つ
金持ち	gold + hold = *rich person*	kane **mo**·chi かね も·ち
持ち上げる	hold + upper = *to lift up*	**mo**·chi a·geru も·ち あ·げる
持物	hold + thing = *one's belongings*	**mochi**·mono もち·もの
気持ち	spirit + hold = *feeling*	KI **mo**·chi キ も·ち

SAMPLE SENTENCE

雪男 は 田中さん を
yuki·otoko wa Tanaka-san o
The Abominable Snowman Tanaka-san
持ち上げました。
mo·chi a·gemashita.
lifted up
= *The Abominable Snowman lifted up Tanaka-san.*

WRITING PRACTICE

COMPONENT 136

PITCHFORK ⺕ 

Fittingly for a pitchfork, this component will always be stabbing through at least one other line in the kanji. The next entry provides an example.

KANJI 136

WRITE

㇆	⺕							書
書								

BUILDING THIS KANJI
Pitchfork ⺕ + **Two** 二(4) + **Pole** | + **Sun** 日(6) = 書

MEANING

Write. This character has to do with all things related to writing, and can suggest such things as books, notes, documents, and calligraphy, amongst others.

REMEMBERING THIS KANJI

Even if you dip them in ink, it is simply not possible to WRITE the Japanese kanji for "**two**" using a **pitchfork** (it makes a triple line) or a **pole** (a single line). Using the **sun** is even worse; it burns the paper and is thus unsuitable for any kind of WRITING.

COMMON PRONUNCIATIONS

Common **ON** reading: **SHO** (ショ)
Common **kun** reading: **ka** (か)

The third and fifth examples below show how this kanji can act like 買. Be aware that the **kun-yomi** is always voiced when it appears in the second position, as it is in the final compound.

kun-yomi suggestion: "**ca**lendar"

Create your **on-yomi** keyword and enter it in the table at the back of the book. After that, write your sentence to remember the **on-yomi** and **kun-yomi** readings in the box below.

LESS COMMON PRONUNCIATIONS

Less common **ON** reading: none
Less common **kun** reading: none

COMMON WORDS AND COMPOUNDS		
書く	*to write*	**ka**·ku か·く
書き入れる	write + enter = *to write in*	**ka**·ki i·reru か·き い·れる
書入れ	write + enter = *an entry*	**kaki** i·re かき い·れ
書道	write + road = *calligraphy*	**SHO**·DŌ ショ·ドウ
前書	before + write = *preface*	mae·**gaki** まえ·がき

SAMPLE SENTENCE

お名前 を こちら へ 書いて 下さい。
o na·mae o kochira e ka·ite kuda·sai.
name here write please
= *Please write your name here.*

WRITING PRACTICE

KANJI 137

SOUND

丶	亠	亠	立	立	产	音	音	音

BUILDING THIS KANJI
Stand 立(112) + **Sun** 日(6) = 音

MEANING
Sound.

REMEMBERING THIS KANJI
Crackling, sizzling, hissing…it's easy, unfortunately, to imagine the SOUNDS that would be produced if someone were **standing** on the **sun**.

COMMON PRONUNCIATIONS
Common **ON** reading: **ON** (オン)
Common **kun** reading: **oto** (おと)

Although it is a mixture of **on-** and **kun-yomi**, the second example below is probably very familiar to you by now. Note also how the meaning of the same compound changes in the example following this, when both kanji are read with their on-yomi.

kun-yomi suggestion: "guan**o to**ast"

Create your **on-yomi** keyword and enter it in the table at the back of the book. After that, write your sentence to remember the **on-yomi** and **kun-yomi** readings in the box below.

LESS COMMON PRONUNCIATIONS
Less common **ON** reading: **IN** (イン)
Less common **kun** reading: **ne** (ね)

COMMON WORDS AND COMPOUNDS		
音	*sound*	**oto** おと
音読み	sound + read = *the **on-yomi***	**ON** yo·mi オン よ·み
音読	sound + read = *reading aloud*	**ON**·DOKU オン·ドク
物音	thing + sound = *a noise*	mono·**oto** もの·おと
足音	leg + sound = *sound of footsteps*	ashi·**oto** あし·おと

SAMPLE SENTENCE

あれ は 水 の 音 だ と 思います。
are wa mizu no oto da to omo·imasu.
that water sound think
= *(I) think that's the sound of water.*

WRITING PRACTICE

COMPONENT 138

SPY 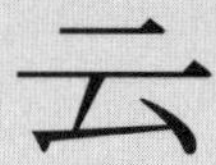 

As with the broken crutch in 厶, the bottom of this component is written with two strokes, not three.

KANJI 138

 **MEET**

ノ	人	亼	亼	会	会			

BUILDING THIS KANJI
Umbrella 𠆢 + **SPY** 云 = 会

MEANING

Meet/Meeting. When found at the end of compounds, this kanji often expresses English words such as "society", "association" and "party".

REMEMBERING THIS KANJI

"What's with the **umbrella**?" she asked on MEETING the **spy**, looking around nervously.

"What do you mean?"

"What do I mean!? The weather's perfect, so why in the world are you under an **umbrella**? Everyone's staring at us!"

"That's enough!" interrupted the **spy**. "You obviously don't know the rules; if you MEET a **spy**, you MEET under an **umbrella**. Everyone knows it's more stylish that way."

COMMON PRONUNCIATIONS

Common **ON** reading: **KAI** (カイ)
Common **kun** reading: **a** (あ)

kun-yomi suggestion: "**a**mbassador"

Create your **on-yomi** keyword and enter it in the table at the back of the book. After that, write your sentence to remember the **on-yomi** and **kun-yomi** readings in the box below.

LESS COMMON PRONUNCIATIONS

Less common **ON** reading: **E** (エ)
Less common **kun** reading: none

COMMON WORDS AND COMPOUNDS		
会う	*to meet*	**a**·u あ·う
会見	meet + see = *interview*	**KAI**·KEN カイ·ケン
大会	large + meet = *convention; tournament*	TAI·**KAI** タイ·カイ
開会	open + meet = *to open a meeting*	KAI·**KAI** カイ·カイ
入会金	enter + meet + gold (money) = *enrollment fee*	NYŪ·**KAI**·KIN ニュウ·カイ·キン

SAMPLE SENTENCE

米国大会 は 九月 にありますか。
BEI·KOKU·TAI·KAI wa KU·GATSU ni arimasu ka.
U.S. tournament September is
= *Is the U.S. tournament in September?*

WRITING PRACTICE

KANJI 139

HEAR

BUILDING THIS KANJI
Gate 門(96) + **Ear** 耳(78) = 聞

MEANING

Hear/Ask. Like "早" (Entry 29), this is another kanji with two unrelated and distinct meanings.

REMEMBERING THIS KANJI

I pressed my **ear** against the **gate**.
"What do you HEAR?" she asked.
"'HEAR ye', 'HEAR ye'," I answered.
"How can I?" she said. "You're in my way."
"No," I said. "I HEAR 'HEAR ye…' oh, forget it."

COMMON PRONUNCIATIONS

Common **ON** reading: **BUN** (ブン)
Common **kun** reading: **ki** (き)

Only the **kun-yomi** appears in the first position.

kun-yomi suggestion: "**key**note address"

Create your **on-yomi** keyword and enter it in the table at the back of the book. After that, write your sentence to remember the **on-yomi** and **kun-yomi** readings in the box below.

LESS COMMON PRONUNCIATIONS

Less common **ON** reading: **MON** (モン)
Less common **kun** reading: none

COMMON WORDS AND COMPOUNDS		
聞こえる (intr)	*to be heard*	**ki**·koeru き·こえる
聞く (tr)	*to hear; to ask*	**ki**·ku き·く
聞き出す	hear + exit = *to find out about*	**ki**·ki da·su き·き だ·す
聞き入れる	hear + enter = *to comply with*	**ki**·ki i·reru き·き い·れる
新聞	new + hear = *newspaper*	SHIN·**BUN** シン·ブン
見聞	see + hear = *information*	KEN·**BUN** ケン·ブン

SAMPLE SENTENCE

夜中 に 物音 を聞きました。
yo·naka ni mono·oto o ki·kimashita.
middle of the night — sound — heard
= (She) heard a sound in the middle of the night.

WRITING PRACTICE

COMPONENT 140

GOAL POSTS 冂 

KANJI 140

央 CENTER

丨	冂	冂	央	央				

BUILDING THIS KANJI
Goal Posts 冂 + **Large (sumo wrestler)** 大(17) = 央

MEANING
Center. Other than the first example (and words derived from it), this kanji is rarely used.

REMEMBERING THIS KANJI
You put a **sumo wrestler** dead CENTER between the **goal posts**, and chances are your team will give up fewer goals. Your opponent, quite simply, will never hit the CENTER of the net.

COMMON PRONUNCIATIONS
Common **ON** reading: **Ō** (オウ)
Common **kun** reading: none

Create your **on-yomi** keyword and enter it in the table at the back of the book. After that, write your sentence to remember the **on-yomi** reading in the box below.

LESS COMMON PRONUNCIATIONS
Less common **ON** reading: none
Less common **kun** reading: none

COMMON WORDS AND COMPOUNDS		
中央	middle + center = *center*	CHŪ·**Ō** チュウ·オウ
中央口	middle + center + mouth = *central exit/entrance*	CHŪ·**Ō**·guchi チュウ·オウ·ぐち

SAMPLE SENTENCE

中央口 で 秋山さん を 見ました。
CHŪ·Ō·guchi de Aki·yama-san o mi·mashita.
central entrance Akiyama-san saw
= *(He) saw Akiyama-san at the central entrance.*

WRITING PRACTICE

CHAPTER 7 REVIEW EXERCISES

A. Please match the following kanji to their meanings.

1. 多	a. Many
2. 物	b. Mother
3. 音	c. Heaven
4. 天	d. Read
5. 花	e. Write
6. 書	f. Thing
7. 読	g. Hear
8. 私	h. Flower
9. 母	i. Private
10. 聞	j. Sound

B. Please match the following meanings to their kanji, and these to their **on** or **kun-yomi**.

1. New	a. 会	1. **Ō** (オウ)
2. Hold	b. 前	2. **wa** (わ)
3. Center	c. 新	3. **KIN** (キン)
4. Road	d. 分	4. **mo** (も)
5. Meet	e. 夜	5. **SHIN** (シン)
6. Axe	f. 央	6. **yoru** (よる)
7. Before	g. 名	7. **a** (あ)
8. Part	h. 持	8. **MEI** (メイ)
9. Name	i. 道	9. **mae** (まえ)
10. Night	j. 斤	10. **DŌ** (ドウ)

C. Please choose the best answer(s) to the following questions.

1. Which of the following kanji have an **on-yomi** of **BUN** (ブン)?
   a. 読
   b. 聞
   c. 分
   d. 母
   e. 物

2. Which of the following readings apply to the kanji 多?
   a. **TA** (タ)
   b. **hana** (はな)
   c. **DŌ** (ドウ)
   d. **michi** (みち)
   e. **ō** (おお)

3. Which of the following readings apply to the kanji 花?
   a. **YA** (ヤ)
   b. **na** (な)
   c. **hana** (はな)
   d. **KA** (カ)
   e. **ON** (オン)

4. I planted a beautiful ___ in a corner of my garden.
   a. 斤
   b. 母
   c. 道
   d. 花
   e. 音

5. Which of the following readings apply to the kanji 物?
   a. **mono** (もの)
   b. **SHŌ** (ショウ)
   c. **SHITSU** (シツ)
   d. **na** (な)
   e. **BUTSU** (ブツ)

D. Please choose the best answer(s) to the following questions.

1. Which is the correct reading of 聞く?
   a. **yu·ku** (ゆ·く)
   b. **ki·ku** (き·く)
   c. **a·ku** (あ·く)
   d. **ka·ku** (か·く)

2. Which is the correct reading of 読む?
   a. **o·mu** (お·む)
   b. **ka·mu** (か·む)
   c. **u·mu** (う·む)
   d. **yo·mu** (よ·む)

3. Which of the following kanji has the most number of strokes?
   a. 前
   b. 物
   c. 書
   d. 夜
   e. 持

4. Which is the correct reading of 書く?
   a. **ka·ku** (か·く)
   b. **ama·ku** (あま·く)
   c. **ki·ku** (き·く)
   d. **shi·ku** (し·く)

5. Which is the correct reading of 新しい?
   a. **atara·shii** (あたら·しい)
   b. **mawa·shii** (まわ·しい)
   c. **utsuku·shii** (うつく·しい)
   d. **ara·shii** (あら·しい)

E. Please match the following compounds and words to their meanings and pronunciations.

1. 金持ち	a. National highway	1. **i·ke bana** (い·け ばな)
2. 新聞	b. An entry	2. **ka·i mono** (か·い もの)
3. 生け花	c. Oneself	3. **na·mae** (な·まえ)
4. 国道	d. Center	4. **kane mo·chi** (かね も·ち)
5. 自分	e. Flower arrangement	5. **JI·BUN** (ジ·ブン)
6. 書入れ	f. Name	6. **NYŪ·KAI·KIN** (ニュウ·カイ·キン)
7. 名前	g. Newspaper	7. **KOKU·DŌ** (コク·ドウ)
8. 中央	h. Enrollment fee	8. **kaki i·re** (かき い·れ)
9. 買い物	i. Rich person	9. **SHIN·BUN** (シン·ブン)
10. 入会金	j. Shopping	10. **CHŪ·Ō** (チュウ·オウ)

CHAPTER 8 (KANJI 141-160)

KANJI 141

NEAR

丿	厂	斤	斤	丶斤	䜣	近		

BUILDING THIS KANJI
Axe 斤 (126) + **Seal** 辶 = 近

MEANING
Near. The sense of "recent" is also incorporated.

REMEMBERING THIS KANJI
Brandishing an **axe**, the **seal** came NEARER and NEARER the waiter's station.
"Don't come NEAR me!" I screamed.
"You ever gonna slip me farmed salmon again?" he said threateningly.
I shouldn't have tried to be sneaky; any **seal** would have known that farmed salmon didn't taste NEARLY as good as wild.

COMMON PRONUNCIATIONS
Common **ON** reading: **KIN** (キン)
Common **kun** reading: **chika** (ちか)

kun-yomi suggestion: "**chica**"

Create your **on-yomi** keyword and enter it in the table at the back of the book. After that, write your sentence to remember the **on-yomi** and **kun-yomi** readings in the box below.

LESS COMMON PRONUNCIATIONS
Less common **ON** reading: none
Less common **kun** reading: none

COMMON WORDS AND COMPOUNDS		
近い	*near*	**chika**·i ちか·い
近づく	*to approach*	**chika**·zuku ちか·づく
近道	near + road = *shortcut*	**chika**·michi ちか·みち
近親	near + parent = *close relative*	**KIN**·SHIN キン·シン
最近	most + near = *recently*	SAI·**KIN** サイ·キン

SAMPLE SENTENCE

新しい 家 は 川 の 近く にあります。
atara·shii ie wa kawa no chika·ku ni arimasu.
new house river near is
= *The new house is near a river.*

WRITING PRACTICE

COMPONENT 142

HAMMER 𠂉

KANJI 142

LOSE

BUILDING THIS KANJI
Hammer 𠂉 + Large (sumo wrestler) 大(17) = 失

MEANING

Lose, in the sense of "mislay". This character often conveys a hint of failure and error, so guard against becoming depressed on seeing it.

REMEMBERING THIS KANJI

LOSING one's belt is obviously the worst thing that can happen to a **sumo wrestler**. Should this occur, the **wrestler** is to strike himself repeatedly with a **hammer** to atone for LOSING face.

COMMON PRONUNCIATIONS

Common **ON** reading: **SHITSU** (シツ)
Common **kun** reading: **ushina** (うしな)

kun-yomi suggestion: "**ooh, she na**pped"

Create your **on-yomi** keyword and enter it in the table at the back of the book. After that, write your sentence to remember the **on-yomi** and **kun-yomi** readings in the box below.

LESS COMMON PRONUNCIATIONS

Less common **ON** reading: none
Less common **kun** reading: none

COMMON WORDS AND COMPOUNDS		
失う	*to lose*	**ushina**·u うしな·う
見失う	see + lose = *to lose sight of*	mi **ushina**·u み うしな·う
失言	lose + say = *slip of the tongue*	**SHITSU**·GEN シツ·ゲン

SAMPLE SENTENCE

大会 で 失言 しました。
TAI·KAI de SHITSU·GEN shimashita.
convention slip of the tongue did
= *(I) made a slip of the tongue at the convention.*

WRITING PRACTICE

KANJI 143

弓 BOW

フ	コ	弓						

MEANING
Bow (the partner to an arrow).

REMEMBERING THIS KANJI
It's a shame about this **BOW** having been run over by a tractor.

COMMON PRONUNCIATIONS
Common **ON** reading: **KYŪ** (キュウ)
Common **kun** reading: **yumi** (ゆみ)

kun-yomi suggestion: "**you, me** and…"

Create your **on-yomi** keyword and enter it in the table at the back of the book. After that, write your sentence to remember the **on-yomi** and **kun-yomi** readings in the box below.

LESS COMMON PRONUNCIATIONS
Less common **ON** reading: none
Less common **kun** reading: none

COMMON WORDS AND COMPOUNDS		
弓	*bow*	**yumi** ゆみ
弓道	bow + road = *(Japanese) archery*	**KYŪ·DŌ** キュウ·ドウ

SAMPLE SENTENCE

前田さん　は　古い　弓　と　美しい
Mae·da-san wa furu·i yumi to utsuku·shii
Maeda-san old bow beautiful
日本刀　を　買いました。
NI·HON·TŌ o ka·imashita.
Japanese sword bought
= *Maeda-san bought an old bow and a beautiful Japanese sword.*

WRITING PRACTICE

COMPONENT 144

SADDLE  

KANJI 144

 **HORSE**

丨	厂	冂	冃	耳	馬	馬	馬	馬
馬								

BUILDING THIS KANJI
Saddle 馬 + Gas Stove 灬 = 馬

MEANING
Horse.

REMEMBERING THIS KANJI
I was devastated when Trigger slipped his **saddle** and bolted off with another HORSE. I waited for him to return, naturally, but it was all in vain: he had left for greener pastures. In the end I hurled his **saddle** onto a **gas stove**; it was hateful to me now, and I didn't want anything to remind me of how fickle a HORSE could be.

COMMON PRONUNCIATIONS
Common **ON** reading: **BA** (バ)
Common **kun** reading: **uma** (うま)

kun-yomi suggestion: "**zoom a**round"

Create your **on-yomi** keyword and enter it in the table at the back of the book. After that, write your sentence to remember the **on-yomi** and **kun-yomi** readings in the box below.

LESS COMMON PRONUNCIATIONS
Less common **ON** reading: none
Less common **kun** reading: **ma** (ま)

COMMON WORDS AND COMPOUNDS		
馬	*horse*	**uma** うま
子馬	child + horse = *colt; pony*	ko·**uma** こ·うま
牛馬	cow + horse = *cows and horses*	GYŪ·**BA** ギュウ·バ
馬具	horse + tool = *harness*	**BA**·GU バ·グ

SAMPLE SENTENCE

馬 と 牛 の どちら が 好き です か。
uma to ushi no dochira ga su·ki desu ka.
horse cow which like
= *Which do you like, horses or cows?*

WRITING PRACTICE

KANJI 145

WEEK

丿	冂	冂	円	円	用	周	周	`周
调	週							

BUILDING THIS KANJI
Around 周(120) + **Seal** 辶 = 週

MEANING
Week.

REMEMBERING THIS KANJI
"It's the same routine every WEEK here at the aquarium," said the **seal**, shrugging. "I swim **around** and **around** 'cause there's nothing else to do."
I nodded. Digging up stories for my magazine "**Seal** WEEKLY", it seemed, was going to be harder than I had thought.

COMMON PRONUNCIATIONS
Common **ON** reading: **SHŪ** (シュウ)
Common **kun** reading: none

Create your **on-yomi** keyword and enter it in the table at the back of the book. After that, write your sentence to remember the **on-yomi** reading in the box below.

LESS COMMON PRONUNCIATIONS
Less common **ON** reading: none
Less common **kun** reading: none

COMMON WORDS AND COMPOUNDS		
週間	week + interval = *week*	**SHŪ**·KAN シュウ·カン
一週間	one + week + interval = *one week*	IS·**SHŪ**·KAN イッ·シュウ·カン
二週間	two + week + interval = *two weeks*	NI·**SHŪ**·KAN ニ·シュウ·カン
週日	week + sun (day) = *weekday*	**SHŪ**·JITSU シュウ·ジツ
先週	precede + week = *last week*	SEN·**SHŪ** セン·シュウ
来週	come + week = *next week*	RAI·**SHŪ** ライ·シュウ

SAMPLE SENTENCE

月曜日 から 二週間 の
GETSU·YŌ·bi kara NI·SHŪ·KAN no
Monday from two weeks
夏休み です
natsu yasu·mi desu.
summer vacation
= *There's a two-week summer vacation from Monday.*

WRITING PRACTICE

KANJI 146

引 PULL

㇕	㇕	弓	引					

BUILDING THIS KANJI
Bow 弓 (143) + **Pole** 丨 = 引

MEANING

Pull. This character also conveys the idea of "attraction" (best seen in the fourth example) and the senses of receding and withdrawing. You will notice it frequently on signs; it indicates "pull" on doors, and "discount" when used with numbers.

REMEMBERING THIS KANJI

A **bow** obviously needs to be PULLED in order to work effectively as a weapon, and the same is true for a **pole**. How so? Well, a catapult is basically a **pole**, and if you think about it, the word "PULL" is actually found in "catapult".

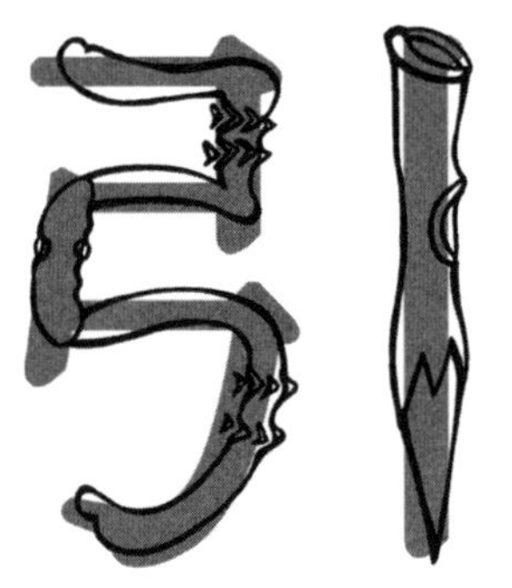

COMMON PRONUNCIATIONS

Common **ON** reading: **IN** (イン)
Common **kun** reading: **hi** (ひ)

As seen in the third example, this is another kanji that can act like 買. The **kun-yomi** can also become voiced in the second position, as happens in the fifth compound. Note, incidentally, that the final word in the sample sentence (引き上げました) has not been encountered before. Try to guess its meaning by looking at the kanji from which it is formed.

kun-yomi suggestion: "**hea**ve"

Create your **on-yomi** keyword and enter it in the table at the back of the book. After that, write your sentence to remember the **on-yomi** and **kun-yomi** readings in the box below.

LESS COMMON PRONUNCIATIONS

Less common **ON** reading: none
Less common **kun** reading: none

COMMON WORDS AND COMPOUNDS		
引く	*to pull*	**hi**·ku ひ·く
引き出す	pull + exit = *to withdraw (something)*	**hi**·ki da·su ひ·き だ·す
引出し	pull + exit = *a withdrawal; a drawer*	**hiki** da·shi ひき だ·し
引力	pull + strength = *gravitation*	**IN**·RYOKU イン·リョク
万引き	ten thousand + pull = *shoplifter*	MAN **bi**·ki マン び·き
引き受ける	pull + receive = *to undertake*	**hi**·ki u·keru ひ·き う·ける
引き上る	pull + upper = *to pull up*	**hi**·ki age·ru ひ·き あげ·る

SAMPLE SENTENCE

やっと 牛 を 川 から 引き上げました。
yatto ushi o kawa kara hi·ki a·gemashita.
finally cow river from pulled up
= *(We) finally pulled the cow from the river.*

WRITING PRACTICE

KANJI 147

SECOND

ノ	二	千	禾	禾	利	利	秒	秒

BUILDING THIS KANJI
Crops 禾 + **Few** 少(45) = 秒

MEANING
Second (of time or arc).

REMEMBERING THIS KANJI
"When there are **few crops**," said the aid worker, "SECONDS count. Food needs to be rushed in, as the population will be growing weaker SECOND by SECOND."

COMMON PRONUNCIATIONS
Common **ON** reading: **BYŌ** (ビョウ)
Common **kun** reading: none

Note that the sample sentence contains one of the less common **on-yomi** for "分" (Entry 124) in the compound "十五分".

Create your **on-yomi** keyword and enter it in the table at the back of the book. After that, write your sentence to remember the **on-yomi** reading in the box below.

LESS COMMON PRONUNCIATIONS
Less common **ON** reading: none
Less common **kun** reading: none

COMMON WORDS AND COMPOUNDS		
一秒	one + second = *one second*	ICHI·**BYŌ** イチ·ビョウ
五秒	five + second = *five seconds*	GO·**BYŌ** ゴ·ビョウ
秒読み	second + read = *countdown*	**BYŌ** yo·mi ビョウ よ·み

SAMPLE SENTENCE

十五分 二十秒 かかりました。
JŪ·GO·FUN NI·JŪ·BYŌ kakarimashita.
fifteen minutes twenty seconds took
= *It took fifteen minutes and twenty seconds.*

WRITING PRACTICE

KANJI 148

甲

SHELL

丨	冂	日	日	甲				

MEANING

Shell. This is another character that rarely appears on its own. Like similar kanji we have encountered, however, it proves valuable as a component.

REMEMBERING THIS KANJI

This is another kanji to which we will give an external meaning – in this case, a fly swatter. Why a fly swatter? Well, you'll need one if you ever go down to the seashore to get SHELLS; flies are all over them at low tide.

COMMON PRONUNCIATIONS

Common **ON** reading: **KŌ** (コウ)
Common **kun** reading: none

Create your **on-yomi** keyword and enter it in the table at the back of the book. After that, write your sentence to remember the **on-yomi** reading in the box below.

LESS COMMON PRONUNCIATIONS

Less common **ON** reading: **KAN** (カン)
Less common **kun** reading: none

COMMON WORDS AND COMPOUND		
手の甲	hand + shell = *back of the hand*	te·no·**KŌ** て·の·コウ

SAMPLE SENTENCE

上田さん	は	手の甲	が	かゆい。
Ue·da-san	**wa**	**te·no·KŌ**	**ga**	**kayui.**
Ueda-san		back of the hand		itchy

= *The back of Ueda-san's hand is itchy.*

WRITING PRACTICE

COMPONENT 149

SKI JUMP

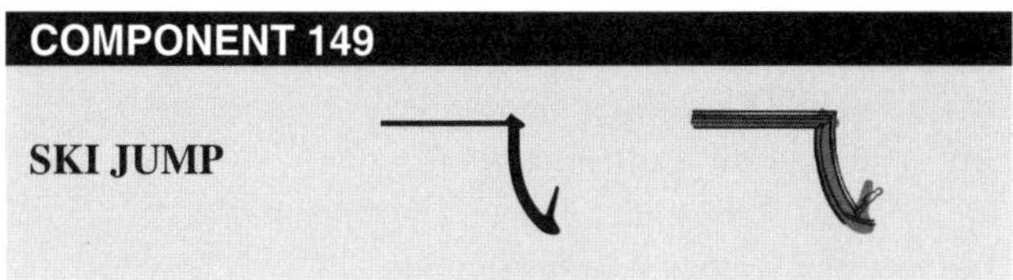

KANJI 149

SPIRIT

BUILDING THIS KANJI
Hammer 𠂉 + One (hamburger patty) 一(3) +
Ski Jump ⺄ + Banana Peels メ = 気

MEANING

This fascinating character encompasses a range of meanings, including the ideas of "spirit", "air", "feeling", and "mood". It is worth spending some time getting to know this kanji; it is found in many common words and expressions.

REMEMBERING THIS KANJI

I wanted to be a **ski-jumper**, but the national team crushed my SPIRIT when they left me off the squad. Oddly, it wasn't long after this that I grew to dislike everything about the sport, and began sabotaging all the facilities I could find. My method was simple: use a **hammer** to drive **hamburger patties** into the **ski jump** so that the athletes would be thrown off course, and leave **banana peels** on the side so that the spectators would slip. Isn't it strange what happens when the SPIRIT moves you?

COMMON PRONUNCIATIONS

Common **ON** reading: **KI** (キ)
Common **kun** reading: none

The sample sentence is an extremely common greeting/question in Japanese. Create your **on-yomi** keyword and enter it in the table at the back of the book. After that, write your sentence to remember the **on-yomi** reading in the box below.

LESS COMMON PRONUNCIATIONS

Less common **ON** reading: **KE** (ケ)
Less common **kun** reading: none

COMMON WORDS AND COMPOUNDS		
気	*spirit*	**KI** キ
元気	basis + spirit = *high spirits*	GEN·**KI** ゲン·キ
人気	person + spirit = *popularity*	NIN·**KI** ニン·キ
電気	electric + spirit = *electricity*	DEN·**KI** デン·キ
天気	heaven + spirit = *the weather*	TEN·**KI** テン·キ
気持ち	spirit + hold = *feeling*	**KI** mo·chi キ も·ち

SAMPLE SENTENCE

元気　です　か。
GEN·KI desu ka.
high spirits
= *How are you?*

WRITING PRACTICE

KANJI 150

TIME

丨	冂	日	日	日一	日十	日土	日圭	時
時								

BUILDING THIS KANJI
Sun 日(6) + **Temple** 寺(104) = 時

MEANING

Time. This character will become familiar to you through its use in the hours of the day (the third and fourth compounds below are examples).

REMEMBERING THIS KANJI

The Incas developed a remarkable system of measuring TIME. The **sun temple** at Machu Picchu was of great importance in this respect, for it marked the exact TIME of the solstices.

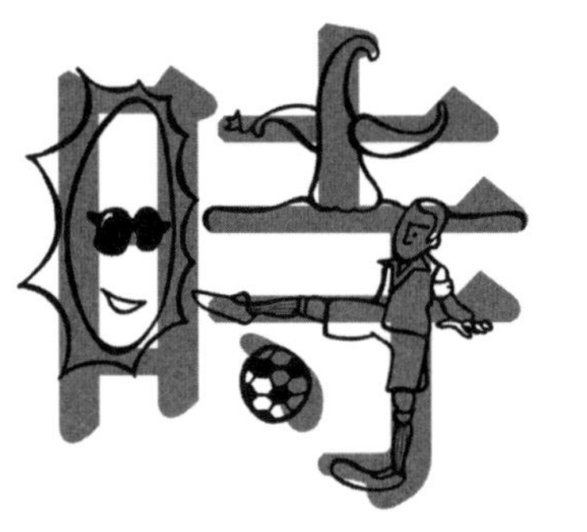

COMMON PRONUNCIATIONS

Common **ON** reading: **JI** (ジ)
Common **kun** reading: **toki** (とき)

Note how the final half of the second compound becomes voiced; this is an occasional feature of repeated compounds.

kun-yomi suggestion: "s**toke ee**ls"

Create your **on-yomi** keyword and enter it in the table at the back of the book. After that, write your sentence to remember the **on-yomi** and **kun-yomi** readings in the box below.

LESS COMMON PRONUNCIATIONS

Less common **ON** reading: none
Less common **kun** reading: none

This irregular reading is very common.

IRREGULAR READING		
時計*	time + measure = *watch; clock*	**to·KEI** と·ケイ

COMMON WORDS AND COMPOUNDS		
時	*time*	**toki** とき
時々	time + time = *sometimes*	**toki·doki** とき·どき
四時	four + time = *four o'clock*	yo·**JI** よ·ジ
九時半	nine + time + half = *nine-thirty*	KU·**JI**·HAN ク·ジ·ハン
同時	same + time = *simultaneous*	DŌ·**JI** ドウ·ジ

SAMPLE SENTENCE

八時半 に 東口 の 近く で
HACHI·JI·HAN ni higashi·guchi no chika·ku de
eight-thirty east entrance near
会いましょう。
a·imashō.
let's meet
= *Let's meet near the east entrance at eight-thirty.*

WRITING PRACTICE

KANJI 151

SPEAK

BUILDING THIS KANJI
Say 言(80) + **Tongue** 舌(110) = 話

MEANING
Speak, along with the ideas of conversations and stories.

REMEMBERING THIS KANJI
"SPEAK freely."

"Though it is on the tip of my **tongue**, pharaoh, I dare not **say** it."

"Then I order you: SPEAK!"

I shriveled inwardly, knowing I would have to **say** it to avoid a **tongue**-lashing, or worse. "All right," I answered, shaking, "if you must know then, yes, it's true: those pants *do* tend to make you look big in the hips."

Pharaoh approached me with his headgear swaying menacingly. "I **say** to you this," he warned. "You will lose that **tongue** should you SPEAK of this further."

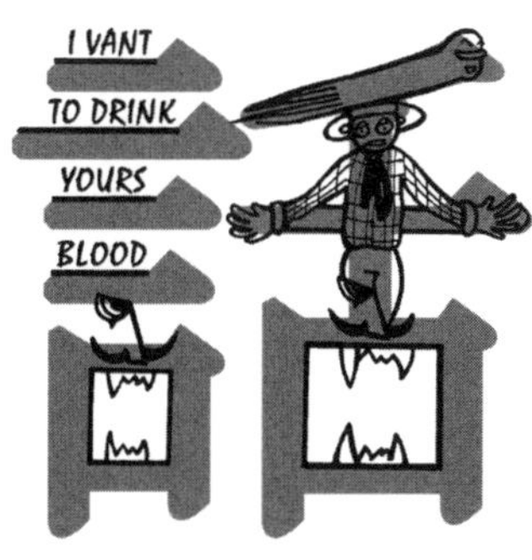

COMMON PRONUNCIATIONS
Common **ON** reading: **WA** (ワ)
Common **kun** readings: **hanashi** (はなし); **hana** (はな)

As in the final example below, the **kun-yomi** for this kanji is always voiced in the second position.

kun-yomi suggestions: "**Hannah shi**elded";
"**Han a**mbassador"

Create your **on-yomi** keyword and enter it in the table at the back of the book. After that, write your sentence to remember the **on-yomi** and **kun-yomi** readings in the box below.

LESS COMMON PRONUNCIATIONS
Less common **ON** reading: none
Less common **kun** reading: none

COMMON WORDS AND COMPOUNDS		
話	*story*	**hanashi** はなし
話す	*to speak*	**hana**·su はな·す
話し好き	speak + like = *talkative*	**hana**·shi zu·ki はな·し ず·き
電話	electric + speak = *telephone*	DEN·**WA** デン·ワ
会話	meet + speak = *conversation*	KAI·**WA** カイ·ワ
立ち話	stand + speak = *chatting while standing*	ta·chi **banashi** た·ち ばなし

SAMPLE SENTENCE

田中さん は フランス語 を 上手 に
Tana·ka-san wa Furansu·GO o JO·zu ni
Tanaka-san French well
話せます。
hana·semasu.
can speak
= *Tanaka-san can speak French well.*

WRITING PRACTICE

KANJI 152

ENGLISH

BUILDING THIS KANJI
Wreath 艹 + **Center** 央(140) = 英

MEANING

Although a secondary meaning relates to "brilliance", this character will be far more familiar to you through its connection with all things English.

REMEMBERING THIS KANJI

To the ENGLISH, there can be only one object at the **center** of a **wreath**: the ENGLISH rose.

COMMON PRONUNCIATIONS

Common **ON** reading: **EI** (エイ)
Common **kun** reading: none

Create your **on-yomi** keyword and enter it in the table at the back of the book. After that, write your sentence to remember the **on-yomi** reading in the box below.

LESS COMMON PRONUNCIATIONS

Less common **ON** reading: none
Less common **kun** reading: none

COMMON WORDS AND COMPOUNDS		
英語	English + words = *English (language)*	**EI**·GO エイ·ゴ
英国	English + country = *England*	**EI**·KOKU エイ·コク
英会話	English + meet + speak = *English conversation*	**EI**·KAI·WA エイ·カイ·ワ
日英	sun + English = *Japan and England*	NICHI·**EI** ニチ·エイ

SAMPLE SENTENCE

英会話	は	日本	で	人気	が
EI·KAI·WA	**wa**	**NI·HON**	**de**	**NIN·KI**	**ga**
English conversation		Japan		popular	

あります。
arimasu.
is

= *English conversation is popular in Japan.*

WRITING PRACTICE

KANJI 153

INSTRUCTION

丶	亠	亠	亖	言	言	言	訁	訓
訓								

BUILDING THIS KANJI
Say 言 (80) + **River** 川 (70) = 訓

MEANING

Instruction. This kanji tends to give a more serious or spiritual sense of teaching to the compounds in which it appears.

REMEMBERING THIS KANJI

INSTRUCTION for **rivers**: *"All right everyone, listen carefully to what I* ***say****. What you want to do is head for the ocean; that means going downhill. Also, keep up a good pace or you'll either turn into a swamp or one of those* ***rivers*** *without a current that everyone laughs at. Oh, and don't be afraid to overflow your banks now and then; if anyone asks what's going on, just* ***say*** *"that's what* ***rivers*** *are supposed to do". Follow these* INSTRUCTIONS *and you'll be fine."*

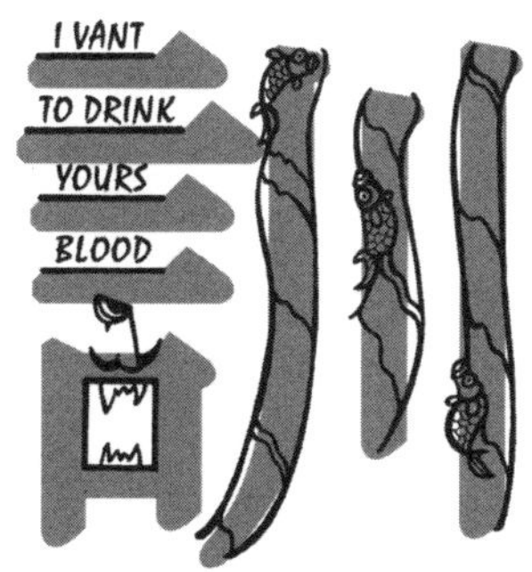

COMMON PRONUNCIATIONS

Common **ON** reading: **KUN** (クン)
Common **kun** reading: none

The first compound below presents another reading with which you may have become familiar. Now create your **on-yomi** keyword and enter it in the table at the back of the book. After that, write your sentence to remember the **on-yomi** reading in the box below.

LESS COMMON PRONUNCIATIONS

Less common **ON** reading: none
Less common **kun** reading: none

COMMON WORDS AND COMPOUNDS		
訓読み	instruction + read = *the* ***kun-yomi***	**KUN** yo·mi クン よ·み
訓話	instruction + speak = *moral discourse*	**KUN**·WA クン·ワ

SAMPLE SENTENCE

これ を 訓読み で 読んで 下さい。
kore o KUN yo·mi de yo·nde kuda·sai.
this kun-yomi read please
= *Please read this with* ***kun-yomi****.*

WRITING PRACTICE

KANJI 154

PUSH

BUILDING THIS KANJI
Finger 扌 + Shell (Fly swatter) 甲 (148) = 押

MEANING

"Push", together with the ideas of "suppression" and "restraint". This kanji also serves as the partner to "引" (Entry 146) on door signs.

REMEMBERING THIS KANJI
OK, then, your **fingers** are now gripping the **fly swatter**. Excellent. The next step is simple: in order to kill the fly, PUSH the **fly swatter** away from you with a PUSHING motion.

COMMON PRONUNCIATIONS

Common **ON** reading: none
Common **kun** reading: **o** (お)

As indicated by the last two examples below, this is another kanji that often shows up in the manner of 買.

kun-yomi suggestion: "**o**rangutan"

Create your sentence to remember the **kun-yomi** reading in the box below.

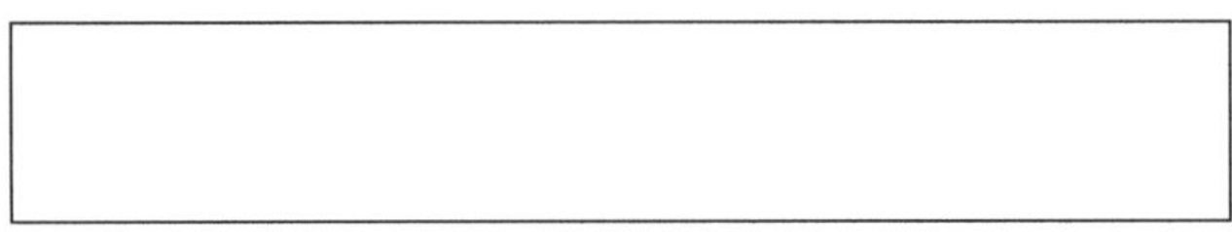

LESS COMMON PRONUNCIATIONS

Less common **ON** reading: **Ō** (オウ)
Less common **kun** reading: none

COMMON WORDS AND COMPOUNDS		
押す	*to push*	**o**·su お·す
押し出す	push + exit = *to push out*	**o**·shi da·su お·し だ·す
押し上げる	push + upper = *to push up*	**o**·shi a·geru お·し あ·げる
押し開ける	push + open = *to push open*	**o**·shi a·keru お·し あ·ける
押入れ	push + enter = *closet*	**oshi** i·re おし い·れ
押売	push + sell = *high-pressure sales*	**oshi**·uri おし·うり

SAMPLE SENTENCE

押入れ の 中 に 物 が 少ない。
oshi i·re no naka ni mono ga suku·nai.
closet middle things few
= *There aren't many things in the closet.*

WRITING PRACTICE

COMPONENT 155

WHIRLING DERVISH 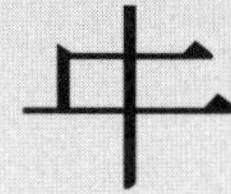 

KANJI 155

 YEAR

ノ	𠂉	亠	午	㐄	年			

BUILDING THIS KANJI
Hammer 𠂉 **+ Whirling Dervish** 㐄 = 年

MEANING
Year.

REMEMBERING THIS KANJI
One of the events at the track and field championships is starting to become controversial: the **hammer** toss. Why? Simply because a **whirling dervish** wins it every YEAR. Athletes unable to whirl as quickly have complained that the **dervishes** have an unfair advantage. YEAR after YEAR of winning, it seems, can bring YEAR after YEAR of envy.

COMMON PRONUNCIATIONS
Common **ON** reading: **NEN** (ネン)
Common **kun** reading: **toshi** (とし)

kun-yomi suggestion: "lot**to shee**t"

Create your **on-yomi** keyword and enter it in the table at the back of the book. After that, write your sentence to remember the **on-yomi** and **kun-yomi** readings in the box below.

LESS COMMON PRONUNCIATIONS
Less common **ON** reading: none
Less common **kun** reading: none

COMMON WORDS AND COMPOUNDS		
年	*year*	**toshi** とし
年上	year + upper = *older*	**toshi**·ue とし·うえ
年下	year + lower = *younger*	**toshi**·shita とし·した
新年	new + year = *the New Year*	SHIN·**NEN** シン·ネン
中年	middle + year = *middle age*	CHŪ·**NEN** チュウ·ネン
一年生	one + year + life = *first-year student*	ICHI·**NEN**·SEI イチ·ネン·セイ

SAMPLE SENTENCE

青木さん は 三年生 です。
Ao·ki-san wa SAN·NEN·SEI desu.
Aoki-san third-year student
= *Aoki-san is a third-year student.*

WRITING PRACTICE

KANJI 156

 COME

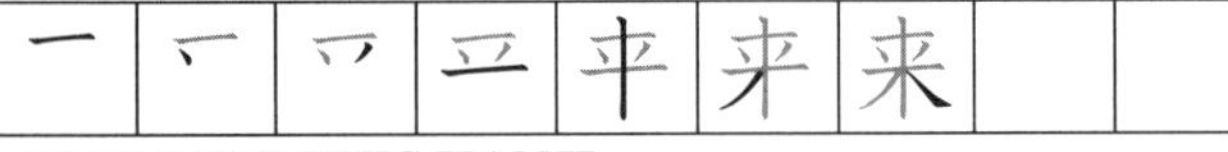

BUILDING THIS KANJI
One (hamburger patty) 一(3) + **Rice** 米(32) = 来

MEANING

Come. As the final four compounds below make clear, the related meaning of "next" is also included.

REMEMBERING THIS KANJI

"COME on, everyone, dig in!"

I didn't want to be rude, but a **hamburger patty** on a pile of uncooked **rice**? COME on! Not to mention the noise we all made as we crunched our way through the grains… Really, it was enough to make me wish I hadn't COME to the **patty** and **rice** festival at all.

COMMON PRONUNCIATIONS

Common **ON** reading: **RAI** (ライ)
Common **kun** reading: **ku** (く)

This character is infamous for being one of only two irregular verbs in Japanese, but whereas "to do" (為る) is rarely presented with its kanji (it is now universally written in **hiragana**), "to come" still is. What this means for us is that the character can be read variously as "**ku**" (く), "**ki**" (き) or "**ko**" (こ), depending on which tense of the verb is being used. The sample sentence offers an example of the polite past tense. Note, however, an important exception in the second compound below (an extremely common word); when following the kanji "出", 来 is always read "**ki**". Lucky for us there are only two odd verbs in Japanese!

kun-yomi suggestion: "**cool**"

Create your **on-yomi** keyword and enter it in the table at the back of the book. After that, write your sentence to remember the **on-yomi** and **kun-yomi** readings in the box below.

LESS COMMON PRONUNCIATIONS

Less common **ON** reading: none
Less common **kun** reading: **ki** (き)

This reading applies to only a pair of words: **ki·tasu** (来たす) "to be forthcoming", and **ki·taru** (来たる) "coming". This latter word is used as an adjective.

COMMON WORDS AND COMPOUNDS		
来る	*to come*	**ku**·ru く·る
出来る	exit + come = *to be able to*	de **ki**·ru で き·る
来週	come + week = *next week*	**RAI**·SHŪ ライ·シュウ
来月	come + moon = *next month*	**RAI**·GETSU ライ·ゲツ
来年	come + year = *next year*	**RAI**·NEN ライ·ネン
来春	come + spring = *next spring*	**RAI**·SHUN ライ·シュン

SAMPLE SENTENCE

先生 は 一週間 前 に 来ました。
SEN·SEI wa IS·SHŪ·KAN mae ni ki·mashita.
teacher one week before came
= *The teacher came a week ago.*

WRITING PRACTICE

COMPONENT 157

CLAW ⺍

KANJI 157

学 STUDY

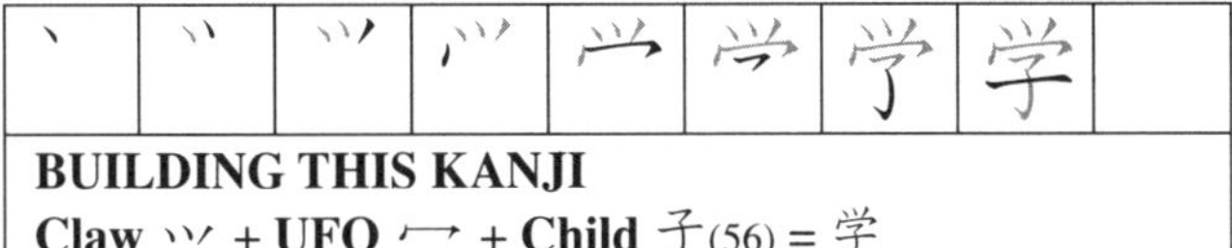

BUILDING THIS KANJI
Claw ⺍ + **UFO** 冖 + **Child** 子(56) = 学

MEANING

This character appears in words related to study and learning. When used as a suffix, it is often equivalent to the English "-ology". The final compound offers such an example.

REMEMBERING THIS KANJI

"I don't want to STUDY," the **child** said. "You can't make me."

"Oh, really?" the teacher replied. "Don't you know what happens to a **child** who doesn't STUDY? A **UFO** flies down to get them."

"Is that so?" said the **child**, now sauntering to the blackboard. "And when the **UFO** arrives, will my screams be like this? Like **claws** scraping down a blackboard?"

"No! Don't do that!"

"Then what happens if I refuse to STUDY?"

"Nothing! You become very successful!"

So it was true, then, thought the other students: there really was no need to STUDY.

COMMON PRONUNCIATIONS

Common **ON** reading: **GAKU** (ガク)
Common **kun** reading: **mana** (まな)

kun-yomi suggestion: "**man an**swer"

Create your **on-yomi** keyword and enter it in the table at the back of the book. After that, write your sentence to remember the **on-yomi** and **kun-yomi** readings in the box below.

LESS COMMON PRONUNCIATIONS

Less common **ON** reading: none
Less common **kun** reading: none

COMMON WORDS AND COMPOUNDS		
学ぶ	*to study*	**mana**·bu まな·ぶ
大学	large + study = *university*	DAI·**GAKU** ダイ·ガク
学生	study + life = *student*	**GAKU**·SEI ガク·セイ
休学	rest + study = *absence from school*	KYŪ·**GAKU** キュウ·ガク
語学	words + study = *linguistics*	GO·**GAKU** ゴ·ガク
生物学	life + thing + study = *biology*	SEI·BUTSU·**GAKU** セイ·ブツ·ガク

SAMPLE SENTENCE

この 家 には 大学生 が 多い。
kono ie ni wa DAI·GAKU·SEI ga ō·i.
this house university students many
= *There are many university students in this house.*

WRITING PRACTICE

KANJI 158

MIND

、	亠	亣	立	立	产	音	音	音
音	意	意	意					

BUILDING THIS KANJI
Sound 音(137) + **Heart** 心(25) = 意

MEANING

Mind/Thought. This abstract character appears in many compounds conveying the ideas of "will", "intention" and "opinion", etc.

REMEMBERING THIS KANJI

Juliet : Take me in your arms, Romeo.
Romeo : My darling.
Juliet : The **sound** of your **heart**…it fills my MIND.
Romeo : Sorry, what's that?
Juliet : My MIND, it's filled with the **sound** of your **heart**.
Romeo : Oh…um…that's great.
Juliet (stepping back) : What do you mean "that's great"? Is that the best you can do? Doesn't this moment inspire anything more eloquent than that?
Romeo : Hey look, I've got a lot on my MIND, OK? Finals are coming up, I've got an important stag hunt this weekend, my cousin's wedding is just around the corner…oh, never MIND.

COMMON PRONUNCIATIONS

Common **ON** reading: **I** (イ)
Common **kun** reading: none

Create your **on-yomi** keyword and enter it in the table at the back of the book. After that, write your sentence to remember the **on-yomi** reading in the box below.

LESS COMMON PRONUNCIATIONS

Less common **ON** reading: none
Less common **kun** reading: none

COMMON WORDS AND COMPOUNDS		
意思	mind + think = *(one's) intent*	**I**·SHI イ・シ
意図	mind + diagram = *(one's) aim*	**I**·TO イ・ト
意外	mind + outside = *unforeseen*	**I**·GAI イ・ガイ
意見	mind + see = *opinion*	**I**·KEN イ・ケン
意気	mind + spirit = *morale*	**I**·KI イ・キ
注意	pour + mind = *attention*	CHŪ·**I** チュウ・イ

SAMPLE SENTENCE

あなた の　意見　が　分かりません。
anata no I·KEN ga wa·karimasen.
you　opinion　don't understand
= *I don't understand your opinion.*

WRITING PRACTICE

KANJI 159

AGAIN

フ	又							

MEANING

Again/Also. Though this character will rarely be encountered on its own (indeed, it is often written in **hiragana**), it does serve as a component in several important kanji. Like other characters we have encountered of this type, we will assign a meaning with a more immediate visual connection: an ironing board.

REMEMBERING THIS KANJI

"Do it AGAIN," ordered the headmistress.

AGAIN and AGAIN I brought out the **ironing board**; AGAIN and AGAIN I failed to get rid of the wrinkles.

COMMON PRONUNCIATIONS

Common **ON** reading: none

Common **kun** reading: **mata** (また)

kun-yomi suggestion: "**mat a**ctivity"

Note how the second kanji in the final example below is voiced. The pronunciation of "来なかった" in the sample sentence, incidentally, is the informal past tense reading of "来". There is no **on-yomi** reading for this character. Create your sentence to remember the **kun-yomi** reading in the box below.

LESS COMMON PRONUNCIATIONS

Less common **ON** reading: none

Less common **kun** reading: none

COMMON WORDS AND COMPOUNDS		
又	*again*	**mata** また
又々	again + again = *once again*	**mata·mata** また·また
又聞き	again + hear = *hearsay*	**mata**·giki また·ぎき

SAMPLE SENTENCE

北川さん　は　又　来なかったよ。

Kita·gawa-san wa mata ko·nakatta.

Kitagawa-san again didn't come

= Kitagawa-san didn't come again!

WRITING PRACTICE

COMPONENT 160

ANTEATER  

KANJI 160

 **RED**

一	十	土				赤		

BUILDING THIS KANJI
Earth 土(87) + **Anteater** 𭕄 = 赤

MEANING
Red.

REMEMBERING THIS KANJI
It's pretty obvious what this **anteater** is doing: looking for RED ants in the RED, RED **earth**.

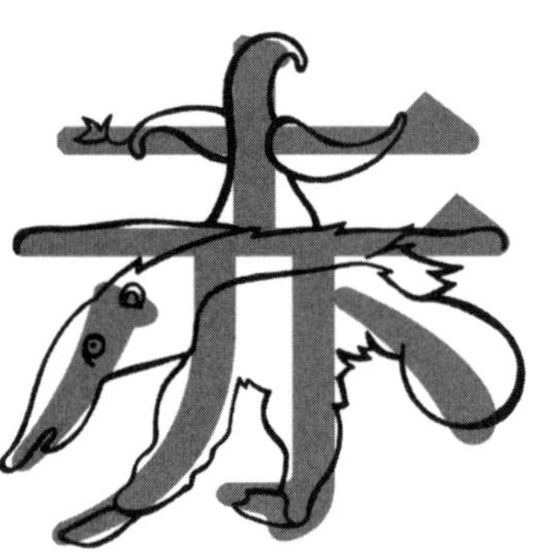

COMMON PRONUNCIATIONS
Common **ON** reading: **SEKI** (セキ)
Common **kun** reading: **aka** (あか)

kun-yomi suggestion: "st**ack a**pples"

Create your **on-yomi** keyword and enter it in the table at the back of the book. After that, write your sentence to remember the **on-yomi** and **kun-yomi** readings in the box below.

LESS COMMON PRONUNCIATIONS
Less common **ON** reading: **SHAKU** (シャク)
Less common **kun** reading: none

COMMON WORDS AND COMPOUNDS		
赤	*red (noun)*	**aka** あか
赤い	*red (adjective)*	**aka**·i あか·い
赤ちゃん	*baby*	**aka**·chan あか·ちゃん
赤道	red + road = *equator*	**SEKI**·DŌ セキ·ドウ

SAMPLE SENTENCE

あの 赤い 花 は 美しい です ね。
ano aka·i hana wa utsuku·shii desu ne.
that red flower beautiful isn't it
= *That red flower is beautiful, isn't it?*

WRITING PRACTICE

CHAPTER 8 REVIEW EXERCISES

A. Please match the following kanji to their meanings.

1. 又	a. Horse
2. 話	b. Again
3. 馬	c. Shell
4. 赤	d. Speak
5. 近	e. Push
6. 訓	f. Pull
7. 引	g. Near
8. 甲	h. Study
9. 押	i. Red
10. 学	j. Instruction

B. Please match the following meanings to their kanji, and these to their **on** or **kun-yomi**.

1. Time	a. 失	1. **toshi** (とし)
2. Year	b. 年	2. **EI** (エイ)
3. Bow	c. 気	3. **SHŪ** (シュウ)
4. Mind	d. 秒	4. **I** (イ)
5. Spirit	e. 来	5. **ushina** (うしな)
6. Come	f. 弓	6. **BYŌ** (ビョウ)
7. Lose	g. 英	7. **RAI** (ライ)
8. Week	h. 意	8. **KI** (キ)
9. Second	i. 週	9. **yumi** (ゆみ)
10. English	j. 時	10. **toki** (とき)

C. Please choose the best answer(s) to the following questions.

1. Which of the following readings apply to the kanji 赤?
   a. **KAN** (カン)
   b. **aka** (あか)
   c. **ON** (オン)
   d. **o** (お)
   e. **SEKI** (セキ)

2. I wasn't popular on my tug-of-war team because I always liked to ___.
   a. 秒
   b. 赤
   c. 近
   d. 押
   e. 年

3. Which of the following readings apply to the kanji 馬?
   a. **BA** (バ)
   b. **NEN** (ネン)
   c. **uma** (うま)
   d. **KI** (キ)
   e. **hana** (はな)

4. Which of the following readings apply to the kanji 近?
   a. **TA** (タ)
   b. **toki** (とき)
   c. **hi** (ひ)
   d. **chika** (ちか)
   e. **KIN** (キン)

5. Which of the following readings apply to the kanji 話?
   a. **hana** (はな)
   b. **YŪ** (ユウ)
   c. **hanashi** (はなし)
   d. **WA** (ワ)
   e. **mi** (み)

D. Please choose the best answer(s) to the following questions.

1. Which is the correct reading of 引く?
   a. **o·ku** (お·く)
   b. **ki·ku** (き·く)
   c. **yu·ku** (ゆ·く)
   d. **hi·ku** (ひ·く)

2. Which is the correct reading of 学ぶ?
   a. **a·bu** (あ·ぶ)
   b. **mana·bu** (まな·ぶ)
   c. **kara·bu** (から·ぶ)
   d. **yo·bu** (よ·ぶ)

3. Which of the following kanji has the most number of strokes?
   a. 週
   b. 馬
   c. 訓
   d. 時
   e. 秒

4. Which is the correct reading of 押す?
   a. **o·su** (お·す)
   b. **ama·su** (あま·す)
   c. **ko·su** (こ·す)
   d. **hi·su** (ひ·す)

5. Which kanji would come next in the following series: 日....週....月....?
   a. 秒
   b. 来
   c. 年
   d. 弓
   e. 引

E. Please match the following compounds and words to their meanings and pronunciations.

1. 週間	a. English (language)	1. **o·shi da·shi** (お·し だ·し)
2. 生物学	b. Week	2. **MAN bi·ki** (マン び·き)
3. 英語	c. Conversation	3. **SEI·BUTSU·GAKU** (セイ·ブツ·ガク)
4. 押し出す	d. Four o'clock	4. **KAI·WA** (カイ·ワ)
5. 来年	e. Feeling	5. **SHŪ·KAN** (シュウ·カン)
6. 四時	f. To push out	6. **RAI·NEN** (ライ·ネン)
7. 赤道	g. Equator	7. **KI mo·chi** (キ も·ち)
8. 万引き	h. Biology	8. **SEKI·DŌ** (セキ·ドウ)
9. 会話	i. Shoplifter	9. **EI·GO** (エイ·ゴ)
10. 気持ち	j. Next year	10. **yo·JI** (よ·ジ)

CHAPTER 9 (KANJI 161-180)

KANJI 161

PUBLIC

BUILDING THIS KANJI
Eight (volcano) 八(19) + **Broken Crutch** 厶 = 公

MEANING

Public. In many instances, this character serves as the opposite to "私" (Entry 131).

REMEMBERING THIS KANJI

The eruption of a **volcano** is a very PUBLIC event, but nobody suffers more than those on **crutches** who are blown off their feet. After all, if you're hobbling along with **broken crutches** as a result of this, you might as well carry a sign that announces "Stay Away: I'm Really Unlucky". It's a very PUBLIC humiliation.

COMMON PRONUNCIATIONS

Common **ON** reading: **KŌ** (コウ)
Common **kun** reading: none

Create your **on-yomi** keyword and enter it in the table at the back of the book. After that, write your sentence to remember the **on-yomi** reading in the box below.

LESS COMMON PRONUNCIATIONS

Less common **ON** reading: **KU** (ク)
Less common **kun** reading: **ōyake** (おおやけ)

COMMON WORDS AND COMPOUNDS		
公有	public + have = *publicly owned*	**KŌ·YŪ** コウ·ユウ
公安	public + ease = *public peace*	**KŌ·AN** コウ·アン
公開	public + open = *open to the public*	**KŌ·KAI** コウ·カイ
公金	public + gold (money) = *public funds*	**KŌ·KIN** コウ·キン
公道	public + road = *public road*	**KŌ·DŌ** コウ·ドウ
公会	public + meet = *public meeting*	**KŌ·KAI** コウ·カイ

SAMPLE SENTENCE

ここ は 公道 です。
koko wa KŌ·DŌ desu.
this public road
= *This is a public road.*

WRITING PRACTICE

KANJI 162

 GOODS

丨	冂	口	口丨	口冂	口口	口口丨	口口冂	品

BUILDING THIS KANJI
Mouth (vampire) 口 (8) + **Mouth (vampire)** 口 (8) + **Mouth (vampire)** 口 (8) = 品

MEANING
This character expresses the idea of "goods" or "articles" in the majority of compounds in which it appears. It can occasionally have the more abstract notion of "refinement"; the fourth and fifth examples below illustrate this aspect of its meaning.

REMEMBERING THIS KANJI
You can imagine the GOODS a trio of **vampires** might have: capes, coffins, hair gel, teeth whiteners, blood pudding…all manner of GOODS, really.

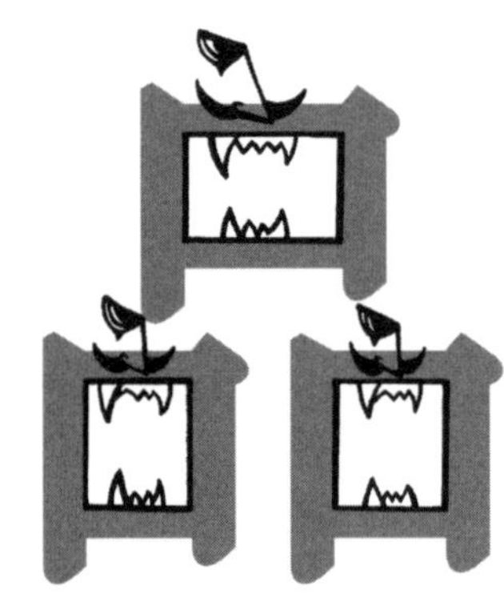

COMMON PRONUNCIATIONS
Common **ON** reading: **HIN** (ヒン)
Common **kun** reading: **shina** (しな)

Note how the second character in example three below has become voiced.

kun-yomi suggestion: "**she na**bbed"

Create your **on-yomi** keyword and enter it in the table at the back of the book. After that, write your sentence to remember the **on-yomi** and **kun-yomi** readings in the box below.

LESS COMMON PRONUNCIATIONS
Less common **ON** reading: none
Less common **kun** reading: none

COMMON WORDS AND COMPOUNDS		
品	*goods*	**shina** しな
品物	goods + thing = *merchandise*	**shina**·mono しな·もの
品切れ	goods + cut = *"out of stock"*	**shina** gi·re しな ぎ·れ
上品	upper + goods = *elegant*	JŌ·**HIN** ジョウ·ヒン
下品	lower + goods = *vulgar*	GE·**HIN** ゲ·ヒン
中古品	middle + old + goods = *secondhand goods*	CHŪ·KO·**HIN** チュウ·コ·ヒン

SAMPLE SENTENCE

下品 な 人 です ね。
GE·HIN na hito desu ne.
vulgar person is
= *(He's) a vulgar person, isn't he?*

WRITING PRACTICE

COMPONENT 163

KANJI 163

市 CITY

丶	亠	亣	市	市				

BUILDING THIS KANJI
Police 亠 + **MUGGER** 巾 = 市

MEANING
City. A secondary meaning relates to "market"; in this sense the character can refer to anything from a simple fair to the idea of a general "business" market. This will be the first of four kanji in Chapter 9 connected with groups of people living in a defined area; moving from larger to smaller units will provide a sense of their relative sizes.

REMEMBERING THIS KANJI
If you've got **police** and **muggers**, chances are you've got yourself a CITY.

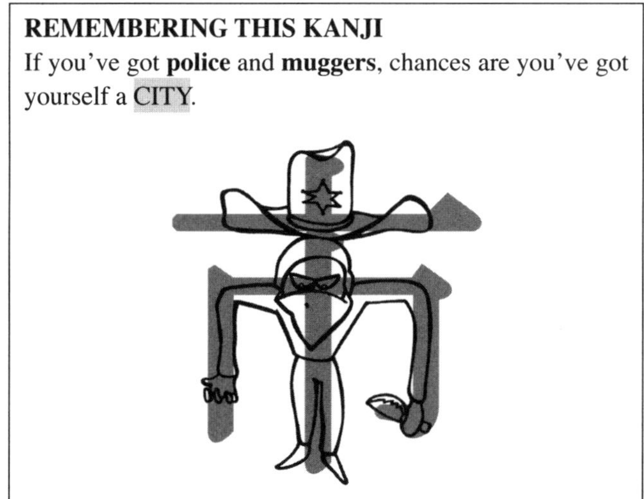

COMMON PRONUNCIATIONS
Common **ON** reading: **SHI** (シ)
Common **kun** reading: none

Create your **on-yomi** keyword and enter it in the table at the back of the book. After that, write your sentence to remember the **on-yomi** reading in the box below.

LESS COMMON PRONUNCIATIONS
Less common **ON** reading: none
Less common **kun** reading: **ichi** (いち)

This **kun-yomi** occurs in compounds when the kanji carries its secondary meaning of "market" or "fair".

COMMON WORDS AND COMPOUNDS		
市	*city*	**SHI** シ
市内	city + inside = *within the city*	**SHI·NAI** シ·ナイ
市外	city + outside = *outside the city*	**SHI·GAI** シ·ガイ
市立	city + stand = *municipal*	**SHI·RITSU** シ·リツ
市有	city + have = *city-owned*	**SHI·YŪ** シ·ユウ

SAMPLE SENTENCE

夜 は 一人 で 市内 を
yoru wa hito·ri de SHI·NAI o
night one person within the city
歩かないで 下さい。
aru·kanaide kuda·sai.
don't walk please
= *Please don't walk alone at night in the city.*

WRITING PRACTICE

KANJI 164

PRIMARY

丶	亠	亍	주	主				

BUILDING THIS KANJI
Jelly Bean ヽ + **King** 王(23) = 主

MEANING
This character conveys a sense of importance and authority; it is used in this vein with both concrete objects and abstract ideas. Note the difference between this kanji and that for "Jewel" in Entry 24 (玉).

REMEMBERING THIS KANJI
The PRIMARY reason a **king** puts a **jelly bean** on his head is to learn from the reaction it generates amongst his subjects. If no one dares tell him it's there, the **king** knows he is ruling PRIMARILY by fear. If it is pointed out to him with a smile, however, he knows he is viewed PRIMARILY with kindness.

COMMON PRONUNCIATIONS
Common **ON** reading: **SHU** (シュ)
Common **kun** reading: **nushi** (ぬし)

kun-yomi suggestion: "**new she**ars"

Create your **on-yomi** keyword and enter it in the table at the back of the book. After that, write your sentence to remember the **on-yomi** and **kun-yomi** readings in the box below.

LESS COMMON PRONUNCIATIONS
Less common **ON** reading: **SU** (ス)
Less common **kun** reading: **omo** (おも)

COMMON WORDS AND COMPOUNDS		
主力	primary + strength = *main force*	**SHU·RYOKU** シュ·リョク
主人公	primary + person + public = *main character*	**SHU·JIN·KŌ** シュ·ジン·コウ
売主	sell + primary = *seller*	uri·**nushi** うり·ぬし
持主	hold + primary = *owner*	mochi·**nushi** もち·ぬし

SAMPLE SENTENCE
主人公 は 有名 な 美人 です。
SHU·JIN·KŌ wa YŪ·MEI na BI·JIN desu.
main character famous beautiful woman
= *The main character is a famously beautiful woman.*

WRITING PRACTICE

KANJI 165

丁 BLOCK

一	丁							

MEANING

The main sense is of a city "block", although more obscure meanings can range from "pages" to "polite". This is a quirky character that shows up often as a component in other kanji.

REMEMBERING THIS KANJI

Let's face it: this looks like a capital "T", so best think of it as an overhead view of a "T" junction marking the intersection of BLOCKS.

COMMON PRONUNCIATIONS

Common **ON** reading: **CHŌ** (チョウ)
Common **kun** reading: none

Create your **on-yomi** keyword and enter it in the table at the back of the book. After that, write your sentence to remember the **on-yomi** reading in the box below.

LESS COMMON PRONUNCIATIONS

Less common **ON** reading: **TEI** (テイ)
Less common **kun** reading: none

COMMON WORDS AND COMPOUNDS		
丁目	block + eye = *city block area*	**CHŌ**·me チョウ·め
二丁目	two + block + eye = *City Block 2*	NI·**CHŌ**·me ニ·チョウ·め
四丁目	four + block + eye = *City Block 4*	yon·**CHŌ**·me よん·チョウ·め

SAMPLE SENTENCE

私 の 新しい 家 は 五丁目 に
watashi no atara·shii ie wa GO·CHŌ·me ni
my new house City Block 5
あります。
arimasu.
is
= *My new house is in City Block 5.*

WRITING PRACTICE

KANJI 166

FRIEND

一	ナ	方	友					

BUILDING THIS KANJI
Superhero ナ + **Again (ironing board)** 又(159) = 友

MEANING
Friend. The first two strokes are written in the same order as Entry 48 ("左").

REMEMBERING THIS KANJI
"I just think you're taking me for granted as a FRIEND," said the **superhero**.

"What do you mean? All I asked you to do was pick up an **ironing board** for me. That's something any FRIEND would do."

"Yeah, but I mean…it's embarrassing to fly with an **ironing board**. I look ridiculous."

"You need to quit worrying about the opinions of others. And don't make that face; I'm telling you this as a FRIEND."

COMMON PRONUNCIATIONS
Common **ON** reading: **YŪ** (ユウ)
Common **kun** reading: **tomo** (とも)

kun-yomi suggestion: "lot**to mo**ment"

Create your **on-yomi** keyword and enter it in the table at the back of the book. After that, write your sentence to remember the **on-yomi** and **kun-yomi** readings in the box below.

LESS COMMON PRONUNCIATIONS
Less common **ON** reading: none
Less common **kun** reading: none

COMMON WORDS AND COMPOUNDS		
友	*friend*	**tomo** とも
友人	friend + person = *friend*	**YŪ·JIN** ユウ·ジン
友好	friend + like = *friendship*	**YŪ·KŌ** ユウ·コウ

SAMPLE SENTENCE

西山さん の 友人 は 南米
Nishi·yama-san no YŪ·JIN wa NAN·BEI
Nishiyama-san friend South America
から 来ました。
kara ki·mashita.
from came
= *Nishiyama-san's friend came from South America*

WRITING PRACTICE

KANJI 167

団 GROUP

丨	冂	冂	冂	冂	団			

BUILDING THIS KANJI
Prison □ + **Tiny (soccer player)** 寸(103) = 団

MEANING
Group. Good luck making sense of the third example below!

REMEMBERING THIS KANJI
When they first arrive in **prison**, **tiny** soccer players will always huddle together in a GROUP. This behavior draws the attention of the regular cons, and a GROUP of them will soon approach the newcomers with welcoming smiles.

COMMON PRONUNCIATIONS
Common **ON** reading: **DAN** (ダン)
Common **kun** reading: none

Create your **on-yomi** keyword and enter it in the table at the back of the book. After that, write your sentence to remember the **on-yomi** reading in the box below.

LESS COMMON PRONUNCIATIONS
Less common **ON** reading: **TON** (トン)
Less common **kun** reading: none

TON is found only in the well-known Japanese word for bedding: **FU·TON** (フ·トン), composed of the kanji 布団 (Spread + Group).

COMMON WORDS AND COMPOUNDS		
一団	one + group = *a group*	ICHI·**DAN** イチ·ダン
団体	group + body = *organization*	**DAN**·TAI ダン·タイ
団子	group + child = *dumpling*	**DAN**·go ダン·ご
入団	enter + group = *joining (a group)*	NYŪ·**DAN** ニュウ·ダン

SAMPLE SENTENCE

内田さん は 団子 が 好き です。
Uchi·da-san wa DAN·go ga su·ki desu.
Uchida-san dumplings likes
= *Uchida-san likes dumplings.*

WRITING PRACTICE

COMPONENT 168

ROWER  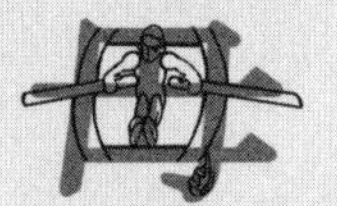

KANJI 168

 **EVERY**

ノ	𠂉	𠂉	𠂉	𠂉	毎			

BUILDING THIS KANJI
Hammer 𠂉 + **Rower** 毌 = 毎

MEANING
Every.

REMEMBERING THIS KANJI
"How long you been a **rower**?"
"A while. I was on the crew that took Caesar to North Africa. You?"
"Just started."
"Well, all you have to remember is this: when the **hammer** comes down, you row. EVERY minute of EVERY hour of EVERY boring day. Not that I'm bitter, though. Like EVERY other guy here, all I want is a little variety in the beat."

COMMON PRONUNCIATIONS
Common **ON** reading: **MAI** (マイ)
Common **kun** reading: none

Note the mix of readings in the last three examples below. Now create your **on-yomi** keyword and enter it in the table at the back of the book. After that, write your sentence to remember the **on-yomi** reading in the box below.

LESS COMMON PRONUNCIATIONS
Less common **ON** reading: none
Less common **kun** reading: **goto** (ごと)

COMMON WORDS AND COMPOUNDS		
毎日	every + sun (day) = *daily*	**MAI**·NICHI マイ・ニチ
毎週	every + week = *weekly*	**MAI**·SHŪ マイ・シュウ
毎月	every + moon (month) = *monthly*	**MAI**·tsuki マイ・つき
毎年	every + year = *yearly*	**MAI**·toshi マイ・とし
毎朝	every + morning = *every morning*	**MAI**·asa マイ・あさ

SAMPLE SENTENCE

私	は	毎朝	父	と	話
watashi	**wa**	**MAI·asa**	**chichi**	**to**	**hanashi**
I		every morning	my father		speak

をします。
o shimasu.
= *I speak with my father every morning.*

WRITING PRACTICE

COMPONENT 169

WEIGHTLIFTER 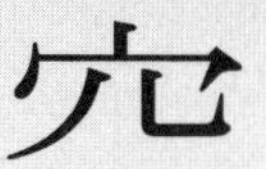 

KANJI 169

 **EMPTY**

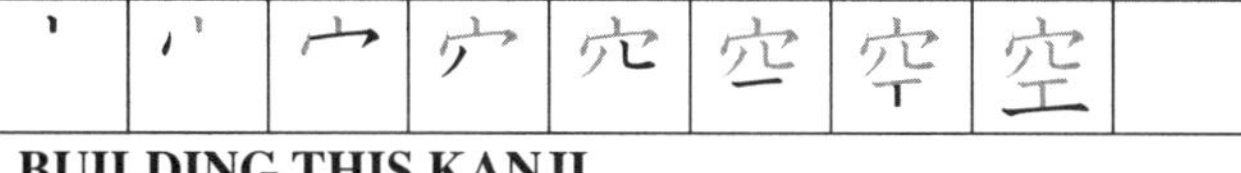

BUILDING THIS KANJI
Weightlifter 穴 + **Craft** 工(47) = 空

MEANING

Empty/Sky. As in English, "empty" can incorporate suggestions of uselessness and futility.

REMEMBERING THIS KANJI

Like a lot of students, I became a **weightlifter** at college and practiced my **craft** well. First up were EMPTY cans – I could curl a lot of those. Next came EMPTY bottles, followed by EMPTY kegs. It was only later that I realized how EMPTY the **craft** of **weightlifting** beer really was.

COMMON PRONUNCIATIONS

Common **ON** reading: **KŪ** (クウ)
Common **kun** readings: **sora** (そら); **kara** (から)

This kanji takes a bit of work, although **KŪ** is by far the most common reading in compounds. **sora**, as shown in the first example, means "sky"; it becomes voiced in the second position (as in the compound following). **kara** occasionally appears in first position with a meaning of "empty", and is a reading you will no doubt be familiar with from the third example.

kun-yomi suggestions: "**soar a**lbatross"; "**cara**mba"

Create your **on-yomi** keyword and enter it in the table at the back of the book. After that, write your sentence to remember the **on-yomi** and **kun-yomi** readings in the box below.

LESS COMMON PRONUNCIATIONS

Less common **ON** reading: none
Less common **kun** reading: **a** (あ)

This reading is used to make the verbs 空く and 空ける (**a·ku and a·keru**). Meaning "to open", these can be thought of as interchangeable with the more common 開く and 開ける (also **a·ku and a·keru**) from Entry 106. A few nouns, however, make use of this kanji exclusively: 空き缶* (**a·ki KAN**) "an empty can", and 空き瓶* (**a·ki BIN**) "an empty bottle", are two examples.

COMMON WORDS AND COMPOUNDS		
空	*sky*	**sora** そら
青空	blue + empty (sky) = *blue sky*	ao·**zora** あお·ぞら
空手	empty + hand = *karate*	**kara**·te から·て
空間	empty + interval = *space*	**KŪ**·KAN クウ·カン
空気	empty + spirit = *air*	**KŪ**·KI クウ·キ

SAMPLE SENTENCE

朝 の 空 は きれい です よ。
asa no sora wa kirei desu yo.
morning sky lovely
= *The morning sky is lovely!*

WRITING PRACTICE

KANJI 170

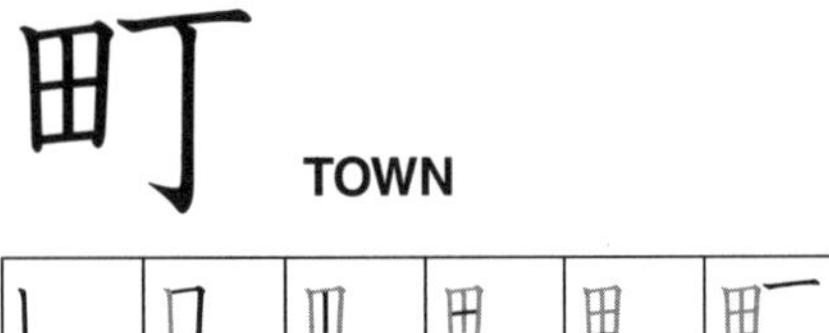

町 TOWN

丨	冂	冂	冊	田	田一	町		

BUILDING THIS KANJI
Rice Field 田 (73) + **Block** 丁 (165) = 町

MEANING
Town. One size smaller than a city is the town, making this the second of our four kanji related to people living in defined locations. This character can also refer on occasion to a "street" or an "alley".

REMEMBERING THIS KANJI
"TOWN! TOWN!"

Strong and clear it resounded over the **rice fields**. From **block** to **block** it was heard in the neighborhoods.

"TOWN! TOWN!"

In all honesty, though, nobody could really see the point of the TOWN crier.

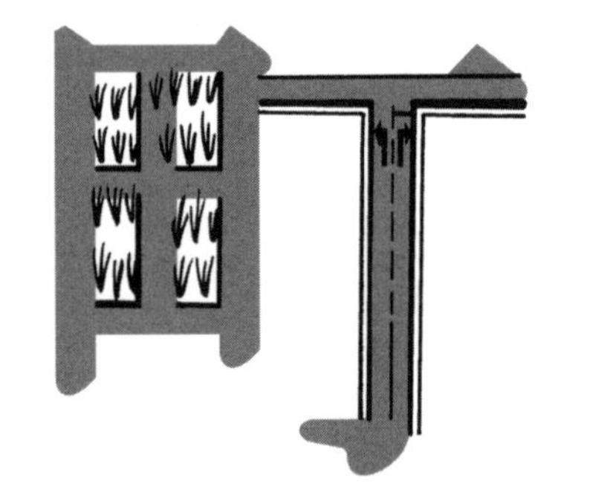

COMMON PRONUNCIATIONS
Common **ON** reading: **CHŌ** (チョウ)
Common **kun** reading: **machi** (まち)

Create your **on-yomi** keyword and enter it in the table at the back of the book. After that, write your sentence to remember the **on-yomi** and **kun-yomi** readings in the box below.

LESS COMMON PRONUNCIATIONS
Less common **ON** reading: none
Less common **kun** reading: none

COMMON WORDS AND COMPOUNDS		
町	*town*	**machi** まち
町内	town + inside = *in the town*	**CHŌ·NAI** チョウ·ナイ
町立	town + stand = *established by the town*	**CHŌ·RITSU** チョウ·リツ
町会	town + meet = *town assembly*	**CHŌ·KAI** チョウ·カイ

SAMPLE SENTENCE
この 町 のラーメンは 有名 です。
kono machi no rāmen wa YŪ·MEI desu.
this town ramen famous
= *This town's ramen is famous.*

WRITING PRACTICE

KANJI 171

DOG

一	ナ	大	犬					

BUILDING THIS KANJI
Large (sumo wrestler) 大(17) + **Jelly Bean** ヽ = 犬

MEANING
Dog.

REMEMBERING THIS KANJI
Only a **jelly bean** dangled next to his head could make a **sumo wrestler** jump up like a DOG.

COMMON PRONUNCIATIONS
Common **ON** reading: **KEN** (ケン)
Common **kun** reading: **inu** (いぬ)

kun-yomi suggestion: "**enu**merate"

Create your **on-yomi** keyword and enter it in the table at the back of the book. After that, write your sentence to remember the **on-yomi** and **kun-yomi** readings in the box below.

LESS COMMON PRONUNCIATIONS
Less common **ON** reading: none
Less common **kun** reading: none

COMMON WORDS AND COMPOUNDS		
犬	*dog*	**inu** いぬ
子犬	child + dog = *puppy*	ko·**inu** こ·いぬ
秋田犬	autumn + rice field + dog = *an Akita dog*	aki·ta·**KEN** あき·た·ケン
愛犬	love + dog = *pet dog*	AI·**KEN** アイ·ケン
愛犬家	love + dog + house = *dog lover*	AI·**KEN**·KA アイ·ケン·カ

SAMPLE SENTENCE
古川さん が 子犬 を 買いました。
Furu·kawa-san ga ko·inu o ka·imashita.
Furukawa-san puppy bought
= *Furukawa-san bought a puppy.*

WRITING PRACTICE

KANJI 172

DEATH

一	ア	万	歹	歹'	死			

BUILDING THIS KANJI
One (top of a bun) 一 (3) + **Evening** 夕 (108) + **Beggar** 匕 = 死

MEANING
Death.

REMEMBERING THIS KANJI
"So how did DEATH arrive for you?" she asked the **beggar**.

"It was weird," he said. "I was begging on my usual corner when I noticed it starting to get dark. "Is it **evening** already?" I wondered. I looked up to check, but realized I was mistaken, that what I had thought was **evening** was actually the **top of a bun** settling over me. Now, you would have thought I'd be scared by this, but I wasn't; the bun was really warm and smelled great, and for the first time in ages I didn't feel hungry. I wasn't afraid of DEATH at all."

COMMON PRONUNCIATIONS
Common **ON** reading: **SHI** (シ)
Common **kun** reading: **shi** (し)

It is a welcome event when both types of reading for a kanji are identical like this; truly, death can sometimes be kind!

kun-yomi suggestion: "**shee**t"

Create your **on-yomi** keyword and enter it in the table at the back of the book. After that, write your sentence to remember the **on-yomi** and **kun-yomi** readings in the box below.

LESS COMMON PRONUNCIATIONS
Less common **ON** reading: none
Less common **kun** reading: none

COMMON WORDS AND COMPOUNDS		
死ぬ	*to die*	**shi**·nu し·ぬ
水死	water + death = *drowning*	SUI·**SHI** スイ·シ
死体	death + body = *dead body*	**SHI**·TAI シ·タイ
死火山	death + fire + mountain = *extinct volcano*	**SHI**·KA·ZAN シ·カ·ザン

SAMPLE SENTENCE

私 の 好き な 馬 は 五年前 に
watashi no su·ki na uma wa GO·NEN·mae ni
my like horse five years ago
死にました。
shi·nimashita.
died
= *My horse that I liked died five years ago.*

WRITING PRACTICE

COMPONENT 173

RAZOR 彳

KANJI 173

GO

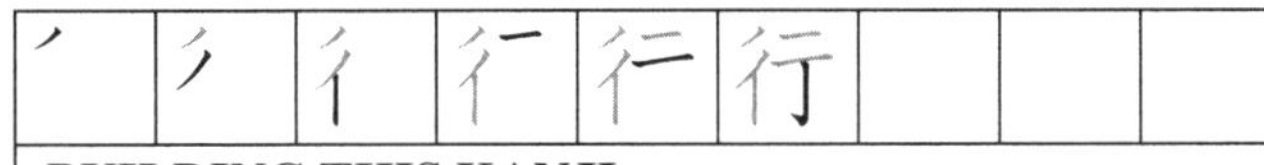

BUILDING THIS KANJI
Razor 彳 + **One (hamburger patty)** 一 (3) +
Block 丁 (165) = 行

MEANING
"Go" is the primary meaning of this character, along with related ideas of "carrying out" or "doing". Far less common is the secondary sense of a "stroke" or "line" of text.

REMEMBERING THIS KANJI
When the **razor** moved into our neighborhood, no one in the **block** knew quite what to do. "How can it fit in with us?" I asked my wife. "GO and invite it to our **block** party," she said. I didn't want to do this, of course, but this turned out to be a great idea, for the **razor** was a big hit when it came time to prepare the **hamburger patties** that day. Shaving each one perfectly, it soon had everyone cheering "GO! GO! GO!" as it worked faster and faster. "You know something, honey?" I said to my wife. "Looks like the **razor's** going to fit in well with our **block** after all. You were right telling me to GO and invite it here."

COMMON PRONUNCIATIONS
Common **ON** reading: **KŌ** (コウ)
Common **kun** readings: **i** (い); **yu** (ゆ)

This is another character for our rogues' gallery of troublesome kanji, and one that merits added attention from the outset. For the general sense of the verb "to go", **i·ku** (い·く) is the choice; **yu·ku** (ゆ·く) is employed far less often and is of most use in a few specific compounds (such as in the second example), or as a suffix meaning "bound for" (as in the third). It can also act like 買, albeit strangely in that on rare occasions it will incorporate yuku as opposed to **yuki**. This is seen in the well-known compound **yuku·e·FU·MEI** (ゆく·え·フ·メイ) 行方不明: "Missing", built from the two words "whereabouts" (Go/Direction*) and "unclear" (Not/Bright).

kun-yomi suggestions: "Egypt"; "Unicorn"

Create your **on-yomi** keyword and enter it in the table at the back of the book. After that, write your sentence to remember the **on-yomi** and **kun-yomi** readings in the box below.

LESS COMMON PRONUNCIATIONS
Less common **ON** readings: **GYŌ** (ギョウ); **AN** (アン)
Less common **kun** reading: **okona** (おこな)

GYŌ is found primarily in compounds relating to this kanji's secondary meaning of "line" or "stroke". Note the irregular compound used at the beginning of the sample sentence (今日); we encountered this word back in Entry 6 (日).

COMMON WORDS AND COMPOUNDS		
行く	*to go*	**i**·ku い·く
行き先	go + precede = *destination*	**yu**·ki saki ゆ·き さき
東京行き	east + capital + go = *bound for Tokyo*	TŌ·KYŌ **yu**·ki トウ·キョウ ゆ·き
夜行	night + go = *night travel*	YA·**KŌ** ヤ·コウ
歩行	walk + go = *walking*	HO·**KŌ** ホ·コウ
歩行者	walk + go + individual = *pedestrian*	HO·**KŌ**·SHA ホ·コウ·シャ

SAMPLE SENTENCE

今日 は 歩行者 が 多い。
kyō wa HO·KŌ·SHA ga ō·i.
today pedestrians many
= There are many pedestrians today.

KANJI 174

TAKE

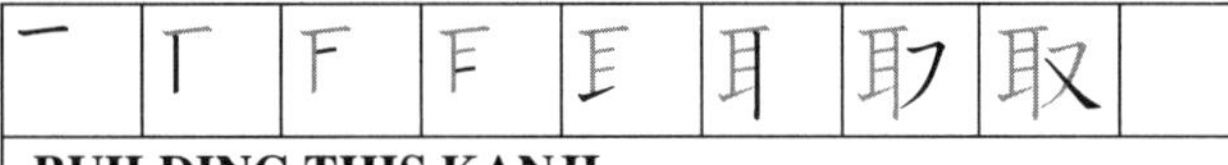

BUILDING THIS KANJI
Ear 耳 (78) + **Again (ironing board)** 又 (159) = 取

MEANING

Take.

REMEMBERING THIS KANJI

The **ear** was nervous.

"Um…I was wondering…" he said to the **ironing board**, "if, uh…"

"Yes?"

"If I could, uh…you know, TAKE you…"

"TAKE me where?"

"TAKE you on a…stroll or something."

The **ironing board** smiled, and for the first time noticed the **ear's** wrinkles; she understood now that he needed her.

"That would be nice," she said. "I'd love for you to TAKE me out."

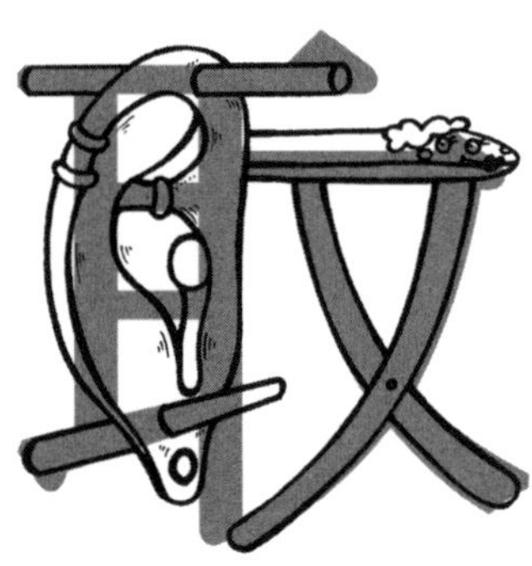

COMMON PRONUNCIATIONS

Common **ON** reading: none
Common **kun** reading: **to** (と)

As the second example below shows, this kanji acts like 買. It can also become voiced in the second position, as shown here in the final compound.

kun-yomi suggestion: "**to**ll"

Create your sentence to remember the **kun-yomi** reading in the box below.

LESS COMMON PRONUNCIATIONS

Less common **ON** reading: **SHU** (シュ)
Less common **kun** reading: none

COMMON WORDS AND COMPOUNDS		
取る	*to take*	**to**·ru と·る
取引	take + pull = *transactions*	**tori**·hiki とり·ひき
取り上げる	take + upper = *to pick up*	**to**·ri a·geru と·り あ·げる
取り入れる	take + enter = *to take in*	**to**·ri i·reru と·り い·れる
取り出す	take + exit = *to take out*	**to**·ri da·su と·り だ·す
気取る	spirit + take = *to put on airs*	KI **do**·ru キ ど·る

SAMPLE SENTENCE

赤とうがらし を 取り出して 下さい。
aka·tōgarashi o to·ri da·shite kuda·sai.
red peppers — take out — please
= *Please take out the red peppers.*

WRITING PRACTICE

KANJI 175

VILLAGE

一	十	才	木	木一	村	村		

BUILDING THIS KANJI
Tree 木(13) + **Tiny (soccer player)** 寸(103) = 村

MEANING

Village. Here we have the third of our four "community" kanji. Keep in mind that this character implies something smaller than a city or town.

REMEMBERING THIS KANJI

As the population of our VILLAGE is **tiny**, the **tiny** soccer players have no one to play with. A suggestion that they use **trees** for opponents, however, was dismissed by everyone. This was hardly surprising given that it was proposed by the VILLAGE idiot.

COMMON PRONUNCIATIONS

Common **ON** reading: **SON** (ソン)
Common **kun** reading: **mura** (むら)

Note that the reading for "人" in the second example is voiced.

kun-yomi suggestion: "**moor a**longside"

Create your **on-yomi** keyword and enter it in the table at the back of the book. After that, write your sentence to remember the **on-yomi** and **kun-yomi** readings in the box below.

LESS COMMON PRONUNCIATIONS

Less common **ON** reading: none
Less common **kun** reading: none

COMMON WORDS AND COMPOUNDS		
村	*village*	**mura** むら
村人	village + person = *villager*	**mura**·bito むら·びと
山村	mountain + village = *mountain village*	SAN·**SON** サン·ソン

SAMPLE SENTENCE

村人 は 小道 に 立っています。
mura·bito wa ko·michi ni ta·tte imasu.
villager path is standing
= *A villager is standing in the path.*

WRITING PRACTICE

KANJI 176

字 CHARACTER

BUILDING THIS KANJI
Pincers 宀 + **Child** 子(56) = 字

MEANING
"Character", in the sense of a Chinese character or letter of an alphabet.

REMEMBERING THIS KANJI
There are various ways of teaching Japanese CHARACTERS to a **child**, but a controversial method in days gone by involved the use of **pincers**. In it, a set of pincers would be suspended menacingly over a **child** practicing kanji. Should a mistake be made with any CHARACTER, the **pincers** would…well, best not describe what happened. Learning CHARACTERS today, quite simply, is a lot less stressful.

COMMON PRONUNCIATIONS
Common **ON** reading: **JI** (ジ)
Common **kun** reading: none

Note that the reading for "引" is voiced in the final example.

Create your **on-yomi** keyword and enter it in the table at the back of the book. After that, write your sentence to remember the **on-yomi** reading in the box below.

LESS COMMON PRONUNCIATIONS
Less common **ON** reading: none
Less common **kun** reading: **aza** (あざ)

COMMON WORDS AND COMPOUNDS		
十字	ten + character = *a cross*	JŪ·**JI** ジュウ·ジ
赤十字	red + ten + character = *the Red Cross*	SEKI·JŪ·**JI** セキ·ジュウ·ジ
字引	character + pull = *dictionary*	**JI**·biki ジ·びき

SAMPLE SENTENCE

多く の 国 で は 赤十字 は
ō·ku no kuni de wa SEKI·JŪ·JI wa
many country Red Cross
大切 です。
TAI·SETSU desu.
important
= *The Red Cross is important in many countries.*

WRITING PRACTICE

COMPONENT 177

SEESAW

KANJI 177

TOOL

丨	冂	冃	冃	目	且	具	具	

BUILDING THIS KANJI
Eye (Cyclops) 目(15) + **Seesaw** 六 = 具

MEANING

Tool/Equipment.

REMEMBERING THIS KANJI

I once got on a **seesaw** with a **Cyclops** and soon found myself stuck in the air. As he was in no hurry to let me down I had to endure watching him eat his lunch as I sat there dangling, which was unpleasant given his manners. Instead of cutlery, he used the only TOOL he had - his club - to do everything from spread butter to roll up pasta. That being said, though, it did work well as a cheese grater, so I suppose he had a point in describing it as a multi-purpose TOOL.

COMMON PRONUNCIATIONS

Common **ON** reading: **GU** (グ)
Common **kun** reading: none

Create your **on-yomi** keyword and enter it in the table at the back of the book. After that, write your sentence to remember the **on-yomi** reading in the box below.

LESS COMMON PRONUNCIATIONS

Less common **ON** reading: none
Less common **kun** reading: none

COMMON WORDS AND COMPOUNDS		
道具	road + tool = *tool*	DŌ·**GU** ドウ·グ
家具	house + tool = *furniture*	KA·**GU** カ·グ
具体	tool + body = *definite; concrete*	**GU**·TAI グ·タイ
馬具	horse + tool = *harness*	BA·**GU** バ·グ

SAMPLE SENTENCE

山下先生 は 新しい 家具 を
Yama·shita-sensei wa atara·shii KA·GU o
(teacher) Yamashita new furniture
買いました。
ka·imashita.
bought
= *Yamashita-sensei bought new furniture.*

WRITING PRACTICE

COMPONENT 178

SPLASH  

This important component usually indicates a character having some connection to water. It will be encountered frequently, being present in more than one hundred of the general-use kanji.

KANJI 178

 **POUR**

丶	冫	氵	氵丶	氵亠	氵亍	氵干	注	

BUILDING THIS KANJI
Splash 氵 + **Primary** 主(164) = 注

MEANING

Pour. In addition to the literal meaning, there is often an implied sense of "directing" something (a gaze or one's attention, for instance) toward an object.

REMEMBERING THIS KANJI

This is how I was taught to POUR:

"When you POUR, your **primary** objective is not to let anything **splash** out. POUR carefully, but POUR confidently. **Splashes** are the **primary** indication that someone does not know how to POUR properly."

COMMON PRONUNCIATIONS

Common **ON** reading: **CHŪ** (チュウ)
Common **kun** reading: **soso** (そそ)

kun-yomi suggestion: "**so-so**"

Create your **on-yomi** keyword and enter it in the table at the back of the book. After that, write your sentence to remember the **on-yomi** and **kun-yomi** readings in the box below.

LESS COMMON PRONUNCIATIONS

Less common **ON** reading: none
Less common **kun** reading: none

COMMON WORDS AND COMPOUNDS		
注ぐ	*to pour*	**soso**·gu そそ·ぐ
注意	pour + mind = *attention*	**CHŪ·I** チュウ·イ
注水	pour + water = *watering*	**CHŪ·SUI** チュウ·スイ
注入	pour + enter = *infusion*	**CHŪ·NYŪ** チュウ·ニュウ
注目	pour + eye = *notice*	**CHŪ·MOKU** チュウ·モク

SAMPLE SENTENCE

犬 に 注意 して 下さい。
inu ni CHŪ·I shite kuda·sai.
dog attention do please
= *Watch out for the dog.*

WRITING PRACTICE

KANJI 179

CHERRY TREE

一	十	才	木	木'	木''	木'''	桜	桜
桜								

BUILDING THIS KANJI
Tree 木(13) + **Claw** ⺍ + **Woman** 女(16) = 桜

MEANING
Cherry tree.

REMEMBERING THIS KANJI
CHERRY TREES are known to exhibit some odd behavior around **women**. When a **woman** approaches, for example, a CHERRY TREE will often extend its **claws** threateningly, and only allow its fruit to be plucked once certain it will be done with a gentle touch. CHERRY TREES, as poets have known for centuries, are very delicate.

COMMON PRONUNCIATIONS
Common **ON** reading: none
Common **kun** reading: **sakura** (さくら)

As the second and third compounds illustrate, this reading is voiced when the kanji appears in the second position.

kun-yomi suggestion: "A **sack? Ooh, wra**p it!"

Create your sentence to remember the **kun-yomi** reading in the box below.

LESS COMMON PRONUNCIATIONS
Less common **ON** reading: **Ō** (オウ)
Less common **kun** reading: none

COMMON WORDS AND COMPOUNDS		
桜	*cherry tree*	**sakura** さくら
山桜	mountain + cherry tree = *wild cherry tree*	yama·**zakura** やま·ざくら
夜桜	night + cherry tree = *cherry trees at night*	yo·**zakura** よ·ざくら

SAMPLE SENTENCE

山桜 は 夜中 で も
yama·zakura wa yo·naka de mo
wild cherry trees middle of the night even
美しかった です。
utsuku·shikatta desu.
were beautiful
= *The wild cherry trees were beautiful even in the middle of the night.*

WRITING PRACTICE

KANJI 180

HAMLET

丨	冂	冃	日	甲	甲	里		

BUILDING THIS KANJI
Shell (Fly swatter) 甲(148) + **Two** 二(4) = 里

MEANING
Hamlet. Here we have the fourth and smallest of our populated units. This character can also signify the countryside in general; not surprisingly, given how small a settlement this kanji implies.

REMEMBERING THIS KANJI
When Hamlet came to our HAMLET, me 'n the other resident were pretty darn excited; the guy was the prince of Denmark, after all. Unfortunately, with only **two** of us in the HAMLET we only had **two fly swatters**, and what with all the flies buzzin' everywhere, I wasn't in any mood to lend him mine. Anyway, rumor has it he told folks back in Elsinore that he didn't much care for our HAMLET. Which strikes me as kind of ironic.

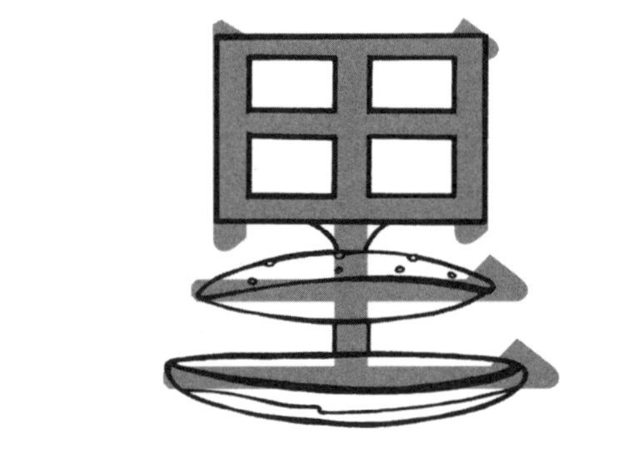

COMMON PRONUNCIATIONS
Common **ON** reading: none
Common **kun** reading: **sato** (さと)

The final compound below reminds us once again that this reading of "人" is always voiced when it appears in the second position

kun-yomi suggestion: "**sat o**penly"

Create your sentence to remember the **kun-yomi** reading in the box below.

LESS COMMON PRONUNCIATIONS
Less common **ON** reading: **RI** (リ)
Less common **kun** readings: none

COMMON WORDS AND COMPOUNDS		
里	*hamlet*	**sato** さと
古里	old + hamlet = *the old hometown*	furu·**sato** ふる·さと
里人	hamlet + person = *country folk*	**sato**·bito さと·びと

SAMPLE SENTENCE

先週 は 古里 へ 行きました。
SEN·SHŪ wa furu·sato e i·kimashita.
last week old hometown went
= *Last week I went to my old hometown.*

WRITING PRACTICE

CHAPTER 9 REVIEW EXERCISES

A. Please match the following kanji to their meanings.

1. 丁	a. Hamlet
2. 死	b. Death
3. 村	c. Take
4. 行	d. Pour
5. 主	e. Goods
6. 取	f. Village
7. 友	g. Block
8. 注	h. Primary
9. 品	i. Friend
10. 里	j. Go

B. Please match the following meanings to their kanji, and these to their **on** or **kun-yomi**.

1. Dog	a. 犬	1. **KŌ** (コウ)
2. Cherry tree	b. 具	2. **MAI** (マイ)
3. Group	c. 公	3. **kara** (から)
4. Every	d. 町	4. **sakura** (さくら)
5. Public	e. 桜	5. **GU** (グ)
6. Character	f. 市	6. **SHI** (シ)
7. City	g. 毎	7. **machi** (まち)
8. Tool	h. 字	8. **inu** (いぬ)
9. Empty	i. 団	9. **DAN** (ダン)
10. Town	j. 空	10. **JI** (ジ)

C. Please choose the best answer(s) to the following questions.

1. Which of the following readings apply to the kanji 村?
   a. **mura** (むら)
   b. **CHŌ** (チョウ)
   c. **SON** (ソン)
   d. **machi** (まち)
   e. **SHI** (シ)

2. Which of the following readings apply to the kanji 友?
   a. **sato** (さと)
   b. **YŪ** (ユウ)
   c. **YŌ** (ヨウ)
   d. **minato** (みなと)
   e. **tomo** (とも)

3. Which of the following readings apply to the kanji 品?
   a. **SHŪ** (シュウ)
   b. **shina** (しな)
   c. **hana** (はな)
   d. **HIN** (ヒン)
   e. **IN** (イン)

4. When springtime rolls around I love to sit under a blooming ___.
   a. 犬
   b. 友
   c. 桜
   d. 具
   e. 注

5. Which of the following readings apply to the kanji 行?
   a. **i** (い)
   b. **KŌ** (コウ)
   c. **yu** (ゆ)
   d. **to** (と)
   e. **KA** (カ)

D. Please choose the best answer(s) to the following questions.

1. Which kanji would come next in the following series: 市....町....村....?
   a. 行
   b. 丁
   c. 空
   d. 里
   e. 具

2. Which is the correct reading of 死ぬ?
   a. **shi·nu** (し·ぬ)
   b. **a·nu** (あ·ぬ)
   c. **chi·nu** (ち·ぬ)
   d. **u·nu** (う·ぬ)

3. Which of the following kanji has the most number of strokes?
   a. 具
   b. 品
   c. 取
   d. 里
   e. 注

4. Which is the correct reading of 注ぐ?
   a. **ama·gu** (あま·ぐ)
   b. **shi·gu** (し·ぐ)
   c. **soso·gu** (そそ·ぐ)
   d. **o·gu** (お·ぐ)

5. Which is the correct reading of 取る?
   a. **mawa·ru** (まわ·る)
   b. **shi·ru** (し·る)
   c. **hi·ru** (ひ·る)
   d. **to·ru** (と·る)

E. Please match the following compounds and words to their meanings and pronunciations.

1. 取り上げる	a. Daily	1. **CHŌ·KAI** (チョウ·カイ)
2. 注意	b. Drowning	2. **KA·GU** (カ·グ)
3. 家具	c. Blue sky	3. **CHŪ·I** (チュウ·イ)
4. 青空	d. Attention	4. **shina·mono** (しな·もの)
5. 毎日	e. Organization	5. **MAI·NICHI** (マイ·ニチ)
6. 主人公	f. Town assembly	6. **DAN·TAI** (ダン·タイ)
7. 品物	g. Furniture	7. **SUI·SHI** (スイ·シ)
8. 団体	h. Merchandise	8. **to·ri a·geru** (と·り あ·げる)
9. 町会	i. Main character	9. **SHU·JIN·KŌ** (シュ·ジン·コウ)
10. 水死	j. To pick up	10. **ao·zora** (あお·ぞら)

CHAPTER 10 (KANJI 181-200)

KANJI 181

GROVE

一	十	オ	木	木一	村	材	林	

BUILDING THIS KANJI
Tree 木(13) + **Tree** 木(13) = 林

MEANING
Grove.

REMEMBERING THIS KANJI
No story needed, as it's easy to see how this character could stand for a small group of trees!

COMMON PRONUNCIATIONS
Common **ON** reading: **RIN** (リン)
Common **kun** reading: **hayashi** (はやし)

As the common Japanese family name in the second example below shows, this reading becomes voiced when not in the first position.

kun-yomi suggestion: "**high ash e**vent"

Create your **on-yomi** keyword and enter it in the table at the back of the book. After that, write your sentence to remember the **on-yomi** and **kun-yomi** readings in the box below.

LESS COMMON PRONUNCIATIONS
Less common **ON** reading: none
Less common **kun** reading: none

COMMON WORDS AND COMPOUNDS		
林	*grove*	**hayashi** はやし
小林さん	small + grove = *Kobayashi-san*	ko·**bayashi**·san こ·ばやし·さん
林道	grove + road = *woodland trail; road*	**RIN**·DŌ リン·ドウ
人工林	person + craft + grove = *planted forest*	JIN·KŌ·**RIN** ジン·コウ·リン
公有林	public + have + grove = *public woodland*	KŌ·YŪ·**RIN** コウ·ユウ·リン

SAMPLE SENTENCE

あの 国 には 公有林 が 少ない。
ano kuni ni wa KŌ·YŪ·RIN ga suku·nai.
that country public woodland few
= *That country has little public woodland.*

WRITING PRACTICE

KANJI 182

FOREST

一	十	才	木					
		森						

BUILDING THIS KANJI
Tree 木(13) + **Grove** 林(181) = 森

MEANING
Forest.

REMEMBERING THIS KANJI
Another wonderfully simple character! You've probably guessed that this kanji implies a larger area of trees than that of the preceding entry.

COMMON PRONUNCIATIONS
Common **ON** reading: **SHIN** (シン)
Common **kun** reading: **mori** (もり)

kun-yomi suggestion: "Ne**mo re**alized"

Create your **on-yomi** keyword and enter it in the table at the back of the book. After that, write your sentence to remember the **on-yomi** and **kun-yomi** readings in the box below.

LESS COMMON PRONUNCIATIONS
Less common **ON** reading: none
Less common **kun** reading: none

COMMON WORDS AND COMPOUNDS		
森	*forest*	**mori** もり
森林	forest + grove = *forests*	**SHIN**·RIN シン·リン
森林学	forest + grove + study = *forestry*	**SHIN**·RIN·GAKU シン·リン·ガク

SAMPLE SENTENCE
森 に 入る 時 は 注意 して 下さい。
mori ni hai·ru toki wa CHŪ·I shite kuda·sai.
forest enter time attention do please
= *Please be careful when going into the forest.*

WRITING PRACTICE

KANJI 183

CLOUD

BUILDING THIS KANJI
Rain 雨(90) + **SPY** 云 = 雲

MEANING

Cloud.

REMEMBERING THIS KANJI

Rain and **spies** are intimately connected with CLOUDS; **rain** for obvious reasons, and **spies** because of their need to operate in CLOUDS of secrecy. These are likely cumulonimbus as opposed to cirrus CLOUDS, though, as the latter are too wispy to provide much cover.

COMMON PRONUNCIATIONS

Common **ON** reading: **UN** (ウン)
Common **kun** reading: **kumo** (くも)

The **kun-yomi** often becomes voiced when not in first position, as here in the second and third compounds.

kun-yomi suggestion: "**coo Mo**zart"

Create your **on-yomi** keyword and enter it in the table at the back of the book. After that, write your sentence to remember the **on-yomi** and **kun-yomi** readings in the box below.

LESS COMMON PRONUNCIATIONS

Less common **ON** reading: none
Less common **kun** reading: none

COMMON WORDS AND COMPOUNDS		
雲	*cloud*	**kumo** くも
雨雲	rain + cloud = *rain cloud*	ama·**gumo** あま·ぐも
雪雲	snow + cloud = *snow cloud*	yuki·**gumo** ゆき·ぐも
星雲	star + cloud = *nebula*	SEI·**UN** セイ·ウン
雲海	cloud + sea = *sea of clouds*	**UN**·KAI ウン·カイ

SAMPLE SENTENCE

雨雲 が 村 の 上 に 掛かって います。

ama·gumo ga mura no ue ni ka·katte imasu.

rain clouds / village / upper / are hanging

= *Rain clouds are hanging over the village.*

WRITING PRACTICE

KANJI 184

BLACK

丨	冂	冃	日	甲	甲	里	里	里
黒	黒							

BUILDING THIS KANJI
Hamlet 里 (180) + **Gas Stove** 灬 = 黒

MEANING
Black.

REMEMBERING THIS KANJI
The introduction of **gas stoves** was problematic for our **hamlet**; nobody was sure how to cook with them, and a lot of food was burnt beyond recognition. The inevitable result was that BLACK smoke drifted everywhere, covering the landscape and **hamlet** with soot. Residents began to grumble. "We should go back to the old ways," some said, "because these **gas stoves** are nothing but trouble. It was a BLACK day when they arrived here".

COMMON PRONUNCIATIONS
Common **ON** reading: **KOKU** (コク)
Common **kun** reading: **kuro** (くろ)

With the exception of the third example, the **kun-yomi** is always voiced in the second position (as it appears in the fourth compound).

kun-yomi suggestion: "**coo ro**sily"

Create your **on-yomi** keyword and enter it in the table at the back of the book. After that, write your sentence to remember the **on-yomi** and **kun-yomi** readings in the box below.

LESS COMMON PRONUNCIATIONS
Less common **ON** reading: none
Less common **kun** reading: none

COMMON WORDS AND COMPOUNDS		
黒	*black (noun)*	**kuro** くろ
黒い	*black (adjective)*	**kuro**·i くろ·い
白黒	white + black = *black-and-white*	shiro·**kuro** しろ·くろ
赤黒い	red + black = *dark red*	aka **guro**·i あか ぐろ·い
黒人	black + person = *a black person*	**KOKU**·JIN コク·ジン

SAMPLE SENTENCE

この 黒い 馬 は 美しい です ね。
kono kuro·i uma wa utsuku·shii desu ne.
this black horse beautiful isn't it
= *This black horse is beautiful, isn't it?*

WRITING PRACTICE

KANJI 185

MIX

丶	亠	亣	六	亣	交			

BUILDING THIS KANJI
Police 亠 + **Father** 父(79) = 交

MEANING

This character conveys a general sense of things mixing in both physical and figurative ways ("associating" with people or "exchanging" words are examples of the latter).

REMEMBERING THIS KANJI

My **father** was a **police** officer who enjoyed throwing MIXERS. Such occasions would always draw an interesting MIX of ranks: corporals, constables, inspectors…they all attended. My **father**, however, would not let anyone else MIX the drinks. "The last thing anyone wants," he said to me, "is a MIX-up with all these guns around."

COMMON PRONUNCIATIONS

Common **ON** reading: **KŌ** (コウ)
Common **kun** reading: **ma** (ま)

kun-yomi suggestion: "**ma**tch"

Create your **on-yomi** keyword and enter it in the table at the back of the book. After that, write your sentence to remember the **on-yomi** and **kun-yomi** readings in the box below.

LESS COMMON PRONUNCIATIONS

Less common **ON** reading: none
Less common **kun** readings: **maji** (まじ); **ka** (か)

COMMON WORDS AND COMPOUNDS		
交ざる (intr)	*to mingle*	**ma**·zaru まざる
交ぜる (tr)	*to mix (something)*	**ma**·zeru まぜる
外交	outside + mix = *foreign policy*	GAI·**KŌ** ガイ·コウ

SAMPLE SENTENCE

あの 国 の 外交 が 分かりません。
ano kuni no GAI·KŌ ga wa·karimasen.
that country foreign policy don't understand
= (I) don't understand that country's foreign policy.

WRITING PRACTICE

KANJI 186

NOT

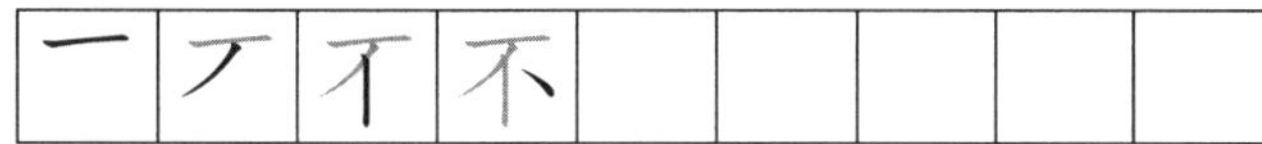

MEANING

Expressing the idea of "not" or "un-", this is an important negating prefix in Japanese.

REMEMBERING THIS KANJI

What is this, you ask? Well, it's NOT a superhero, it's NOT a giraffe, and it's NOT a figure skater. It's just… NOT like anything, really.

COMMON PRONUNCIATIONS

Common **ON** reading: **FU** (フ)
Common **kun** reading: none

Note how this kanji can function as a prefix with complete words, as it does below in the final example [the base compound for this word (親切) was presented in Entry 118].

Create your **on-yomi** keyword and enter it in the table at the back of the book. After that, write your sentence to remember the **on-yomi** reading in the box below.

LESS COMMON PRONUNCIATIONS

Less common **ON** reading: **BU** (ブ)
Less common **kun** readings: none

COMMON WORDS AND COMPOUNDS		
不意	not + mind = *unexpectedly*	**FU·I** フ·イ
不安	not + ease = *uneasy*	**FU·AN** フ·アン
不明	not + bright = *unclear*	**FU·MEI** フ·メイ
不死	not + death = *immortal*	**FU·SHI** フ·シ
不親切	not + parent + cut = *unkind*	**FU·SHIN·SETSU** フ·シン·セツ

SAMPLE SENTENCE

小林さん の 意図 は 不明 です。
Ko·bayashi·san no I·TO wa FU·MEI desu.
Kobayashi-san aim unclear
= *Kobayashi-san's aim is unclear.*

WRITING PRACTICE

COMPONENT 187

FRUSTRATION  

As will be seen in the following entry, this component is written with three strokes.

KANJI 187

 **AFTER**

BUILDING THIS KANJI
Razor 彳 + **Frustration** 幺 + **Running Chicken** 夂 = 後

MEANING

After/Later/Behind. These meanings apply to the ideas of both physical location and time.

REMEMBERING THIS KANJI

A butcher's lament:

"Am I **frustrated**? Yeah, I'm **frustrated**. I just spent an hour chasing AFTER a **running chicken** with a **razor**. Why? 'Cause a customer wanted shaved chicken, that's why! And then AFTER I got it for them, they complained about the taste of the AFTER shave!"

COMMON PRONUNCIATIONS

Common **ON** readings: **KŌ** (コウ); **GO** (ゴ)
Common **kun** readings: **ato** (あと); **ushi** (うし)

This can be a tough character to master, but is not as fearsome as might be expected given its many readings. Look for **KŌ** in the first position; **ato** and **ushi·ro** (this reading is always accompanied by **ro**) appear far less frequently here, and **GO** pops up in only a few words. In second position, morever, the reading will invariably be **GO**.

It is worth having another look at the compounds for "前" in Chapter 7 (Entry 133), to see how the fourth, fifth and sixth examples given there "pair up" with the three below.

kun-yomi suggestions: "**at O**klahoma"; "**Ooh, she**…"

Create your **on-yomi** keyword and enter it in the table at the back of the book. After that, write your sentence to remember the **on-yomi** and **kun-yomi** readings in the box below.

LESS COMMON PRONUNCIATIONS

Less common **ON** reading: none
Less common **kun** readings: **nochi** (のち); **oku** (おく)

COMMON WORDS AND COMPOUNDS		
後	*after*	**ato** あと
後ろ	*behind*	**ushi**·ro うし·ろ
後年	after + year = *in later years*	**KŌ**·NEN コウ·ネン
後半	after + half = *second half*	**KŌ**·HAN コウ·ハン
後者	after + individual = *the latter*	**KŌ**·SHA コウ·シャ
午後	noon + after = *P.M.; afternoon*	GO·**GO** ゴ·ゴ

SAMPLE SENTENCE

後 で 友人 と 東京 へ 行きます。
ato de YŪ·JIN to TŌ·KYŌ e i·kimasu.
after friend with Tokyo go
= *Afterward, I'll go to Tokyo with a friend.*

WRITING PRACTICE

KANJI 188

MOST

BUILDING THIS KANJI
Sun 日(6) + **Take** 取(174) = 最

MEANING
Most. Note how the first stroke of "ear" has been lengthened.

REMEMBERING THIS KANJI
So the ear was finally able to **take** the ironing board on a date, and luckily for him it turned out to be the MOST wonderful, MOST picturesque day. Not to mention the MOST romantic, too, for when the **sun** grew overly hot, the ear stretched himself out so that the ironing board would be shaded. He really was a MOST chivalrous ear when it came to **taking** care of a date.

COMMON PRONUNCIATIONS
Common **ON** reading: **SAI** (サイ)
Common **kun** reading: none

Create your **on-yomi** keyword and enter it in the table at the back of the book. After that, write your sentence to remember the **on-yomi** reading in the box below.

LESS COMMON PRONUNCIATIONS
Less common **ON** reading: none
Less common **kun** readings: **motto** (もっと); **mo** (も)

COMMON WORDS AND COMPOUNDS		
最小	most + small = *smallest*	**SAI**·SHŌ サイ・ショウ
最少	most + few = *fewest*	**SAI**·SHŌ サイ・ショウ
最高	most + tall = *highest; the best*	**SAI**·KŌ サイ・コウ
最古	most + old = *oldest*	**SAI**·KO サイ・コ
最新	most + new = *newest*	**SAI**·SHIN サイ・シン
最後	most + after = *the last*	**SAI**·GO サイ・ゴ

SAMPLE SENTENCE

この 天気 は 最高 です よ。
kono TEN·KI wa SAI·KŌ desu yo.
this weather the best is
= *This weather is fantastic!*

WRITING PRACTICE

KANJI 189

FAT

一	ナ	大	太					

BUILDING THIS KANJI
Large (sumo wrestler) 大(17) + **Jelly Bean** ヽ = 太

MEANING
Fat/Thick. Note the difference between this character and "犬" (Entry 171).

REMEMBERING THIS KANJI
This is what happens when a **sumo wrestler** gets too FAT: try as he might, he can't even bend down to pick up a **jelly bean** lying between his feet.

COMMON PRONUNCIATIONS
Common **ON** reading: **TAI** (タイ)
Common **kun** reading: **futo** (ふと)

kun-yomi suggestion: "**who to**ld"

Create your **on-yomi** keyword and enter it in the table at the back of the book. After that, write your sentence to remember the **on-yomi** and **kun-yomi** readings in the box below.

LESS COMMON PRONUNCIATIONS
Less common **ON** reading: **TA** (タ)
Less common **kun** reading: none

COMMON WORDS AND COMPOUNDS		
太い	*fat; thick*	**futo**·i ふと·い
太る	*to grow fat*	**futo**·ru ふと·る
太子	fat + child *= crown prince*	**TAI**·SHI タイ·シ

SAMPLE SENTENCE

私 は 冬休み に とても 太った。
watashi wa fuyu yasu·mi ni totemo futo·tta.
I winter vacation really grew fat
= I really put on weight during winter vacation.

WRITING PRACTICE

KANJI 190

CAR

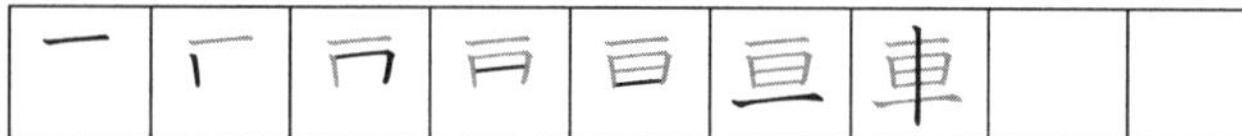

MEANING

Car. As the compounds below indicate, this character can also refer to a wide range of other vehicles. No story required.

COMMON PRONUNCIATIONS

Common **ON** reading: **SHA** (シャ)
Common **kun** reading: **kuruma** (くるま)

kun-yomi suggestion: "**coo rheuma**tism"

Create your **on-yomi** keyword and enter it in the table at the back of the book. After that, write your sentence to remember the **on-yomi** and **kun-yomi** readings in the box below.

LESS COMMON PRONUNCIATIONS

Less common **ON** reading: none
Less common **kun** reading: none

COMMON WORDS AND COMPOUNDS		
車	*car; vehicle*	**kuruma** くるま
電車	electric + car = *(electric) train*	DEN·**SHA** デン·シャ
空車	empty + car = *(taxi) "for hire"*	KŪ·**SHA** クウ·シャ
車内	car + inside = *inside the car*	**SHA**·NAI シャ·ナイ
中古車	middle + old + car = *used car*	CHŪ·KO·**SHA** チュウ·コ·シャ

SAMPLE SENTENCE

中村さん は 中古車 を 買いました。
Naka·mura-san wa CHŪ·KO·SHA o ka·imashita.
Nakamura-san used car bought
= *Nakamura-san bought a used car.*

WRITING PRACTICE

COMPONENT 191

STROLLER  

KANJI 191

 **RECEIVE**

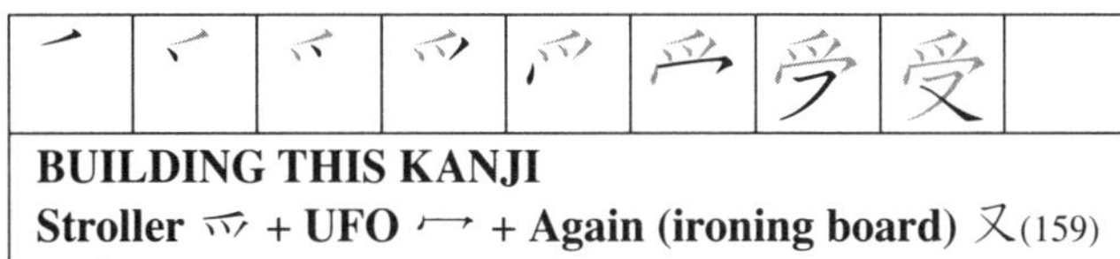

BUILDING THIS KANJI
Stroller ⺥ + UFO 冖 + Again (ironing board) 又(159) = 受

MEANING
Receive/Accept. This interesting character encompasses a wide range of meanings having to do with the idea of reception; "taking" an exam, "undergoing" an operation, or "suffering" injuries are several examples.

REMEMBERING THIS KANJI
The **ironing board** longed to have a miniature **ironing board** in the worst way, but still hadn't RECEIVED the adoption papers. As the wait dragged on, she began to have visions of a **UFO** descending with a **stroller**: "We have your **ironing board**," a voice would announce, "will you RECEIVE it?". "I will RECEIVE it, yes" she always answered, "I will".

COMMON PRONUNCIATIONS
Common **ON** reading: **JU** (ジュ)
Common **kun** reading: **u** (う)

The third and fourth examples below show this to be another kanji sharing the pronunciation characteristics of 買.

kun-yomi suggestion: "**oo**long tea"

Create your **on-yomi** keyword and enter it in the table at the back of the book. After that, write your sentence to remember the **on-yomi** and **kun-yomi** readings in the box below.

LESS COMMON PRONUNCIATIONS
Less common **ON** reading: none
Less common **kun** reading: none

COMMON WORDS AND COMPOUNDS		
受ける	*to receive; to accept*	**u**·keru う·ける
受け取る	receive + take = *to receive*	**u**·ke to·ru う·け と·る
受取	receive + take = *receipt*	**uke**·tori うけ·とり
受取人	receive + take + person = *recipient*	**uke**·tori·NIN うけ·とり·ニン
引き受ける	pull + receive = *to undertake*	hi·ki **u**·keru ひ·き う·ける
受注	receive + pour = *receipt of an order*	**JU**·CHŪ ジュ·チュウ

SAMPLE SENTENCE

田中さん は 新しい 本 を受け取りました。
Ta·naka-san wa atara·shii HON o u·ke to·rimashita.
Tanaka-san new book received
= *Tanaka-san received a new book.*

WRITING PRACTICE

KANJI 192

EVIL

ノ	メ	凶	凶					

BUILDING THIS KANJI
Banana Peels メ + Garbage Can 凵 = 凶

MEANING

Take care: this unpleasant character relates exclusively to evil and misfortune.

REMEMBERING THIS KANJI

EVIL comes in all forms. Environmentalists, for example, regard **banana peels** in a **garbage can** as EVIL, as this is a telltale sign of someone being uninterested in composting.

COMMON PRONUNCIATIONS

Common **ON** reading: **KYŌ** (キョウ)
Common **kun** reading: none

Create your **on-yomi** keyword and enter it in the table at the back of the book. After that, write your sentence to remember the **on-yomi** reading in the box below.

LESS COMMON PRONUNCIATIONS

Less common **ON** reading: none
Less common **kun** reading: none

COMMON WORDS AND COMPOUNDS		
凶年	evil + year = *a bad year*	**KYŌ**·NEN キョウ·ネン
凶行	evil + go = *violence*	**KYŌ**·KŌ キョウ·コウ

SAMPLE SENTENCE

凶年 だ そう です。
KYŌ·NEN da sō desu.
bad year seems
= *Apparently it's a bad year.*

WRITING PRACTICE

KANJI 193

SEA

丶	冫	氵	氵	氵	汇	氵	海	海

BUILDING THIS KANJI
Splash 氵 + **Every** 毎(168) = 海

MEANING
Sea.

REMEMBERING THIS KANJI
Q. Which SEA **splashes every** shoreline in the Caribbean?
A. a) The SEA of Confusion?
b) The SEA of Tranquility?
c) The Caribbean SEA?

COMMON PRONUNCIATIONS
Common **ON** reading: **KAI** (カイ)
Common **kun** reading: **umi** (うみ)

Recall that the fifth example below was presented early in Chapter 2; we've come a long way since then!

kun-yomi suggestion: "**to me**"

Create your **on-yomi** keyword and enter it in the table at the back of the book. After that, write your sentence to remember the **on-yomi** and **kun-yomi** readings in the box below.

LESS COMMON PRONUNCIATIONS
Less common **ON** reading: none
Less common **kun** reading: none

COMMON WORDS AND COMPOUNDS		
海	*sea*	**umi** うみ
海水	sea + water = *sea water*	**KAI**·SUI カイ·スイ
海図	sea + diagram = *nautical chart*	**KAI**·ZU カイ·ズ
雲海	cloud + sea = *sea of clouds*	UN·**KAI** ウン·カイ
海王星	sea + king + star = *Neptune (planet)*	**KAI**·Ō·SEI カイ·オウ·セイ
北海道	north + sea + road = *Hokkaido*	HOK·**KAI**·DŌ ホッ·カイ·ドウ

SAMPLE SENTENCE

夏休み に 北海道 へ 行きました。
natsu yasu·mi ni HOK·KAI·DŌ e i·kimashita.
summer vacation Hokkaido went
= *(We) went to Hokkaido for summer vacation.*

WRITING PRACTICE

KANJI 194

SCHOOL

一	十	才	木	木'	木亠	木亠'	木六	木六ノ
校								

BUILDING THIS KANJI
Tree 木(13) + **Mix** 交(185) = 校

MEANING

School. A secondary meaning related to "proofreading" shows up in only a few compounds.

REMEMBERING THIS KANJI

When **trees** attend SCHOOL, they are often required to **mix** with other species. This can be problematic; maple **trees** refuse to take exams with evergreens, for example, and thus drag down test scores for the SCHOOL as a whole. This, as we know, is a traditional source of tension; when it comes to SCHOOL, some argue, coniferous and deciduous **trees** simply cannot **mix**.

COMMON PRONUNCIATIONS

Common **ON** reading: **KŌ** (コウ)
Common **kun** reading: none

Note how "学" in the second example "doubles up" with 校, and how this remains constant in the other compounds in which this word occurs.

Create your **on-yomi** keyword and enter it in the table at the back of the book. After that, write your sentence to remember the **on-yomi** reading in the box below.

LESS COMMON PRONUNCIATIONS

Less common **ON** reading: none
Less common **kun** reading: none

COMMON WORDS AND COMPOUNDS		
校外	school + outside = *off-campus*	**KŌ**·GAI コウ·ガイ
学校	study + school = *school*	GAK·**KŌ** ガッ·コウ
小学校	small + study + school = *elementary school*	SHŌ·GAK·**KŌ** ショウ·ガッ·コウ
中学校	middle + study + school = *junior high school*	CHŪ·GAK·**KŌ** チュウ·ガッ·コウ
高校	tall + school = *high school*	KŌ·**KŌ** コウ·コウ
女学校	woman + study + school = *girls' school*	JO·GAK·**KŌ** ジョ·ガッ·コウ

SAMPLE SENTENCE

あの 女 の 子 は 高校
ano onna no ko wa KŌ·KŌ
that woman child high school
二年生 です。
NI·NEN·SEI desu.
second year student
= *That girl is a second-year high school student.*

WRITING PRACTICE

KANJI 195

LEG

						足		

BUILDING THIS KANJI
Mouth (vampire) 口(8) + **Good Figure Skater** ⺊ + **Person** 人(2) = 足

MEANING

Confusingly for English speakers, this character can signify both "leg" and "foot". A secondary meaning relates to the sense of "suffice".

REMEMBERING THIS KANJI

Even a **good figure skater** can mess up on occasion, and the kanji here provides an example of this happening. The steps are easy to follow: 1. **Vampire** flies onto **good figure skater**; 2. Figure skater is distracted, lands awkwardly on the **person** skating with her (this takes place during a pairs competition); 3. Said **person** breaks LEG.

COMMON PRONUNCIATIONS

Common **ON** reading: **SOKU** (ソク)
Common **kun** reading: **ashi** (あし)

Note that "取" is voiced in the fouth example.

kun-yomi suggestion: "**ash eat**ing"

Create your **on-yomi** keyword and enter it in the table at the back of the book. After that, write your sentence to remember the **on-yomi** and **kun-yomi** readings in the box below.

LESS COMMON PRONUNCIATIONS

Less common **ON** reading: none
Less common **kun** reading: **ta** (た)

IRREGULAR READING		
裸足*	naked + leg = *barefoot*	**hadashi** はだし

COMMON WORDS AND COMPOUNDS		
足	*leg; foot*	**ashi** あし
足首	leg + neck = *ankle*	**ashi**·kubi あし·くび
足音	leg + sound = *sound of footsteps*	**ashi**·oto あし·おと
足取り	leg + take = *one's gait*	**ashi** do·ri あし ど·り
土足	earth + leg = *with shoes on*	DO·**SOKU** ド·ソク
足元注意	leg + basis + pour + mind = *"watch your step"*	**ashi**·moto·CHŪ·I あし·もと·チュウ·イ

SAMPLE SENTENCE

足音 を 聞きました か。
ashi·oto o ki·kimashita ka.
sound of footsteps heard
= *Did you hear footsteps?*

WRITING PRACTICE

COMPONENT 196

TRIPOD ノ|ヽ 

KANJI 196

糸 THREAD

く	幺	幺	糸	糸	糸			

BUILDING THIS KANJI
Frustration 幺 + **Tripod** ノ|ヽ = 糸

MEANING
Thread. You will become very familiar with this character over time; it appears as a component in more than sixty other kanji.

REMEMBERING THIS KANJI
If you want to get a sense of **frustration**, try doing anything with a **tripod** made out of THREAD. The moment you use it with a camera, the THREAD collapses and ruins your shot. As a support for painting, though, it's even worse: the **tripod** falls over and leaves a bunch of THREAD stuck in your masterpiece.

COMMON PRONUNCIATIONS
Common **ON** reading: none
Common **kun** reading: **ito** (いと)

Note that "口" is voiced in the second example.

kun-yomi suggestion: "**eat o**nly"

Create your sentence to remember the **kun-yomi** reading in the box below.

LESS COMMON PRONUNCIATIONS
Less common **ON** reading: **SHI** (シ)
Less common **kun** reading: none

COMMON WORDS AND COMPOUNDS		
糸	*thread*	**ito** いと
糸口	thread + mouth = *beginning; clue*	**ito**·guchi いと·ぐち

SAMPLE SENTENCE

青い　糸　が　あります　か。
ao·i ito ga arimasu ka.
blue thread is
= Is there any blue thread?

WRITING PRACTICE

KANJI 197

SAME

丨	冂	冂	冂	同	同			

BUILDING THIS KANJI
Gorilla 冂 **+ One (hamburger patty)** 一(3) +
Mouth (vampire) 口(8) = 同

MEANING
Same.

REMEMBERING THIS KANJI
As a vegetarian, a **gorilla's** diet is always the SAME: fruits, nuts and berries. A **vampire**, too, is only interested in having the SAME meal over and over: the blood of living creatures. It should come as no surprise, therefore, that a **gorilla** and **vampire** will react the SAME way if a **hamburger patty is placed between them** – neither will want it.

COMMON PRONUNCIATIONS
Common **ON** reading: **DŌ** (ドウ)
Common **kun** reading: **ona** (おな)

Remember that **ona** (おな) differs from **onna** (おんな), a reading for "女" in Entry 16.

kun-yomi suggestion: "**o, na**sty!"

Create your **on-yomi** keyword and enter it in the table at the back of the book. After that, write your sentence to remember the **on-yomi** and **kun-yomi** readings in the box below.

LESS COMMON PRONUNCIATIONS
Less common **ON** reading: none
Less common **kun** reading: none

COMMON WORDS AND COMPOUNDS		
同じ	*same*	**ona**·ji おな·じ
同意	same + mind = *agreement*	**DŌ**·I ドウ·イ
同一	same + one = *identical*	**DŌ**·ITSU ドウ·イツ
同時	same + time = *simultaneous*	**DŌ**·JI ドウ·ジ
同化	same + change = *assimilation*	**DŌ**·KA ドウ·カ
同行者	same + go + individual = *traveling companion*	**DŌ**·KŌ·SHA ドウ·コウ·シャ

SAMPLE SENTENCE

私 と 中村さん は 同時 に
watashi to Naka·mura-san wa DŌ·JI ni
I Nakamura-san simultaneous
来ました。
ki·mashita.
came
= *Nakamura-san and I arrived at the same time.*

WRITING PRACTICE

KANJI 198

NOON

ノ	𠂉	二	午					

BUILDING THIS KANJI
Hammer 𠂉 + Ten (scarecrow) 十(28) = 午

MEANING
Noon.

REMEMBERING THIS KANJI
Everyone feels sorry for a **scarecrow** at NOON, as NOON is when the heat starts to pound on him like a **hammer**.

COMMON PRONUNCIATIONS
Common **ON** reading: **GO** (ゴ)
Common **kun** reading: none

Create your **on-yomi** keyword and enter it in the table at the back of the book. After that, write your sentence to remember the **on-yomi** reading in the box below.

LESS COMMON PRONUNCIATIONS
Less common **ON** reading: none
Less common **kun** reading: none

COMMON WORDS AND COMPOUNDS		
午前	noon + before = *A.M.; morning*	**GO**·ZEN ゴ·ゼン
午後	noon + after = *P.M.; afternoon*	**GO**·GO ゴ·ゴ
午前中	noon + before + middle = *all morning*	**GO**·ZEN·CHŪ ゴ·ゼン·チュウ

SAMPLE SENTENCE
午前 八時 に 高校 へ 行きます。
GO·ZEN HACHI·JI ni KŌ·KŌ e i·kimasu.
A.M. eight o'clock high school go
= I go to high school at 8 A.M.

WRITING PRACTICE

KANJI 199

LOVE

BUILDING THIS KANJI
Stroller ⺫ + **UFO** 冖 + **Heart** 心(25) +
Running Chicken 夂 = 愛

MEANING

Love. After an entry for "evil", space had to be made for this character!

REMEMBERING THIS KANJI

LOVE, as we know, is profound, and the components in this kanji all have a connection to its secrets. A **stroller** can be filled through LOVE, a **UFO** is as mysterious as LOVE, a **heart** is the symbol of LOVE, and a **running chicken**… well, a **running chicken** has clearly been set free by someone who LOVES chickens.

COMMON PRONUNCIATIONS

Common **ON** reading: **AI** (アイ)
Common **kun** reading: none

Create your **on-yomi** keyword and enter it in the table at the back of the book. After that, write your sentence to remember the **on-yomi** reading in the box below.

LESS COMMON PRONUNCIATIONS

Less common **ON** reading: none
Less common **kun** reading: none

The following is a very common irregular reading.

IRREGULAR READING		
可愛い*	possible + love = *cute*	KA·**WAI**·i カ·ワイ·い

COMMON WORDS AND COMPOUNDS		
愛好	love + like = *love; like*	**AI**·KŌ アイ·コウ
愛犬	love + dog = *pet dog*	**AI**·KEN アイ·ケン
愛犬家	love + dog + house = *dog lover*	**AI**·KEN·KA アイ·ケン·カ
愛鳥家	love + bird + house = *bird lover*	**AI**·CHŌ·KA アイ·チョウ·カ
愛国心	love + country + heart = *patriotism*	**AI**·KOKU·SHIN アイ·コク·シン

SAMPLE SENTENCE

本田さん　は　愛鳥家　として　有名　です。
Hon·da-san wa AI·CHŌ·KA toshite YŪ·MEI desu.
Honda-san　bird lover　as　famous
= *Honda-san is famous as a bird lover.*

WRITING PRACTICE

KANJI 200

SEPARATE

BUILDING THIS KANJI
Police 亠 + **Evil** 凶(192) + **Gorilla** 冂 +
Broken Crutch 厶 + **Squirrels** 隹 = 離

MEANING
Separate/Leave. This is one the most complicated-looking of all the kanji, but as you are now familiar with each its components, even a ferocious character like this can be tackled with confidence.

REMEMBERING THIS KANJI
A warning: *never* try to SEPARATE the **squirrels**, as they will offer violent resistance should you try. The **police** once made an effort, of course, but the **squirrels** SEPARATED them from their weapons and committed an act of such unspeakable **evil** that it cannot be related here. The **police** then sent in a **gorilla** to do their dirty work, but as the **broken crutch** indicates, this maneuver failed miserably as well. In the end, everyone was forced to agree that it was best not to SEPARATE the **squirrels** at all.

COMMON PRONUNCIATIONS
Common **ON** reading: **RI** (リ)
Common **kun** reading: **hana** (はな)

Note how the reading of this character has become voiced in the third compound.

kun-yomi suggestions: "**Han a**mulet"

Create your **on-yomi** keyword and enter it in the table at the back of the book. After that, write your sentence to remember the **on-yomi** and **kun-yomi** readings in the box below.

LESS COMMON PRONUNCIATIONS
Less common **ON** reading: none
Less common **kun** reading: none

COMMON WORDS AND COMPOUNDS		
離れる (intr)	*to separate; to leave*	**hana**·reru はな·れる
離す (tr)	*to separate (something)*	**hana**·su はな·す
離れ離れ	separate + separate = *scattered; separated*	**hana**·re **bana**·re はな·れ ばな·れ
切り離す	cut + separate = *to cut off*	ki·ri **hana**·su き·り はな·す
分離	part + separate = *separation*	BUN·**RI** ブン·リ
離村	separate + village = *rural exodus*	**RI**·SON リ·ソン

SAMPLE SENTENCE

山 で その 親子 は 離れ離れ
yama de sono oya·ko wa hana·re bana·re
mountain that parent and child separated
に なってしまいました。
ni natte shimaimashita.
ended up

= *That parent and child ended up getting separated on the mountain.*

WRITING PRACTICE

CHAPTER 10 REVIEW EXERCISES

A. Please match the following kanji to their meanings.

1. 雲 a. Separate
2. 午 b. After
3. 交 c. Sea
4. 後 d. Same
5. 海 e. Mix
6. 太 f. Black
7. 離 g. Receive
8. 受 h. Cloud
9. 黒 i. Noon
10. 同 j. Fat

B. Please match the following meanings to their kanji, and these to their **on** or **kun-yomi**.

1. Not	a. 林	1. **SAI** (サイ)
2. School	b. 最	2. **ashi** (あし)
3. Grove	c. 足	3. **KŌ** (コウ)
4. Car	d. 不	4. **mori** (もり)
5. Love	e. 凶	5. **AI** (アイ)
6. Leg	f. 糸	6. **hayashi** (はやし)
7. Forest	g. 車	7. **KYŌ** (キョウ)
8. Evil	h. 愛	8. **ito** (いと)
9. Most	i. 森	9. **FU** (フ)
10. Thread	j. 校	10. **kuruma** (くるま)

C. Please choose the best answer(s) to the following questions.

1. Which of the following readings apply to the kanji 離?
   a. **YŪ** (ユウ)
   b. **mori** (もり)
   c. **RYŌ** (リョウ)
   d. **hana** (はな)
   e. **RI** (リ)

2. Which of the following readings apply to the kanji 太?
   a. **futo** (ふと)
   b. **DAI** (ダイ)
   c. **inu** (いぬ)
   d. **TA** (タ)
   e. **ō** (おお)

3. I was going to win the marathon, but got a massive cramp in my ____.
   a. 雲
   b. 車
   c. 森
   d. 愛
   e. 足

4. Which of the following readings apply to the kanji 海?
   a. **mizu** (みず)
   b. **umi** (うみ)
   c. **KAI** (カイ)
   d. **kawa** (かわ)
   e. **KŌ** (コウ)

5. Which of the following readings apply to the kanji 後?
   a. **ushi** (うし)
   b. **KŌ** (コウ)
   c. **SHŌ** (ショウ)
   d. **ato** (あと)
   e. **GO** (ゴ)

D. Please choose the best answer(s) to the following questions.

1. . Which is the correct reading of 交ぜる?
   a. **ora·zeru** (おら·ぜる)
   b. **ko·zeru** (こ·ぜる)
   c. **ma·zeru** (ま·ぜる)
   d. **a·zeru** (あ·ぜる)

2. Which is the correct reading of 同じ?
   a. **ona·ji** (おな·じ)
   b. **ara·ji** (あら·じ)
   c. **aka·ji** (あか·じ)
   d. **u·ji** (う·じ)

3. Which of the following kanji has the most number of strokes?
   a. 後
   b. 雲
   c. 最
   d. 愛
   e. 黒

4. Which is the correct reading of 受ける?
   a. **a·keru** (あ·ける)
   b. **u·keru** (う·ける)
   c. **tata·keru** (たた·ける)
   d. **oda·keru** (おだ·ける)

5. Which is the correct reading of 黒い?
   a. **shiro·i** (しろ·い)
   b. **ao·i** (あお·い)
   c. **aka·i** (あか·い)
   d. **kuro·i** (くろ·い)

E. Please match the following compounds and words to their meanings and pronunciations.

1. 分離	a. Smallest	1. **DŌ·I** (ドウ·イ)
2. 赤黒い	b. To undertake	2. **ashi·kubi** (あし·くび)
3. 同意	c. Afternoon	3. **KAI·Ō·SEI** (カイ·オウ·セイ)
4. 海王星	d. Unclear	4. **GO·GO** (ゴ·ゴ)
5. 引き受ける	e. Agreement	5. **KŌ·KŌ** (コウ·コウ)
6. 最小	f. High school	6. **SAI·SHŌ** (サイ·ショウ)
7. 足首	g. Neptune (planet)	7. **BUN·RI** (ブン·リ)
8. 不明	h. Dark red	8. **hi·ki u·keru** (ひ·き う·ける)
9. 午後	i. Separation	9. **FU·MEI** (フ·メイ)
10. 高校	j. Ankle	10. **aka guro·i** (あか ぐろ·い)

CUMULATIVE REVIEW EXERCISES FOR CHAPTERS 1 - 10

A. Please match the following kanji to their meanings.

1. 家		a. Electric
2. 干		b. Country
3. 先		c. Mother
4. 母		d. Spirit
5. 空		e. Dry
6. 国		f. House
7. 太		g. Precede
8. 有		h. Fat
9. 電		i. Empty
10. 気		j. Have

B. Which kanji does not belong in the group?

1. a. 日	b. 週	c. 年	d. 首	e. 秒
2. a. 赤	b. 外	c. 青	d. 白	e. 黒
3. a. 春	b. 秋	c. 注	d. 冬	e. 夏
4. a. 市	b. 里	c. 高	d. 町	e. 村
5. a. 金	b. 馬	c. 牛	d. 鳥	e. 犬
6. a. 東	b. 南	c. 西	d. 北	e. 干
7. a. 舌	b. 売	c. 目	d. 足	e. 耳
8. a. 鳥	b. 午	c. 夕	d. 朝	e. 夜
9. a. 車	b. 寺	c. 門	d. 花	e. 道
10. a. 美	b. 好	c. 愛	d. 天	e. 凶

C. Identify the kanji having the most number of strokes.

1. a. 出	b. 主	c. 右	d. 央	e. 百
2. a. 車	b. 学	c. 持	d. 押	e. 周
3. a. 道	b. 週	c. 桜	d. 黒	e. 校
4. a. 字	b. 図	c. 来	d. 英	e. 糸
5. a. 秋	b. 思	c. 書	d. 品	e. 前
6. a. 雲	b. 鳥	c. 開	d. 新	e. 朝
7. a. 年	b. 私	c. 気	d. 甲	e. 母
8. a. 注	b. 夜	c. 音	d. 訓	e. 具
9. a. 掛	b. 時	c. 雪	d. 海	e. 最
10. a. 親	b. 離	c. 読	d. 語	e. 一

D. Please list the following kanji in the order indicated (alphabetical).

1. Dog / Fat / Heaven / Large / Lose
   a. 大　　d. 天
   b. 犬　　e. 失
   c. 太

2. Come / Half / Mix / Rice / Tree
   a. 来　　d. 半
   b. 米　　e. 交
   c. 木

3. Block / Dry / Noon / Not / Thousand
   a. 午　　d. 不
   b. 干　　e. 千
   c. 丁

4. Father / Heaven / Mix / School / Stand
   a. 天　　d. 校
   b. 交　　e. 立
   c. 父

5. Complete / Jewel / King / Pour / Primary
   a. 主　d. 王
   b. 注　e. 全
   c. 玉

6. Basis / Meet / Part / Public / Same
   a. 同　d. 会
   b. 公　e. 元
   c. 分

7. Precede / Read / Receive / Red / Sell
   a. 受　d. 読
   b. 売　e. 赤
   c. 先

8. Mind / New / Parent / Sound / Stand
   a. 親　d. 意
   b. 新　e. 立
   c. 音

9. Character / City / Ease / House / Study
   a. 学　d. 家
   b. 字　e. 市
   c. 安

10. Buy / Neck / Road / Shellfish / Tool
   a. 具　d. 買
   b. 道　e. 貝
   c. 首

E. Please choose the best answer to the following questions.

1. I often see monks when I walk past that ____.
   a. 星　d. 電
   b. 馬　e. 寺
   c. 足

2. The samurai made a menacing gesture with his ___.
   a. 花　d. 川
   b. 車　e. 牛
   c. 刀

3. What is the worst thing to find waiting for you on your doorstep?
   a. 金　d. 鳥
   b. 品　e. 死
   c. 親

4. Romeo was troubled. How could he demonstrate his ___ for Juliet?
   a. 凶　d. 愛
   b. 太　e. 田
   c. 具

5. It's so quiet and peaceful in the middle of this ___!
   a. 森　d. 肉
   b. 犬　e. 火
   c. 月

F. Please choose the best answer(s) to the following questions.

1. As 小 is to 大, 少 is to ___.
   a. 多　d. 外
   b. 人　e. 主
   c. 名

2. As 読 is to 書, 押 is to ___.
   a. 有　d. 引
   b. 交　e. 休
   c. 買

3. As 内 is to 外, 私 is to ___.
   a. 毎　d. 元
   b. 公　e. 取
   c. 不

4. As 上 is to 下, 前 is to ___.
   a. 本　d. 山
   b. 生　e. 後
   c. 最

5. As 林 is to 森, 好 is to ___.
   a. 赤　d. 先
   b. 愛　e. 図
   c. 心

G. Please choose the best answer to the following questions.

1. Which is the correct reading of 行く?
   a. **a·ku** (あ·く)
   b. **i·ku** (い·く)
   c. **fu·ku** (ふ·く)
   d. **ta·ku** (た·く)

2. Which is the correct reading of 切る?
   a. **tabe·ru** (たべ·る)
   b. **ino·ru** (いの·る)
   c. **a·ru** (あ·る)
   d. **ki·ru** (き·る)

3. Which is the correct reading of 会う?
   a. **a·u** (あ·う)
   b. **o·u** (お·う)
   c. **muka·u** (むか·う)
   d. **i·u** (い·う)

4. Which is the correct reading of 近い?
   a. **chika·i** (ちか·い)
   b. **ao·i** (あお·い)
   c. **kata·i** (かた·い)
   d. **aka·i** (あか·い)

5. Which is the correct reading of 話す?
   a. **wata·su** (わた·す)
   b. **furu·su** (ふる·す)
   c. **hana·su** (はな·す)
   d. **ta·su** (た·す)

6. Which is the correct reading of 赤い?
   a. **furu·i** (ふる·い)
   b. **taka·i** (たか·い)
   c. **ō·i** (おお·い)
   d. **aka·i** (あか·い)

7. Which is the correct reading of 少し?
   a. **suko·shi** (すこ·し)
   b. **haya·shi** (はや·し)
   c. **ara·shi** (あら·し)
   d. **hana·shi** (はな·し)

8. Which is the correct reading of 古い?
   a. **kuro·i** (くろ·い)
   b. **shiro·i** (しろ·い)
   c. **furu·i** (ふる·い)
   d. **usu·i** (うす·い)

9. Which is the correct reading of 聞く?
   a. **hi·ku** (ひ·く)
   b. **ki·ku** (き·く)
   c. **a·ku** (あ·く)
   d. **ara·ku** (あら·く)

10. Which is the correct reading of 押す?
   a. **hana·su** (はな·す)
   b. **u·su** (う·す)
   c. **ama·su** (あま·す)
   d. **o·su** (お·す)

H. Please match the following compounds and words to their meanings and pronunciations.

1. 有名	a. Exit	1. **TA·DOKU·KA** (タ·ドク·カ)
2. 多読家	b. Talkative	2. **NYŪ·KAI·KIN** (ニュウ·カイ·キン)
3. 出口	c. Famous	3. **BI·KA** (ビ·カ)
4. 同行者	d. The four seasons	4. **ta·chi i·ru** (た·ち い·る)
5. 書き入れる	e. "Watch Your Step"	5. **ka·ki i·reru** (か·き い·れる)
6. 午前	f. Traveling companion	6. **GAI·KŌ** (ガイ·コウ)
7. 立ち入る	g. Patriotism	7. **GO·ZEN** (ゴ·ゼン)
8. 春夏秋冬	h. Well-read person	8. **YŪ·MEI** (ユウ·メイ)
9. 美化	i. Beautification	9. **hana·shi zu·ki** (はな·し ず·き)
10. 足元注意	j. Fireworks	10. **hana·bi** (はな·び)
11. 外交	k. Morning (a.m.)	11. **de·guchi** (で·ぐち)
12. 愛国心	l. Enrollment fee	12. **SHUN·KA·SHŪ·TO** (シュン·カ·シュウ·トウ)
13. 話し好き	m. To go into	13. **AI·KOKU·SHIN** (アイ·コク·シン)
14. 入会金	n. Foreign policy	14. **DŌ·KŌ·SHA** (ドウ·コウ·シャ)
15. 花火	o. To write in	15. **ashi·moto·CHŪ·I** (あし·もと·チュウ·イ)

ANSWER KEY FOR EXERCISES

CHAPTER 1

Section A

1. e　2. c　3. g　4. i　5. b
6. f　7. a　8. j　9. h　10. d

Section B

1. g – 8　2. j – 5　3. a – 10　4. i – 7　5. b – 3
6. h – 9　7. c – 1　8. f – 2　9. d – 6　10. e – 4

Section C

1. b/c/d　2. c　3. d/e　4. a/d　5. a/c/e

Section D

1. d　2. e　3. b　4. d　5. b

Section E

1. f – 4　2. j – 9　3. a – 6　4. e – 5　5. b – 10
6. i – 2　7. h – 1　8. d – 7　9. c – 3　10. g - 8

CHAPTER 2

Section A

1. c　2. j　3. f　4. h　5. e
6. a　7. i　8. g　9. d　10. b

Section B

1. d – 10　2. f – 4　3. a – 2　4. j – 9　5. h – 1
6. b – 3　7. g – 8　8. e – 7　9. c – 6　10. i – 5

Section C

1. a/b/d　2. a/b/d/e　3. b/d　4. d　5. a/b/c/d/e

Section D

1. b　2. c　3. a　4. d　5. c

Section E

1. g – 1　2. j – 6　3. a – 10　4. f – 3　5. i – 7
6. c – 2　7. h – 9　8. d – 5　9. b – 8　10. e - 4

CHAPTER 3

Section A

1. d　2. h　3. j　4. b　5. i
6. g　7. c　8. f　9. a　10. e

Section B

1. i – 10　2. f – 2　3. d – 3　4. c – 7　5. a – 1
6. g – 8　7. b – 9　8. j – 4　9. h – 5　10. e – 6

Section C

1. a/d　2. e　3. c/d　4. a/b/d　5. b/c/d

Section D

1. b　2. b　3. a　4. c　5. d

Section E

1. d – 6　2. b – 4　3. h – 2　4. j – 7　5. c – 9
6. f – 1　7. i – 5　8. g – 10　9. e – 3　10. a – 8

CHAPTER 4

Section A

1. c　2. j　3. f　4. h　5. b
6. g　7. d　8. i　9. a　10. e

Section B

1. f – 4　2. c – 9　3. i – 2　4. g – 8　5. a – 6
6. j – 3　7. e – 7　8. d – 1　9. h – 5　10. b – 10

Section C

1. a/b　2. b/c　3. a/d/e　4. d　5. b/e

Section D

1. d　2. b　3. c　4. d　5. a

Section E

1. c – 9　2. h – 6　3. f – 8　4. a – 3　5. j – 1
6. e – 10　7. i – 4　8. d – 7　9. g – 2　10. b – 5

CHAPTER 5

Section A

1. h　2. b　3. e　4. g　5. c
6. j　7. f　8. i　9. d　10. a

Section B

1. d – 10　2. e – 5　3. a – 1　4. j – 3　5. g – 8
6. i – 6　7. b – 4　8. f – 9　9. h – 2　10. c – 7

Section C

1.c/e　2. a/b/d　3. e　4. d　5. b/d/e

Section D

1. b 2. c 3. d 4. b 5. d

Section E

1. f – 4 2. d – 7 3. h – 3 4. a – 9 5. c – 6
6. j – 8 7. e – 10 8. g – 1 9. b – 5 10. i – 2

CUMULATIVE REVIEW FOR CHAPTERS 1 - 5

Section A

1. f 2. d 3. i 4. a 5. h
6. c 7. j 8. e 9. g 10. b

Section B

1. c (not a body part)
2. a (not a person)
3. b (not something found in nature)
4. e (not a plant or animal)
5. a (not a direction)
6. d (not a number)
7. b (not a number)
8. c (not of water)
9. a (not a verb of motion)
10. h (not one of the kanji for days of the week)

Section C

1. b 2. d 3. a 4. d 5. e
6. c 7. a 8. b 9. e 10. c

Section D

1. d/c/a/e/b 2. b/d/a/e/c
3. c/e/d/a/b 4. c/b/e/a/d
5. a/e/d/c/b 6. b/c/d/e/a
7. e/c/a/d/b 8. a/d/b/e/c
9. c/b/d/a/e 10. b/a/d/e/c

Section E

1. e 2. b 3. d 4. d 5. c

Section F

1. a/b/e 2. a/b/d/e/f/g
3. a/b/c 4. a/b/c/d/e/g
5. a/b/c/e

Section G

1. b 2. a 3. d 4. d 5. b
6. c 7. a 8. c 9. b 10. d

Section H

1. k – 3 2. e – 10 3. h – 14 4. m – 6 5. b – 12
6. f – 4 7. c – 9 8. n – 15 9. l – 7 10. g – 13
11. i – 2 12. o – 8 13. a – 5 14. j – 11 15. d – 1

CHAPTER 6

Section A

1. f 2. c 3. g 4. a 5. b
6. e 7. i 8. j 9. d 10. h

Section B

1. i – 7 2. f – 2 3. h – 6 4. c – 10 5. a – 5
6. j – 3 7. d – 8 8. e – 9 9. g – 4 10. b – 1

Section C

1.b/e 2. a/d 3. c 4. d/e 5. a/c

Section D

1. d 2. c 3. a 4. a 5. b/d

Section E

1. g – 3 2. d – 10 3. h – 1 4. j – 7 5. i – 5
6. b – 6 7. a – 4 8. e – 8 9. f – 2 10. c – 9

CHAPTER 7

Section A

1. a 2. f 3. j 4. c 5. h
6. e 7. d 8. i 9. b 10. g

Section B

1. c – 5 2. h – 4 3. f – 1 4. i – 10 5. a – 7
6. j – 3 7. b – 9 8. d – 2 9. g – 8 10. e – 6

Section C

1. b/c 2. a/e 3. c/d 4. d 5. a/e

Section D

1. b 2. d 3. c 4. a 5. a

Section E

1. i – 4 2. g – 9 3. e – 1 4. a – 7 5. c – 5
6. b – 8 7. f – 3 8. d – 10 9. j – 2 10. h – 6

CHAPTER 8

Section A

1. b 2. d 3. a 4. i 5. g
6. j 7. f 8. c 9. e 10. h

Section B

1. j – 10 2. b – 1 3. f – 9 4. h – 4 5. c – 8
6. e – 7 7. a – 5 8. i – 3 9. d – 6 10. g – 2

Section C

1. b/e 2. d 3. a/c 4. d/e 5. a/c/d

Section D

1. d 2. b 3. a 4. a 5. c

Section E

1. b – 5 2. h – 3 3. a – 9 4. f – 1 5. j – 6
6. d – 10 7. g – 8 8. i – 2 9. c – 4 10. e – 7

CHAPTER 9

Section A

1. g 2. b 3. f 4. j 5. h
6. c 7. i 8. d 9. e 10. a

Section B

1. a – 8 2. e – 4 3. i – 9 4. g – 2 5. c – 1
6. h – 10 7. f – 6 8. b – 5 9. j – 3 10. d – 7

Section C

1. a/c 2. b/e 3. b/d 4. c 5. a/b/c

Section D

1. d 2. a 3. b 4. c 5. d

Section E

1. j – 8 2. d – 3 3. g – 2 4. c – 10 5. a – 5
6. i – 9 7. h – 4 8. e – 6 9. f – 1 10. b – 7

CHAPTER 10

Section A

1. h 2. i 3. e 4. b 5. c
6. j 7. a 8. g 9. f 10. d

Section B

1. d – 9 2. j – 3 3. a – 6 4. g – 10 5. h – 5
6. c – 2 7. i – 4 8. e – 7 9. b – 1 10. f – 8

Section C

1. d/e 2. a/d 3. e 4. b/c 5. a/b/d/e

Section D

1. c 2. a 3. d 4. b 5. d

Section E

1. i – 7 2. h – 10 3. e – 1 4. g – 3 5. b – 8
6. a – 6 7. j – 2 8. d – 9 9. c – 4 10. f – 5

CUMULATIVE REVIEW FOR CHAPTERS 1 - 10

Section A

1. f 2. e 3. g 4. c 5. i
6. b 7. h 8. j 9. a 10. d

Section B

1. d (not a time measurement)
2. b (not a color)
3. c (not a season)
4. c (not a population center)
5. a (not an animal)
6. e (not a direction)
7. b (not a body part)
8. a (not a time of the day)
9. d (not a man-made object)
10. e (not a positive thing)

Section C

1. e 2. c 3. a 4. d 5. c
6. d 7. b 8. d 9. e 10. b

Section D

1. b/c/d/a/e 2. a/d/e/b/c
3. c/b/a/d/e 4. c/a/b/d/e
5. e/c/d/b/a 6. e/d/c/b/a
7. c/d/a/e/b 8. d/b/a/c/e
9. b/e/c/d/a 10. d/c/b/e/a

Section E

1. e 2. c 3. e 4. d 5. a

Section F

1. a 2. d 3. b 4. e 5. b

Section G

1. b 2. d 3. a 4. a 5. c
6. d 7. a 8. c 9. b 10. d

Section H

1. c – 8 2. h – 1 3. a – 11 4. f – 14 5. o – 5
6. k – 7 7. m – 4 8. d – 12 9. i – 3 10. e – 15
11. n – 6 12. g – 13 13. b – 9 14. l – 2 15. j – 10

INDEX 1: STROKE COUNT

1 Stroke

一 3

2 Strokes

人 2
二 4
八 19
十 28
九 39
七 44
力 63
入 94
刀 117
又 159
丁 165

3 Strokes

山 1
三 5
口 8
女 16
大 17
小 20
上 30
下 31
工 47
子 56
千 65
川 70
干 81
士 84
土 87
万 89
寸 103
夕 108
弓 143

4 Strokes

日 6
月 11
木 13
五 14
中 18
六 22
王 23
心 25
内 34
止 43
少 45
円 52
元 53
火 59
水 61
手 67
化 69
父 79
牛 100
切 118
天 123
分 124
斤 126
引 146
公 161
友 166
犬 171
不 186
太 189
凶 192
午 198

5 Strokes

白 7
四 10
目 15
玉 24
右 35
半 38
左 48
古 58
冬 60
本 68
北 72
田 73
出 98
生 99
外 109
立 112
母 130
央 140
失 142
甲 148
市 163
主 164

6 Strokes

回 9
全 27
早 29
米 32
自 33
有 36
肉 37
百 51
好 57
安 62
休 66
耳 78
寺 104
先 105
舌 110
西 116
名 129
多 134
会 138
気 149
年 155
団 167
毎 168
死 172
行 173
字 176
交 185
糸 196
同 197

7 Strokes

貝 21
見 42
体 71
男 74
言 80
売 92
図 111
花 128
私 131
近 141
来 156
赤 160
町 170
村 175
里 180
車 190
足 195

8 Strokes

明 12
国 26
京 41
歩 55
東 76
金 82
青 86
雨 90
者 93
門 96
周 120
物 125
夜 132
英 152
押 154
学 157
空 169
取 174
具 177
注 178
林 181
受 191

9 Strokes

春 40
南 46
首 54
思 77
美 101
星 114
秋 115
前 133
持 135
音 137
秒 147
品 162
後 187
海 193

10 Strokes

高 49
夏 64
家 75
島 102
書 136
馬 144
時 150
訓 153
桜 179
校 194

11 Strokes

掛 88
雪 95
鳥 107
週 145
黒 184

12 Strokes

買 50
朝 85
間 97
開 106
道 122
森 182
雲 183
最 188

13 Strokes

電 91
新 127
話 151
意 158
愛 199

14 Strokes

語 83
読 121
聞 139

16 Strokes

親 113

18 Strokes

曜 119
離 200

INDEX 2: KANJI NAMES

After 後 187
Again 又 159
Around 周 120
Autumn 秋 115
Axe 斤 126

Basis 元 53
Beautiful 美 101
Before 前 133
Bird 鳥 107
Black 黒 184
Block 丁 165
Blue 青 86
Body 体 71
Bow 弓 143
Bright 明 12
Buy 買 50

Capital 京 41
Car 車 190
Center 央 140
Change 化 69
Character 字 176
Cherry tree 桜 179
Child 子 56
Circle 円 52
City 市 163
Cloud 雲 183
Come 来 156
Complete 全 27
Country 国 26
Cow 牛 100
Craft 工 47
Cut 切 118

Day of the Week 曜 119
Death 死 172
Diagram 図 111
Dog 犬 171
Dry 干 81

Ear 耳 78
Early 早 29
Earth 土 87
Ease 安 62
East 東 76
Eight 八 19
Electric 電 91
Empty 空 169
English 英 152
Enter 入 94
Evening 夕 108
Every 毎 168
Evil 凶 192
Exit 出 98
Eye 目 15

Fat 太 189
Father 父 79
Few 少 45
Fire 火 59
Five 五 14
Flower 花 128
Forest 森 182
Four 四 10
Friend 友 166

Gate 門 96
Gentleman 士 84
Go 行 173
Gold 金 82
Goods 品 162
Group 団 167
Grove 林 181

Half 半 38
Hamlet 里 180
Hand 手 67
Hang 掛 88
Have 有 36
Hear 聞 139
Heart 心 25
Heaven 天 123
Hold 持 135
Horse 馬 144
House 家 75
Hundred 百 51

Individual 者 93
Inside 内 34
Instruction 訓 153
Interval 間 97
Island 島 102

Jewel 玉 24

King 王 23

Large 大 17
Left 左 48
Leg 足 195
Life 生 99
Like 好 57
Lose 失 142
Love 愛 199
Lower 下 31

Main 本 68
Man 男 74
Many 多 134
Meat 肉 37
Meet 会 138
Middle 中 18
Mind 意 158
Mix 交 185
Moon 月 11
Morning 朝 85
Most 最 188
Mother 母 130
Mountain 山 1
Mouth 口 8

Name 名 129
Near 近 141
Neck 首 54
New 新 127
Night 夜 132
Nine 九 39
Noon 午 198
North 北 72
Not 不 186

Old 古 58
One 一 3
Open 開 106
Outside 外 109

Parent 親 113
Part 分 124
Person 人 2
Pour 注 178
Precede 先 105
Primary 主 164
Private 私 131
Public 公 161
Pull 引 146
Push 押 154

Rain 雨 90
Read 読 121
Receive 受 191
Red 赤 160
Rest 休 66
Rice 米 32
Rice Field 田 73
Right 右 35

River 川 70
Road 道 122
Rotate 回 9

Same 同 197
Say 言 80
School 校 194
Sea 海 193
Second 秒 147
See 見 42
Self 自 33
Sell 売 92
Separate 離 200
Seven 七 44
Shell 甲 148
Shellfish 貝 21
Six 六 22
Small 小 20
Snow 雪 95
Sound 音 137
South 南 46
Speak 話 151
Spirit 気 149
Spring 春 40
Stand 立 112
Star 星 114
Stop 止 43
Strength 力 63
Study 学 157
Summer 夏 64
Sun 日 6
Sword 刀 117

Take 取 174
Tall 高 49
Temple 寺 104
Ten 十 28
Ten Thousand 万 89
Thing 物 125
Think 思 77
Thousand 千 65
Thread 糸 196
Three 三 5
Time 時 150
Tiny 寸 103
Tongue 舌 110
Tool 具 177
Town 町 170
Tree 木 13
Two 二 4

Upper 上 30

Village 村 175
Walk 歩 55
Water 水 61
Week 週 145
West 西 116
White 白 7
Winter 冬 60
Woman 女 16
Words 語 83
Write 書 136

Year 年 155

INDEX 3: ROMAJI

a	明	12
a	上	30
a	有	36
a	開	106
a	会	138
a	空	169
AI	愛	199
aida	間	97
aka	明	12
aka	赤	160
aki	明	12
aki	秋	115
ama	雨	90
ama	天	123
ame	雨	90
ame	天	123
AN	安	62
AN	行	173
ao	青	86
arata	新	127
aru	歩	55
asa	朝	85
ashi	足	195
atara	新	127
ato	後	187
ayu	歩	55
aza	字	176
ba	化	69
BA	馬	144
BAI	貝	21
BAI	買	50
BAI	売	92
BAN	万	89
BEI	米	32
BI	美	101
BO	母	130
BOKU	木	13
BOKU	目	15
BU	歩	55
BU	分	124
BU	不	186
BUN	分	124
BUN	聞	139
BUTSU	物	125
BYAKU	白	7
BYŌ	秒	147
chi	千	65
chichi	父	79
chii	小	20
chika	近	141
chikara	力	63
CHŌ	朝	85
CHŌ	鳥	107
CHŌ	丁	165
CHŌ	町	170
CHŪ	中	18
CHŪ	注	178
da	出	98
DAI	大	17
DAI	内	34
DAN	男	74
DAN	団	167
de	出	98
DEN	田	73
DEN	電	91
DO	土	87
DŌ	道	122
DŌ	同	197
DOKU	読	121
E	会	138
EI	英	152
EN	円	52
FU	歩	55
FU	父	79
FU	不	186
FUN	分	124
furu	古	58
futa	二	4
futo	太	189
fuyu	冬	60
GAI	外	109
GAKU	学	157
GAN	元	53
GATSU	月	11
GE	下	31
GE	夏	64
GE	外	109
GEN	元	53
GEN	言	80
GETSU	月	11
GO	五	14
GO	語	83
GO	後	187
GO	午	198
GON	言	80
goto	毎	168
GU	具	177
GYŌ	行	173
GYOKU	玉	24
GYŪ	牛	100
ha	生	99
HACHI	八	19
haha	母	130
hai	入	94
haka	図	111
HAKU	白	7
HAN	半	38
hana	花	128
hana	話	151
hana	離	200
hanashi	話	151
haru	春	40
haya	早	29
hayashi	林	181
hazu	外	109
hi	日	6
hi	火	59
hi	干	81
hi	引	146
hidari	左	48
higashi	東	76
HIN	品	162
hira	開	106
hito	人	2
hito	一	3
ho	火	59
ho	干	81
HO	歩	55
hoka	外	109
HOKU	北	72
HON	本	68
hoshi	星	114
HYAKU	百	51
i	言	80
i	入	94
i	生	99
i	行	173
I	意	158
ichi	市	163
ICHI	一	3
ie	家	75
IN	音	137
IN	引	146
inu	犬	171
ito	糸	196
itsu	五	14
ITSU	一	3

JI 自 33
JI 耳 78
JI 寺 104
JI 持 135
JI 時 150
JI 字 176
JIN 人 2
JITSU 日 6
JITSU 十 28
JO 女 16
JŌ 上 30
JU 受 191
JŪ 中 18
JŪ 十 28

ka 日 6
ka 買 50
ka 掛 88
ka 書 136
ka 交 185
KA 下 31
KA 火 59
KA 夏 64
KA 化 69
KA 家 75
KA 花 128
kado 門 96
kai 貝 21
KAI 回 9
KAI 開 106
KAI 会 138
KAI 海 193
kami 上 30
KAN 千 81
KAN 間 97
KAN 甲 148
kana 金 82
kane 金 82
kara 空 169
karada 体 71
kata 語 83
katana 刀 117
katari 語 83
kawa 川 70
KE 化 69
KE 家 75
KE 気 149
KEI 京 41
KEN 見 42
KEN 間 97
KEN 犬 171
ki 木 13
ki 生 99
ki 切 118
ki 聞 139
ki 来 156
KI 気 149
KIN 金 82
KIN 斤 126
KIN 近 141
kita 北 72
ko 木 13
ko 小 20
ko 子 56
KO 古 58
KŌ 口 8
KŌ 工 47
KŌ 高 49
KŌ 好 57
KŌ 甲 148
KŌ 公 161
KŌ 行 173
KŌ 交 185
KŌ 後 187
KŌ 校 194
kokono 九 39
kokoro 心 25
KOKU 国 26
KOKU 黒 184
kome 米 32
KON 金 82
kono 好 57
koto 言 80
ku 来 156
KU 口 8
KU 九 39
KU 工 47
KU 公 161
KŪ 空 169
kubi 首 54
kuchi 口 8
kuda 下 31
kumo 雲 183
KUN 訓 153
kuni 国 26
kuro 黒 184
kuruma 車 190
KYŌ 京 41
KYŌ 凶 192
KYŪ 九 39
KYŪ 休 66
KYŪ 弓 143

ma 目 15
ma 間 97
ma 馬 144
ma 交 185
machi 町 170
mae 前 133
MAI 米 32
MAI 毎 168
maji 交 185
MAN 万 89
mana 学 157
maru 円 52
mata 又 159
matta 全 27
matto 全 27
mawa 回 9
me 目 15
me 女 16
MEI 明 12
MEI 名 129
mi 三 5
mi 見 42
mi- 三 5
michi 道 122
migi 右 35
mimi 耳 78
MIN 明 12
minami 南 46
mizu 水 61
mizuka 自 33
mo 持 135
mo 最 188
MOKU 木 13
MOKU 目 15
MON 門 96
MON 聞 139
mono 者 93
mono 物 125
mori 森 182
moto 下 31
moto 元 53
moto 本 68
MOTSU 物 125
motto 最 188
mu 六 22
mu- 六 22
mui 六 22
mura 村 175
MYŌ 明 12
MYŌ 名 129

na 名 129
NAI 内 34
naka 中 18
naka 半 38
nama 生 99
NAN 南 46
NAN 男 74
nana 七 44
nano 七 44
natsu 夏 64
ne 音 137
NEN 年 155
NI 二 4
NICHI 日 6

nii	新	127
NIKU	肉	37
NIN	人	2
nishi	西	116
nobo	上	30
nochi	後	187
nushi	主	164
NYO	女	16
NYŌ	女	16
NYŪ	入	94
o	小	20
o	下	31
o	生	99
o	押	154
ō	大	17
ō	多	134
Ō	王	23
Ō	央	140
Ō	押	154
Ō	桜	179
ōyake	公	161
okona	行	173
oku	後	187
omo	思	77
omo	主	164
ON	音	137
ona	同	197
onna	女	16
oto	音	137
otoko	男	74
oya	親	113
RAI	来	156
RI	里	180
RI	離	200
RIKI	力	63
RIKU	六	22
RIN	林	181
RITSU	立	112
ROKU	六	22
RYOKU	力	63
RYŪ	立	112
sa	下	31
SA	左	48
SAI	西	116
SAI	切	118
SAI	最	188
saki	先	105
sakura	桜	179
SAN	山	1
SAN	三	5
sato	里	180
SATSU	早	29
SEI	青	86
SEI	生	99
SEI	星	114
SEI	西	116
SEKI	夕	108
SEKI	赤	160
SEN	千	65
SEN	川	70
SEN	先	105
SETSU	雪	95
SETSU	切	118
SHA	者	93
SHA	車	190
SHAKU	赤	160
shi	死	172
SHI	四	10
SHI	自	33
SHI	止	43
SHI	子	56
SHI	思	77
SHI	士	84
SHI	私	131
SHI	市	163
SHI	死	172
SHI	糸	196
SHICHI	七	44
shima	島	102
shimo	下	31
SHIN	心	25
SHIN	親	113
SHIN	新	127
SHIN	森	182
shina	品	162
shira	白	7
shiro	白	7
shita	下	31
shita	舌	110
shita	親	113
SHITSU	失	142
SHO	書	136
SHŌ	小	20
SHŌ	上	30
SHŌ	少	45
SHŌ	青	86
SHŌ	生	99
SHŌ	星	114
SHU	首	54
SHU	手	67
SHU	主	164
SHU	取	174
SHŪ	秋	115
SHŪ	周	120
SHŪ	週	145
SHUN	春	40
SHUTSU	出	98
SŌ	早	29
SOKU	足	195
SON	村	175
sora	空	169
soso	注	178
soto	外	109
su	好	57
SU	子	56
SU	主	164
SUI	水	61
SUI	出	98
suko	少	45
suku	少	45
SUN	寸	103
ta	手	67
ta	田	73
ta	立	112
ta	足	195
TA	多	134
TA	太	189
TAI	大	17
TAI	体	71
TAI	太	189
taka	高	49
tama	玉	24
te	手	67
TEI	体	71
TEI	丁	165
TEN	天	123
tera	寺	104
to	十	28
to	止	43
to	取	174
TO	土	87
TO	図	111
tō	十	28
TŌ	冬	60
TŌ	東	76
TŌ	島	102
TŌ	刀	117
TŌ	読	121
TŌ	道	122
toki	時	150
TOKU	読	121
tomo	友	166
TON	団	167
tori	鳥	107
toshi	年	155
tsuchi	土	87
tsuki	月	11
u	売	92
u	生	99
u	受	191
U	右	35
U	有	36
U	雨	90

uchi	内	34
ue	上	30
uma	馬	144
umi	海	193
UN	雲	183
ushi	牛	100
ushi	後	187
ushina	失	142
utsuku	美	101
uwa	上	30
wa	分	124
WA	話	151
watakushi	私	131
watashi	私	131
ya	八	19
ya	家	75
YA	夜	132
ya-	八	19
yama	山	1
yasu	安	62
yasu	休	66
yo	四	10
yo	読	121
yo	夜	132
yo-	四	10
yō	八	19
YŌ	曜	119
yon	四	10
yoru	夜	132
yu	行	173
yū	夕	108
YŪ	右	35
YŪ	有	36
YŪ	友	166
yuki	雪	95
yumi	弓	143
ZEN	全	27
ZEN	前	133
ZETSU	舌	110
ZU	図	111

INDEX 4: HIRAGANA/KATAKANA

Reading	Kanji	No.
あ	明	12
あ	上	30
あ	有	36
あ	開	106
あ	会	138
あ	空	169
アイ	愛	199
あいだ	間	97
あお	青	86
あか	明	12
あか	赤	160
あき	明	12
あき	秋	115
あさ	朝	85
あざ	字	176
あし	足	195
あたら	新	127
あと	後	187
あま	雨	90
あま	天	123
あめ	雨	90
あめ	天	123
あゆ	歩	55
あらた	新	127
ある	歩	55
アン	安	62
アン	行	173
イ	意	158
い	言	80
い	入	94
い	生	99
い	行	173
いえ	家	75
イチ	一	3
いち	市	163
イツ	一	3
いつ	五	14
いと	糸	196
いぬ	犬	171
イン	音	137
イン	引	146
ウ	右	35
ウ	有	36
ウ	雨	90
う	売	92
う	生	99
う	受	191
うえ	上	30
うし	牛	100
うし	後	187
うしな	失	142
うち	内	34
うつく	美	101
うま	馬	144
うみ	海	193
うわ	上	30
ウン	雲	183
エ	会	138
エイ	英	152
エン	円	52
お	小	20
お	下	31
お	生	99
お	押	154
オウ	王	23
オウ	央	140
オウ	押	154
オウ	桜	179
おお	大	17
おお	多	134
おおやけ	公	161
おく	後	187
おこな	行	173
おと	音	137
おとこ	男	74
おな	同	197
おも	思	77
おも	主	164
おや	親	113
オン	音	137
おんな	女	16
カ	下	31
カ	火	59
カ	夏	64
カ	化	69
カ	家	75
カ	花	128
か	日	6
か	買	50
か	掛	88
か	書	136
か	交	185
カイ	回	9
カイ	開	106
カイ	会	138
カイ	海	193
かい	貝	21
ガイ	外	109
ガク	学	157
かた	語	83
かたな	刀	117
かたり	語	83
ガツ	月	11
かど	門	96
かな	金	82
かね	金	82
かみ	上	30
から	空	169
からだ	体	71
かわ	川	70
カン	干	81
カン	間	97
カン	甲	148
ガン	元	53
キ	気	149
き	木	13
き	生	99
き	切	118
き	聞	139
き	来	156
きた	北	72
キュウ	九	39
キュウ	休	66
キュウ	弓	143
ギュウ	牛	100
キョウ	京	41
キョウ	凶	192
ギョウ	行	173
ギョク	玉	24
キン	金	82
キン	斤	126
キン	近	141
ク	口	8
ク	九	39
ク	工	47
ク	公	161
く	来	156
グ	具	177
クウ	空	169
くだ	下	31
くち	口	8
くに	国	26
くび	首	54
くも	雲	183
くるま	車	190
くろ	黒	184
クン	訓	153
ケ	化	69
ケ	家	75
ケ	気	149
ゲ	下	31
ゲ	夏	64
ゲ	外	109
ケイ	京	41
ゲツ	月	11
ケン	見	42

ケン	間	97
ケン	犬	171
ゲン	元	53
ゲン	言	80
コ	古	58
こ	木	13
こ	小	20
こ	子	56
ゴ	五	14
ゴ	語	83
ゴ	後	187
ゴ	午	198
コウ	口	8
コウ	工	47
コウ	高	49
コウ	好	57
コウ	甲	148
コウ	公	161
コウ	行	173
コウ	交	185
コウ	後	187
コウ	校	194
コク	国	26
コク	黒	184
ここの	九	39
こころ	心	25
こと	言	80
ごと	毎	168
この	好	57
こめ	米	32
コン	金	82
ゴン	言	80
サ	左	48
さ	下	31
サイ	西	116
サイ	切	118
サイ	最	188
さき	先	105
さくら	桜	179
サツ	早	29
さと	里	180
サン	山	1
サン	三	5
シ	四	10
シ	自	33
シ	止	43
シ	子	56
シ	思	77
シ	士	84
シ	私	131
シ	市	163
シ	死	172
シ	糸	196
し	死	172
ジ	自	33
ジ	耳	78
ジ	寺	104
ジ	持	135
ジ	時	150
ジ	字	176
した	下	31
した	舌	110
した	親	113
シチ	七	44
シツ	失	142
ジツ	日	6
ジツ	十	28
しな	品	162
しま	島	102
しも	下	31
シャ	者	93
シャ	車	190
シャク	赤	160
シュ	首	54
シュ	手	67
シュ	主	164
シュ	取	174
ジュ	受	191
シュウ	秋	115
シュウ	周	120
シュウ	週	145
ジュウ	中	18
ジュウ	十	28
シュツ	出	98
シュン	春	40
ショ	書	136
ジョ	女	16
ショウ	小	20
ショウ	上	30
ショウ	少	45
ショウ	青	86
ショウ	生	99
ショウ	星	114
ジョウ	上	30
しら	白	7
しろ	白	7
シン	心	25
シン	親	113
シン	新	127
シン	森	182
ジン	人	2
ス	子	56
ス	主	164
す	好	57
ズ	図	111
スイ	水	61
スイ	出	98
すく	少	45
すこ	少	45
スン	寸	103
セイ	青	86
セイ	生	99
セイ	星	114
セイ	西	116
セキ	夕	108
セキ	赤	160
セツ	雪	95
セツ	切	118
ゼツ	舌	110
セン	千	65
セン	川	70
セン	先	105
ゼン	全	27
ゼン	前	133
ソウ	早	29
ソク	足	195
そそ	注	178
そと	外	109
そら	空	169
ソン	村	175
タ	多	134
タ	太	189
た	手	67
た	田	73
た	立	112
た	足	195
だ	出	98
タイ	大	17
タイ	体	71
タイ	太	189
ダイ	大	17
ダイ	内	34
たか	高	49
たま	玉	24
ダン	男	74
ダン	団	167
ち	千	65
ちい	小	20
ちか	近	141
ちから	力	63
ちち	父	79
チュウ	中	18
チュウ	注	178
チョウ	朝	85
チョウ	鳥	107
チョウ	丁	165
チョウ	町	170
つき	月	11
つち	土	87
て	手	67
で	出	98
テイ	体	71
テイ	丁	165
てら	寺	104
テン	天	123
デン	田	73
デン	電	91
ト	土	87

ト	図	111
と	十	28
と	止	43
と	取	174
ド	土	87
トウ	冬	60
トウ	東	76
トウ	島	102
トウ	刀	117
トウ	読	121
トウ	道	122
ドウ	道	122
ドウ	同	197
とお	十	28
とき	時	150
トク	読	121
ドク	読	121
とし	年	155
とも	友	166
とり	鳥	107
トン	団	167
な	名	129
ナイ	内	34
なか	中	18
なか	半	38
なつ	夏	64
なな	七	44
なの	七	44
なま	生	99
ナン	南	46
ナン	男	74
ニ	二	4
にい	新	127
ニク	肉	37
にし	西	116
ニチ	日	6
ニュウ	入	94
ニョ	女	16
ニョウ	女	16
ニン	人	2
ぬし	主	164
ね	音	137
ネン	年	155
のち	後	187
のぼ	上	30
は	生	99
バ	馬	144
ば	化	69
はい	入	94
バイ	貝	21
バイ	買	50
バイ	売	92
はか	図	111
ハク	白	7
はず	外	109
ハチ	八	19
はな	花	128
はな	話	151
はな	離	200
はなし	話	151
はは	母	130
はや	早	29
はやし	林	181
はる	春	40
ハン	半	38
バン	万	89
ひ	日	6
ひ	火	59
ひ	干	81
ひ	引	146
ビ	美	101
ひがし	東	76
ひだり	左	48
ひと	人	2
ひと	一	3
ヒャク	百	51
ビャク	白	7
ビョウ	秒	147
ひら	開	106
ヒン	品	162
フ	歩	55
フ	父	79
フ	不	186
ブ	歩	55
ブ	分	124
ブ	不	186
ふた	二	4
ブツ	物	125
ふと	太	189
ふゆ	冬	60
ふる	古	58
フン	分	124
ブン	分	124
ブン	聞	139
ベイ	米	32
ホ	歩	55
ほ	火	59
ほ	干	81
ボ	母	130
ほか	外	109
ホク	北	72
ボク	木	13
ボク	目	15
ほし	星	114
ホン	本	68
ま	目	15
ま	間	97
ま	馬	144
ま	交	185
マイ	米	32
マイ	毎	168
まえ	前	133
まじ	交	185
また	又	159
まち	町	170
まった	全	27
まっと	全	27
まな	学	157
まる	円	52
まわ	回	9
マン	万	89
み	三	5
み	見	42
みぎ	右	35
みず	水	61
みずか	自	33
みち	道	122
みっ	三	5
みなみ	南	46
みみ	耳	78
ミョウ	明	12
ミョウ	名	129
ミン	明	12
む	六	22
むい	六	22
むっ	六	22
むら	村	175
め	目	15
め	女	16
メイ	明	12
メイ	名	129
も	持	135
も	最	188
モク	木	13
モク	目	15
モツ	物	125
もっと	最	188
もと	下	31
もと	元	53
もと	本	68
もの	者	93
もの	物	125
もり	森	182
モン	門	96
モン	聞	139
ヤ	夜	132
や	八	19
や	家	75
やす	安	62
やす	休	66
やっ	八	19
やま	山	1
ゆ	行	173
ユウ	右	35
ユウ	有	36
ユウ	友	166
ゆう	夕	108
ゆき	雪	95

ゆみ	弓	143
よ	四	10
よ	読	121
よ	夜	132
ヨウ	曜	119
よう	八	19
よっ	四	10
よる	夜	132
よん	四	10
ライ	来	156
リ	里	180
リ	離	200
リキ	力	63
リク	六	22
リツ	立	112
リュウ	立	112
リョク	力	63
リン	林	181
ロク	六	22
ワ	話	151
わ	分	124
わたくし	私	131
わたし	私	131

ON-YOMI KEYWORD TABLE

ON-YOMI		KEYWORD(s)
AI	アイ	
AN	アン	
BA	バ	
BAI	バイ	
BAN	バン	
BEI	ベイ	
BI	ビ	
BO	ボ	
BOKU	ボク	
BU	ブ	
BUN	ブン	
BUTSU	ブツ	
BYAKU	ビャク	
BYŌ	ビョウ	
CHŌ	チョウ	
CHŪ	チュウ	
DAI	ダイ	
DAN	ダン	
DEN	デン	
DO	ド	
DŌ	ドウ	
DOKU	ドク	
E	エ	
EI	エイ	
EN	エン	
FU	フ	
FUN	フン	
GAI	ガイ	

ON-YOMI		KEYWORD(s)
GAKU	ガク	
GAN	ガン	
GATSU	ガツ	
GE	ゲ	
GEN	ゲン	
GETSU	ゲツ	
GO	ゴ	
GON	ゴン	
GU	グ	
GYŌ	ギョウ	
GYOKU	ギョク	
GYŪ	ギュウ	
HACHI	ハチ	
HAKU	ハク	
HAN	ハン	
HIN	ヒン	
HO	ホ	
HOKU	ホク	
HON	ホン	
HYAKU	ヒャク	
I	イ	
ICHI	イチ	
IN	イン	
ITSU	イツ	
JI	ジ	
JIN	ジン	
JITSU	ジツ	
JO	ジョ	
JŌ	ジョウ	
JU	ジュ	
JŪ	ジュウ	

ON-YOMI		KEYWORD(s)
KA	カ	
KAI	カイ	
KAN	カン	
KE	ケ	
KEI	ケイ	
KEN	ケン	
KI	キ	
KIN	キン	
KO	コ	
KŌ	コウ	
KOKU	コク	
KON	コン	
KU	ク	
KŪ	クウ	
KUN	クン	
KYŌ	キョウ	
KYŪ	キュウ	
MAI	マイ	
MAN	マン	
MEI	メイ	
MIN	ミン	
MOKU	モク	
MON	モン	
MOTSU	モツ	
MYŌ	ミョウ	
NAI	ナイ	
NAN	ナン	
NEN	ネン	
NI	ニ	
NICHI	ニチ	
NIKU	ニク	

ON-YOMI		KEYWORD(s)
NIN	ニン	
NYO	ニョ	
NYŌ	ニョウ	
NYŪ	ニュウ	
Ō	オウ	
ON	オン	
RAI	ライ	
RI	リ	
RIKI	リキ	
RIKU	リク	
RIN	リン	
RITSU	リツ	
ROKU	ロク	
RYOKU	リョク	
RYŪ	リュウ	
SA	サ	
SAI	サイ	
SAN	サン	
SATSU	サツ	
SEI	セイ	
SEKI	セキ	
SEN	セン	
SETSU	セツ	
SHA	シャ	
SHAKU	シャク	
SHI	シ	
SHICHI	シチ	
SHIN	シン	
SHITSU	シツ	
SHO	ショ	
SHŌ	ショウ	

ON-YOMI		KEYWORD(s)
SHU	シュ	
SHŪ	シュウ	
SHUN	シュン	
SHUTSU	シュツ	
SŌ	ソウ	
SOKU	ソク	
SON	ソン	
SU	ス	
SUI	スイ	
SUN	スン	
TA	タ	
TAI	タイ	
TEI	テイ	
TEN	テン	
TO	ト	
TŌ	トウ	
TOKU	トク	
TON	トン	
U	ウ	
UN	ウン	
WA	ワ	
YA	ヤ	
YŌ	ヨウ	
YŪ	ユウ	
ZEN	ゼン	
ZETSU	ゼツ	
ZU	ズ	